The Inclusive Pulpit Journal

Resources for Community Church Worship

The Inclusive Pulpit Journal
Resources for Community Church Worship

Published by
Community Church Press
21116 Washington Parkway
Frankfort, Illinois 60423-3112
Phone: (815) 464-5690
Fax:(815) 464-5692
Email: iccc60423@sbcglobal.net
Web: http://www.icccusa.com/

ISBN: 978-0-9638451-8-4

Printed and bound in the United States of America

The Inclusive Pulpit Journal
Resources for Community Church Worship

Volume 17, Summer, 2012

Edited by
Larry and Carolyn Dipboye

The International Council of Community Churches

With offices located in Frankfort, Illinois, The International Council of Community Churches is a network of interdenominational, community churches located throughout the United States and in seventeen countries around the world devoted to the prayer of Christ, "that they all may be one." Its primary purpose is to be a grassroots demonstration that the ecumenical spirit works.

The International Council of Community Churches is affiliated with the World Council of Churches, the National Council of Churches, and Churches Uniting in Christ.

Our Mission
As people devoted to following Christ we are committed
- *To community*
- *To treasuring diversity*
- *To living our faith in service and love.*

Our Vision
- *To affirm individual freedom of conscience*
- *To protect and promote congregational self-determination*
- *To proclaim that the love of God, which unites, can overcome any division*
- *To be an integral partner in the worldwide ecumenical movement.*

Contact ICCC at 21116 Washington Parkway, Frankfort, Illinois 60423-3112. Phone: (815) 464-5690, Fax: (815) 464-5692, Email: iccc60423@sbcglobal.net. Information about the Community Church Press and other publications may be found at our website, http://www.icccusa.com/.

Contents

Sermons

Poetry

Prayer

Special Occasions

Council Minister's Foreword

"There were giants in the earth in those days." The passing of another giant of faith brings the names back to mind. Some of them we knew and embraced; others had passed from human sight before our time. They were pioneers of faith and leaders in loving kindness. They spoke in vibrant shouts and quiet whispers and most of all in acts of compassion. I will not list names here, because I would be sure to neglect or forget one or more whose witness and ministry made your life more full. Those giants of faith are the ones on whose shoulders we stand, looking forward and upward toward the vision of a celestial city not made with hands. For each of those giants we give thanks to the God who made them and who re-makes us.

Those of us whose privilege and burden it is to preach know how profound our challenge is: to speak a word of truth in our own time and place even as they did in theirs. We are called, as they were, to be prophets in the most profound sense, to speak a word for God in the sanctuary and in the marketplace, to speak God's word of justice and mercy to those who need comfort and to those who dwell in it.

The 2012 issue of *The Inclusive Pulpit* reveals the joy, the sorrow, and above all the authenticity that is distilled in a sermon. As I have read the lines of each preacher's work, I have been drawn to that which was unsaid and still communicated – the Word between the lines. As you read each sermon, please take the time to do so slowly and carefully so that the Word may speak to you.

Sermons are the reflection and the expression of things both evanescent and eternal. The ethos, the atmosphere, the year's culture (as in "corporate culture") all shimmer in the atmosphere for a while and then dissipate. Decades from now some of the references will seem obscure, and some of the similes and metaphors will certainly

9

appear quaint. But the central themes will be ever fresh and always relevant. The truths communicated will not change. So it is a good thing that the Council publishes an annual homiletic collection as a witness to the present day, and as a legacy of faith communicated to generations yet to come.

So enjoy! And if the preachers have done their work well this year, as I know they have, you will be hungering and thirsting for more in 2013's collection.

Don Ashmall, Council Minister

Editors' Preface

We have been reading sermons from ICCC churches for six years as editors of *Inclusive Pulpit Journal*. We are struck by the wide variety of sermons that happen every Sunday in ICCC churches. Even when sermons happen to flow from the same biblical text, the interpretation, the approach, and often the conclusions are distinctly different. For example, compare Paul Drake's sermon on page 64 with Ron Stephens' sermon on page 134, both from the same text.

Friends, whether we like it or not, there is a lot of difference among us. ICCC sermons probably sound a lot like the cacophony coming from the disciples at Pentecost. We are obviously a community of churches rather than a Church or a Denomination in the institutional sense of those words.

We do not look or believe exactly alike. In addition to worship style, our congregations present significant diversity in age, appearance, gender, language, dialect, and culture, to mention only a sample of our distinguishing characteristics. Could it be that Christians committed to the prayer of Jesus, "that they may be one, as we are one," do not think or believe in lockstep as if we were all cut from the exact same block? Without question, Jesus knew as he prayed for his disciples that Peter was not at all like his brother Andrew and that Thomas was going to ask a lot of questions before he decided to follow and that Judas would always be a maverick. The Twelve for whom Jesus prayed and the churches that grew out of that prayer were a lot like us. They were distinctly different from one another. You might even call them a hodgepodge. But all had decided to follow Jesus.

Jesus' prayer for unity could not have been a call for enforced conformity on that ragtag family of disciples whom he called "friends." They were diverse. They had always been unique. They

11

would always be different from the world and from each other. I suspect Jesus was praying for something better than a military organization or a pecking order.

A few centuries of trial and error in church experience says that Jesus was praying for *community*, not *conformity*. He knew that his disciples would need to respect difference in order to work together, that they would have to learn how to love someone who is not always lovely, and that they would need to abandon force as the means to accomplish the Christian mission. They would have to be children of the new commandment that we associate with Maundy Thursday, "Love one another as I have loved you." They would have to become one body in Christ, members one of another, and understand Paul's metaphor of body parts to apply to the diversity of the Spirit's gifts among the brothers and sisters.

Through the centuries, Christians have misconstrued the prayer of Jesus. On occasions, Churches have been obsessed with issues of orthodoxy (doctrinal uniformity), orthopraxy (behavioral uniformity), and institutional obedience. As every student of church history knows, holy wars have often been the effect of attempts to enforce conformity; and the *koinonia*/communion of the Spirit has been the missing quality of these institutions.

After six years of reading ICCC sermons, the editors are bragging, not complaining, about the diversity of our churches and of our pulpits. As you read, we hope that you can take as much pleasure in our diversity and in expanding your experience of Christian worship as we have.

The Editors

Larry and Carolyn Dipboye
108 Wimberly Lane, Oak Ridge, Tennessee 37831-8126
Phone: 865 483-6752
Email: Ldipboye@gmail.com

Acknowledgements

We are grateful to the pastors, preachers, and friends of ICCC churches who have graciously provided manuscripts suitable for publication in this volume of *Inclusive Pulpit*.

The members of ICCC Community Church Press Editorial Board read the sermons submitted for the Inclusive Pulpit and determine the winner of Dr. Charles A. Trentham Homiletics Award each year. We are grateful to the members of the Board Richard Griffith (Moderator), Robert Puckett, Nicholas Brame, Dorothy Bascom, Bob Harris, Donald Ashmall, and William Samuels, who have served with the editors in selecting the sermon which best reflects the spirit and values of the Community Church movement. The Charles A. Trentham Award is announced each year at the annual conference banquet. Award guidelines and a list of previous recipients can be found on pages 167-168.

In Loving Memory
2012 ICCC President Paul R. Drake
Who passed from this life
April 12, 2012

The messages Paul left for friends and family are far more authentic and more profound than any word we might offer in his behalf. The gospel that he lived will continue to live in his beloved International Council of Community Churches.

Paul Drake addressed his battle with cancer in his *Inclusive Pulpit* sermons "Keep Hope Alive" in 2011 and "Ready or Not, Here He Comes!" in this volume. His pastoral message below in the April Newsletter of The Community Church of Little Neck addresses the meaning of Easter for all of us. Paul died on April 12, four days after Easter.

From the Pastor's Desk   ***April 2012***

"When the Sabbath was over, Mary Magdalene, and Mary the mother of James, and Salome bought spices, so that they might go and anoint him. And very early on the first day of the week, when the sun had risen, they went to the tomb. They had been saying to one another, 'Who will roll away the stone for us from the entrance to the tomb?' When they looked up, they saw that the stone, which was very large, had already been rolled back. As they entered the tomb, they saw a young man, dressed in a white robe, sitting on the right side; and they were alarmed. But he said to them, 'Do not be alarmed; you are looking for Jesus of Nazareth, who was crucified. He has been raised; he is not here. Look, there is the place they laid him. But go, tell his disciples and Peter that he is going ahead of you to Galilee; there you will see him, just as he told you.'" (Mark 16:1-7, NRSV)

Dear Friends in Christ,

We are preparing to celebrate what is for Christians the most important holiday of this or any year. Easter the day of the Resurrection of Jesus Christ our Lord is the seminal event of the Christian faith. Without it, there would be no reason to take any particular notice of the birth of one obscure Jewish boy born to poor

16

parents who weren't even married to each other at the time; there would be no Christian observance of Pentecost to commemorate the sending of the Holy Spirit to the believers; no Epiphany, since why would God bother to reveal to anyone the birth of one more failed Messiah figure; no Lent, no Advent, etc. In short, without the Resurrection, there would be no Christianity as we know it.

I am finding that thinking and talking about the Resurrection and eternal life takes on a whole new level of meaning when you realize that you may be entering that eternal life yourself sooner rather than later. As I deal with a diagnosis of cancer that, barring a miracle in answer to the prayers of so many, is considered incurable, particularly as I am now beginning to experience more symptoms of it and have just enrolled in our local Hospice program, belief in Jesus as the Resurrection and the Life is no longer an academic exercise for me, but something very real, personal, and existential. Interestingly enough, I have discovered that my faith is more vital and dynamic than I ever realized it was which is making this whole process of coping with the reality and increasing imminence of death easier than I ever imagined it could be.

As pastor and members of a congregation that we have variously described as more "mainstream," "progressive, "even "liberal" than some, there are those who probably assume our faith is more intellectual and less vital than that of our more "evangelical" brothers and sisters. (Note from the quotation marks that I am reluctant to use these labels even for descriptive purposes, because I generally find them to be both inadequate and inaccurate, but I am forced into it because we lack more precise language to use to describe the very real differences that exist within the Christian faith.)

What I am finding for myself, however, is that while I may be somewhat more prone than some Christians to question my beliefs, having done so has helped me solidify what I believe in such a way that I am absolutely convinced of it with all my heart, soul, mind, and strength, and therefore more committed to it and more easily comforted by it than if I believed with just my heart or just my head. Having head and heart both engaged yields an unshakeable faith that is sustaining me even as I realize that the day when I will see Jesus face-to-face is drawing ever closer for me.

Just to give one example of what I mean, I will share that in the past Karen and I have had some frank discussions with each other about whether or not we believe the Resurrection was a real event or perhaps more of an expression of the longing of the earliest followers of Jesus for him to remain alive and with them, even though he had been put to death on a Roman cross. I have always been a little more convinced of the reality of the Resurrection myself, but both of us have always ended up saying that, in terms of our faith, it doesn't really matter so much whether it was a literal, factual event or a more symbolic reminder of the underlying Truth that Christ is alive in our hearts. I can now tell you, without a doubt, that either way, I have no doubt whatsoever that Christ has been raised from the dead and that because he lives, I shall live also. While I may have arrived at that belief by a bit more convoluted path than many, I am absolutely committed to the Truth of it with every fiber of my being. And that is what is making it possible for me to continue to preach the Good News and do what I can to share it with those around me, even (or perhaps especially) with what I increasingly realize may be my very last breath.

This Easter, as we celebrate the Resurrection of Our Lord during a Sunrise service in the courtyard and at our normal Family Worship Hour, my sermon will be every bit as much for me as for each of you. I hope you will join me in worshipping the One who is the Resurrection and the Life this Easter. And I assure you, with everything I am and everything I have, that Christ is risen indeed! Alleluia! Amen.

 Yours in Christ,

Pastor Paul Drake

Sermons

Get Real

Delivered at an ecumenical Lenten worship service of St. Christopher Catholic Church, Bridgeport, Michigan, April, 2011

Donald H. Ashmall, *Council Minister*
International Council of Community Churches,
former pastor, Bridgeport Community Church

I have to begin this evening by telling you one of my strangest memories of this particular church–of St. Christopher Church–and attending an ecumenical worship service here. On that particular occasion, the clergy were all seated up front. The liturgy called for a time when the fragrance of burning incense would be borne upwards just as our prayers ascend unto God; and in order to illustrate the lesson that the prayers of all God's people are lifted together unto the gates of heaven itself, all of the congregation were invited to come forward one by one to place a bit of frankincense onto the burner.

Now, I'm sure that my memory about that time of worship is not exactly accurate in all respects; but, at least in my recollection, the incense burner had a diameter roughly that of a thirty gallon trash can; and there was a heap of about three and a half pounds of charcoal glowing at the bottom of it. And the whole setup was about four feet in front of where I was sitting. The ushers directed the congregation to come up, one by one, and to take a tiny shovel and to dip it into the incense and place the raw material onto the coals.

The first few people to come forward were Catholics, and they took just a few grains each and reverently placed them into the incense burner. Then came some Lutherans, and they followed suit, placing just a few grains of frankincense onto the coals. And then came some Community Church people, about fifteen of them in a

21

row; and when they got up front, they used that tiny shovel like a sugar scoop. They picked up as much incense as they could and then dumped it onto the burning charcoal. On they came, one after another, each one it seemed to me trying to scoop up a larger amount than the person before and pour it onto the fire.

When the Lutherans and the Catholics ever so carefully placed their bits of incense onto the coals, tendrils of sweet smelling smoke ascended with the prayers of the people. By the time the first bunch of Community Church people got done, the place was looking like fog rolling in off the Cass River. Instead of going up, the smoke was rolling out of the burner horizontally and coming in my direction in great billowing clouds.

Now we all know, especially at an ecumenical service of worship, that the clergy are supposed to be on their best behavior and look and act in ways that are respectable and pious. But let me tell you, it's hard to act like you're pious when you're choking and gagging on frankincense smoke. And the Community Church people kept coming, and they kept dumping incense on the burner, three-quarters of a pound at a time. And the smoke kept pouring out in my direction. And I found that it did inspire me to pray. And what I prayed was, "Enough with the Community Church people; Lord send me some Catholics; send me some Lutherans, please!"

Now, why am I telling you this story? The point of the story is not in what happened in worship, but what happened, or rather, what didn't happen during the after-worship coffee hour. I'm there with tears still running down my face, and everybody is pretending it's just religious ecstasy.

Some of the Community Church people are realizing they may have gone just a bit overboard with the incense, and they're not sure whether they're supposed to be amused or appalled at the results. Whoever is in charge of the incense inventory at St. Christopher is realizing that we've just used up eight months' worth in one hour, and is trying to figure out how much to reorder, and whether or not it can wait until next week.

And *nobody* said a word. That coffee hour on that occasion was afflicted as so many of our ecumenical meetings are, by terminal niceness. We are so polite and kind and trying not to offend so much, that butter won't melt in our mouths, and nobody will ever catch us saying anything other than nice things.

We don't trust ourselves, we don't trust one another, we don't trust God enough to break through the niceness and speak about those things that really matter to us. We fear that if we ever get down to those things that are real that make a difference in our hearts and in our guts that the earth will crack open beneath us like rotten ice on the river on a warm spring day, and we will be lost in it. We really don't believe that God will sustain us in our honesty, so instead, we're just nice.

But the God who sustained Abraham and Sarah, the God who spoke through the angel to Mary, the God who proclaimed out of the heavens the very identity of Jesus, that God is powerful enough to sustain us and keep us when we tell the truth and seek the truth in our own time and place. But we sure don't act like it.

How are you? *"Oh, I'm fine."* My granddaughter is pregnant out of wedlock, and we're awaiting the biopsy report on my spleen, and my wife is depressed, and my dog just died. *"Oh, I'm fine."*

How's retirement going for you? *"Oh, just great."* I'm bored out of my skull, I'm driving my wife crazy following her around all day, I've discovered I don't have any real hobbies, and I'm wondering if all that's left for me is just waiting to die. *"Oh, just great."*

What if we suddenly got honest with one another? What if I began every conversation with you by asking: "What is *the* most important thing you and I need to talk about today?"[1] And what if you skipped the niceness and told me?

"What is *the* most important thing you and I need to talk about today?" *Oh, I don't know.* "Well, what *would* it be if you did know?"

Talk about scary, and yet, what's the alternative? You've been dealing with the alternatives throughout this season's series of worship services and sermons.[2] You've been talking about toning down the horrid, horrible rhetoric that seems to be all around us these days. And do you know the "heart reason" why that hateful noise seems to surround us? It's because people's hearts and guts are hurting for any of a thousand reasons. But rather than deal with the hurt, we spew it out onto others in the form of hatred and vicious bile.

Inside ourselves, the child who is within is in pain. The real answer to the pain is bearing one another's burdens, and discovering God's presence in that sharing: "What is *the* most important thing you and I need to talk about today?" Maybe it's a joy, but so often it's a sorrow or a worry or a fear or a wearing, crushing burden. "What is *the* most important thing you and I need to talk about today?" We aren't sure we want to know the answer.

Do you remember the story about Jesus and the woman at the well? The Ashmall revised and condensed version goes something like this: Jesus stops by a Samaritan village to get a drink of water at the village well. A woman shows up in the middle of the day to get water. That's an unusual time, because most women get the water early in the morning before it gets too hot outside. But there she is, and there he is, and they have a conversation.

If you ever take the time to read the New Testament account, you will discover that the report about the conversation is very disjointed mainly because Jesus keeps wanting to talk about the woman, and she keeps trying to sidetrack the encounter onto something else. She brings up social customs, and she tries a theological argument about whether the temple should be in Jerusalem or in Samaria. She wants to derail the conversation with anything else she can think of.

And Jesus keeps bringing her back to the most important thing she needs to be talking about that day, her own life and her own self. It's a battle to get the woman off the tangents to face herself. Only when she deals with the important stuff within does she find healing and hope.

You and I? We are the woman at the well. We fight it all the way. We squirm and twist and try to lead ourselves and others on tangents. "What is *the* most important thing you and I need to talk about today?" No, no! Anything but that! We'd rather rail about Obama or the tea party or the Middle East or anything rather than face the real issues of our hearts and our guts. We'd rather carry on about the economy or the town government or our neighbors or our in-laws. Or, if we're at an inter-church gathering, we want to put on our masks of niceness and hold it all inside. Just don't–please don't–ask us about our very selves.

"What is *the* most important thing you and I need to talk about today?" I have good news for you. In spite of what you may think, you can handle it, whatever "it" is. More important, God can handle it. God is bigger than it is, whatever "it" is. A loving God will not give you more than you can take–even if it, whatever "it" is, is scary beyond belief to you. You are a child of God, and God does not abandon God's children. Whatever "it" is–that most important thing that you really need to talk about–you and God can handle it together.

"What is *the* most important thing you and I need to talk about today?" There is no room for silly, insulting rhetoric in that question or in its answer. There is no room for niceness either. There is only truth. Ask the question. Answer it. Open yourself to the truth. For by God's grace, the truth will set you free.

Will you do it? Will you ask the question? Will you answer it? "What is *the* most important thing you and I need to talk about today?"

> "Change our hearts this time,
> your word says it can be.
> Change our minds this time,
> your life could make us free.
> We are the people your call sets apart.
> Lord, this time change our hearts." [3]

This time when we get out there in the coffee hour, let's not be nice. Let's talk about it, whatever "it" is. "What is *the* most important thing you and I need to talk about today?"

---

[1] For an in-depth treatment of in-depth conversation, see Susan Scott, *Fierce Conversations*, Berkley Publishing Group, 2002. ISBN 0-670-03124-0.

[2] The Bridgeport, MI 2011 ecumenical worship series for Lent used as its thematic inspiration Richard Mouw's *Uncommon Decency; Christian Civility in an Uncommon World*, InterVarsity Press, 2010. ISBN 978-0-8308-3309-2

[3] Lyrics by Rory Cooney ©.

Be Strong and Have Courage

Isaac Appiah, *Apostolic Christian Missions*
P. O. Box KJ 713, Kejetia Kumasi
Ghana, West Africa.

As Christians, there are times in our lives that we feel very weak and discouraged especially in difficulties. When this happens, go on your knees and pray to God. Read the scriptures, and let the Holy Spirit minister to you and renew your strength, (Isaiah 40:31).

Verse 31: "But they that wait upon the lord shall renew their strength, they shall mount up with wings as eagles, they shall run and not be weary, and shall walk and not faint."

The following scriptures confirm that as Christians, we need not faint or be discouraged.

1. Because it is the Lord that is always with you, and he will go before you. (Deuteronomy 31:6-8; 22-23)

Verse 6. "Be strong and of a good courage, fear not, nor be afraid of them: for the Lord thy God, he it is that doth go with thee, he will not fail thee nor forsake thee."

2. The Lord is always with us if we keep His commandments, read the Bible and do what it says.

Joshua 1:7: "Only be thou strong and very courageous, that thou mayest observe to do according to all the law, which Moses my servant commanded thee: turn not from it to the right hand or to the left, that thou mayest prosper whithersoever thou goest."

1 John 3:23-24: "And this is his commandment, That we should believe on the name of his Son Jesus Christ, and love one another, as he gave us commandment. And he that keepeth his commandments dwelleth in him, and he in him. And hereby we know that he abideth in us, by the Spirit which he hath given us."

3. The Lord will fight your enemies for you.

Joshua 10:25: "And Joshua said unto them fear not, nor be dismayed, be strong and of good courage for thus shall the Lord do to all your enemies against whom ye fight."

1 Chronicles 28:20: "And David said to Solomon his son, Be strong and of good courage, and do it: fear not, nor be dismayed: for the LORD God, even my God, will be with thee; he will not fail thee, nor forsake thee, until thou hast finished all the work for the service of the house of the LORD."

Isaiah 35:3-4: "Strengthen ye the weak hands, and confirm the feeble knees. Say to them that are of a fearful heart, Be strong, fear not: behold, your God will come with vengeance, even God with a recompense; he will come and save you."

4. We need to encourage one another. Isaiah 4:6: "They helped everyone his neighbor; and everyone said to his brother, Be of good courage."

5. By fasting and seeking the Lord, he will strengthen us.

Daniel10:2-3: "In those days I Daniel was mourning three full weeks. I ate no pleasant bread, neither came flesh nor wine in my mouth, neither did I anoint myself at all, till three whole weeks were fulfilled."

Isaac Appiah - Be Strong and Have Courage

Psalm 27:14: "Wait on the Lord. Be of good courage and he shall strengthen thine heart: be of good courage and he shall strengthen your heart, all ye that hope in the Lord."

In all things we must act like men/women of God and "Be strong." Be strong in God, the grace of Jesus Christ and in the power of His Might!

1 Corinthians 16:13: "Watch ye, stand fast in the faith, quit you like men, be strong."

2 Timothy 2:1: "Thou therefore, my son, be strong in the grace that is in Christ Jesus."

Ephesians 6:10: "Finally, my brethren, be strong in the Lord, and in the power of his might."

AMEN!

What Are You Doing Here?

1 Kings 19:9-18

Rhonda Abbott Blevins, *Associate Pastor*
Tellico Village Community Church
Loudon, Tennessee

O h my! When God asks a question, watch out! To Elijah, God asks a question not once but twice. "What are you doing here, Elijah?" Watch out, Elijah. God isn't done with you yet.

So the story goes something like this. Our hero Elijah is running for his life from the villainous Queen Jezebel. You may remember what happened on Mt. Carmel. Jezebel had led the Israelites in the way of Baal worship. She had killed off many of the Lord's prophets, so Elijah confronted her husband, King Ahab, told him to assemble all the prophets of Baal together for a dual to the end, so to speak, so that the people of Israel would choose once and for all whom they would worship. So King Ahab assembled 450 prophets of Baal together on Mt. Carmel. On two separate altars two bulls would be placed. They would call on their respective gods to set fire to the altar. Whichever God responded, that would be the God Israel would worship. So the prophets of Baal went first. They danced. They prayed. They shouted, "Answer us!" (Nothing). Morning came and went (Nothing), on through the midday (Nothing). Then evening fell (Nothing).

Then it was Elijah's turn, the lone prophet of Yahweh. The bull was laid upon the altar in much the same way. But he added a little twist. He poured twelve large jars of water over the sacrifice just for a little drama. He prayed. The fire of the Lord fell. The people rejected Baal and offered their worship to Yahweh. Then Elijah had the 450 prophets of Baal slaughtered just for good measure. Well, Jezebel didn't take too kindly to her prophets being killed, so she sent a text message to Elijah saying she would have his head on a platter. She was just the kind of woman to keep her promise. So Elijah ran for his life, for forty days and forty nights, until he found a cave at Mt. Horeb. Scared, tired, alone, he spent the night in that cave; and that's where we find him in today's lection, hiding out in a cave.

Do you ever feel like Elijah? Do you ever feel like hiding out in a cave? Every now and then, doesn't it feel like Jezebel's minions are after you, trying to kill you, and you simply want to find a safe place far away from your troubles and hide out? Now Elijah was no coward. Mt. Carmel proved that. He was anything but yellow. But sometimes, like for Elijah, it seems that we fight and we fight and eventually we're all out of fight.

We just want to run away and hide. And if what the poet said is true, there is a time for everything, then certainly there is a time for hiding: when threats are real, when mental and physical health are at stake, when healing is needed. There is a time for hiding and there is a time to come out of hiding. That's when the Lord says, "What are you doing in here?"

Did you notice the pity party Elijah offered as an answer? "Nobody likes me, everybody hates me, and it's all your fault, God." So God showed Elijah a little something– not in the wind, not in the earthquake, not in the fire, not in any of the usual ways God showed up in theophanies. God came in the silence. But Elijah missed it.

God asked again, "What are you doing here?" Elijah, having missed God's self-revelation, repeated his same old whine: "Nobody likes me, everybody hates me, and it's all your fault." All this finger-pointing didn't seem to faze God. God is used to that, you know. Ignoring Elijah's complaint, God simply tells him, "Hey Elijah, move along. I've got a job for you to do. Come out of the cave, Elijah. I'm not done with you yet."

Rhonda Blevins - What Are You Doing Here?

I get this story. This week I got it more than ever before. I've read this story many times. I've even preached it a time or two. But this week I felt like Elijah, wanting nothing more than to hide out in a cave, far, far away from everyone and everything. It was just one of those terrible, horrible, no-good, very bad weeks. Has anyone ever had a week like that, a week where nothing seems to go right? My cat got sick, had to take her to the vet. A bill came due that I wasn't expecting. I burned myself getting something out of the oven. (I know! I was surprised to learn I had one too!) And to top it all off, someone hurt my feelings. Awwwww!

By Thursday, I was ready to crawl off into a cave with a good book and a cup of coffee and have myself a humdinger of a pity-party. And I did for about a day. But then God reminded me, "Hey Blevins, move along. I've got a job for you to do." You see, my name was right there on the preaching lineup. All I wanted to do was feel sorry for myself, but God had a word for the people. "Come out of the cave, Rhonda. I'm not done with you yet." Well, here I am. I guess God isn't done with me yet. And God isn't done with us yet.

You know this story about Elijah is remarkable because it seems that he goes from the highest of the high to the lowest of the low. From brazen, victorious, and strong on Mt. Carmel in one scene to fearful, defeated, and weak on Mt. Horeb. There's quite a striking resemblance to our church right now. Back in December, we opened the doors to this beautiful new sanctuary–the result of tremendous sacrifice of time, talent, and treasure of so many of you. When I think about all that went into this incredible accomplishment, I am simply dumbfounded. You did an absolutely amazing thing. God will be honored here for untold decades. Future generations of Christians will marvel at what you've done together. What an incredible feat!

But I wonder if the elation of December has given way to the doldrums of August. The victory on Mt. Carmel has left us weary and tired. It's tempting to feel as if our work is now done. But God have mercy on us if we built this beautiful sanctuary just so that we'd have a bigger cave to hide in! Can you hear God now? "Hey church! Move along. I've got a job for you to do!" Do you remember my saying, "There's a time for hiding and a time to come out of hiding?" "Come out of the cave, Community Church! I'm not done with you yet."

God's not done with me. God's not done with us. And God's not done with you. I've got a friend who serves as a pastor in metro Atlanta, kind of a rough part of town the way he describes it. A while back, this homeless man stood outside when church let out on Sunday mornings, asking for money. Some folks gave him money, so guess what happened the next week. He was back, asking for more money. This went on for a while, and some folks from the church befriended him. They learned his name was Mike. They invited Mike to church. They made him feel welcomed. They showed him love and friendship. Eventually, Mike was baptized and became a member of that church. My pastor friend was so proud of his people for being the presence of Christ in Mike's life. Not too long after Mike's baptism, my friend was at home with his family in the church parsonage, when a knock came at the door. It was Mike. What do you think was my friend's assumption? He thought Mike was there for a handout. That wasn't the case at all. Instead, Mike handed my friend a plastic bag, filled with coins. Mike was offering his tithe to the church, ten per cent of what he had collected on the street that week. My friend's first instinct was to decline the gift, knowing that Mike needed those coins more than the church needed them. But he quickly thought better and accepted the gift, knowing that it was important to demonstrate the worth, the inherent value, of Mike's gift.

You see, Mike had something important to offer. If Mike, one of the "least of these" has something important to offer, what does that mean for you and for me? There's not a single person here who doesn't have some kind thing to do, some healing word to say, some good to give. But we're kind of like the people in the TV show, "Hoarders." We keep our deeds, our compliments, and our gifts stored away in our caves, as if they'll do us any good in there. "Come out of the cave, my child! I'm not done with you yet."

33

Back to our scripture lesson: Elijah was obedient to the Lord's prompting. He found the young Elisha and invested him with the prophetic office. He spent the rest of his earthly life, some seven or eight years mentoring him and quite literally walking with him in the journey. Those seven or eight years paid off. Elisha served the Lord as a prophet to Israel for roughly sixty years, long after Elijah's whirlwind trip to heaven. Job well done, Elijah! Time well spent! Much better than hanging out with a bunch of bats!

Well, when God asks a question, watch out! When God asked Elijah "What are you doing here?" it quickly led to "Come out of the cave. I'm not done with you yet!" So I close with a time of silence, following all the noise. In this moment of silent reflection, I invite that same question to resonate within you. "What are you doing here?"

Superman vs. Son of Man

Kevin C. Brown, *Lead Pastor*
Bellevue First Congregational UCC
Bellevue, WA 98004

It was 1934 and America was struggling with the detritus of the Great Depression. The revolutionary left believed that capitalism was about to collapse, and fascism was challenging democracy as the government of choice. In the midst of this difficult time, young Jerry Siegel arose after a sleepless night. He ran over to see his friend Joe Shuster, and they worked all day until they had finished writing and illustrating twelve newspaper strips. After many rejections, Detective Comics bought the idea and helped them launch a new comic book. On the pages of Action Comics in April, 1938, Superman made his debut. The Man of Steel quickly became an icon for "truth, justice, and the American way" and, since that time, has been portrayed in newspapers, theater, books, radio, television, and movies. Such status clearly reflects a Modernist American mythos, that of the rugged and independent individual who, despite rocky beginnings and innumerable hardships, overcomes all obstacles; Superman is the quintessential American success story: "a foreigner who comes to America and is more successful here than he could ever be anywhere else" (John Byrne, Time, March 14, 1988). No one really knows about his past or even his present; he must live a double life as Clark Kent/Superman. He is an orphan. He honors Midwestern American values; "I'm just a boy from Kansas," he says in the fiftieth Anniversary issue of Action Comics. But he is a hero to the whole world, reflecting American exceptionalism. He has a past that haunts him (look out for Kryptonite, the remains of his home world), and he is vulnerable (Lana Lang, Lois Lane, Lex Luther, and a host of other LL's) but ultimately he overcomes all obstacles to save the day.

Kevin Brown - Superman vs. Son of Man

This myth of the Superman, while perhaps owing some debt to Nietzsche, is really part and parcel of American culture. Nineteenth century literature emphasized the concept of rugged independence and self-sufficiency, and the mythos grew during the twentieth century with characters such as Superman, Batman, Wonder Woman, the Green Hornet, Captain America, and Spiderman. And, yes, I was a comic book nut as a kid. Just last week I was quoting something from Green Lantern to Lisa; and, as she listened, she assumed the same concerned pastoral look I affect when I am listening to someone while thinking, "Is he nuts?"

Each generation invents its own version of the superhero, but the story line is always the same: a mysterious stranger shows up in town, is distrusted by the ruling powers (malevolent in nature) but befriended by outcasts (the town drunk, the saloon girl/hooker, or the feisty orphan) who are noble at heart but so overwhelmed that they have lost the courage to fight. The Mysterious Stranger does not seek trouble but his own forthrightness brings trouble to him, as he refuses the constant entreaties of the Powers to join and serve them. In the end, the Mysterious Stranger must display courage and stand up for others and the rightness of the cause, regardless of the personal cost. There is a confrontation with the Powers: the Mysterious stranger struggles valiantly and at the last minute, though wounded himself, receives the unexpected help of others and wins the ultimate victory.

So, what has Superman to do with Jesus Christ? I have come to believe that Superman, or at least our desire for Superman style celebrity, has everything to do with the profound religious mis-interpretation of Jesus Christ the Son of Man. In spite of all our intellectual and scientific advances, we humans still bump up against the outer boundary of our own self-sufficiency. Where do we turn when our skills, technology, and intellect no longer serve to answer our questions or solve our problems, when we reach the end of our tether and cry out for Superman, the savior of the damsel in distress, the misguided man, or the innocent child? What do we do when Superman does not show up, when no matter how faithfully we serve

36

or how sincerely we pray, pain does not depart, sadness does not dissolve, and riches do not abound? Does faith disappear only to be replaced by anger and cynicism? We thus return once more to our Advent query, "Who is Jesus Christ for us today?" with an added caveat, Superman or Son of Man?

The human impulse, demonstrated so frequently in fundamental and evangelical religious traditions, answers the Jesus question with no less than the Superman answer. Images abound: Jesus is my personal savior; Jesus heals all my ills; Jesus carries me when I cannot walk. We have allowed a vocal, fear-centered understanding of our Christian faith to reign. We in the progressive church have become the outcasts in the narrative of the Mysterious Stranger. We have been overwhelmed by the sheer volume of the Powers. We have lost our will to fight and, through our silence, we have surrendered to those who would manipulate and misuse the Faith for their own ends.

But wait; there is more to the narrative of the Mysterious Stranger! Remember that in the myth the Mysterious Stranger is not invulnerable (not even Superman is completely invulnerable). In the final battle between good and evil, the Mysterious Stranger is wounded and requires the help of the drunk, the saloon girl, the townsfolk, who, because of the courage and sacrifice of the Mysterious Stranger and because of their relationship with the Mysterious Stranger, arm themselves with whatever little they possess and step in to do battle with the Powers. They do not save themselves, and the Mysterious Stranger does not save them by himself, but together in mutual relationship they achieve salvation. The Mysterious Stranger serves as catalyst for the people to act with courage for others.

Jesus Christ as Son of Man is most definitely not a superman, but a symbol of humanity itself with all its strengths and weaknesses, joys and sorrows. It represents Jesus' claim not of superiority, but of humility. Jesus as Son of Man is not otherworldly, rescuing from on high, but entirely this worldly, providing transformation through his

37

love and sacrifice. Jesus is dressed in the sobriquet Son of Man, not as an eschatological title relating to the end of the world as claimed by those on the far right; but as Son of Man, Jesus declares his full humanity, his relationship, his complete mutuality with, not separation from, human beings in all their frailty.

We must define Jesus not by function but by relationship, the *who* question. *Who* is not just Bonhoeffer's question, but the question in the rock opera Jesus Christ Superstar as well: "Jesus Christ, Jesus Christ, Who are you? What have you sacrificed?" Who is Jesus Christ is an especially important question in light of the Superman versus Son of Man dialectic found in so much right wing Christian rhetoric today. Right wing religion wants to make of Jesus a superman, which is really just another mask for a god who exists at the boundary of our knowledge and ability, whose job is to answer our questions, fill in the gaps of our understanding, and take care of us when we are at the end of our tether. Just as cub reporter Jimmy Olson pushes his signal watch whenever there is a need for Superman, we hit our "Help me Jesus!" button when we don't know what else to do. We make of Jesus a function, not a person, a celebrity to be worshiped instead of a savior to be followed. We sing with Judas: "Jesus Christ, Superstar! We hope that you are what they say you are!"

When we confuse Superman with Son of Man, we continue to answer the *what* question. We come to church seeking the *what*, trying to learn how to be good. So relationship, the *who* is replaced by practice the *what*. We want to know what to believe, what rituals to perform, what to do within the public sphere so that we can be good. But *what* is simply a form of works righteousness, which is to believe that with the right knowledge, the correct *what*, we can imitate Jesus and transform the world through our actions–the Modernist belief. We make gods of ourselves, relying on our own works, whether ritualistic or social, for transformation, thus redeeming the world through our own efforts and once more pushing God to the boundary edge. We humans continue to stand as the central focus, striving to learn what we can do to earn personal salvation, which in itself is based on individualism; thus, *I* remains the central focus. Tell me what I can do so I can be good. This is ethics as an inviolate principle, the Modernist approach rather than ethics as a will-of-God question, which is relational.

Ethics as a principle seeks a single, ultimate answer to a question. For example, if we were to say that lying is always wrong and telling the truth always right, we have established truth-telling as an inviolate ethical principle. By the way, the ninth commandment does not say, "Thou shalt not lie"; it focuses on a particularly pernicious, specific form of lying, that is, bearing false witness.

If then faced by a concrete situation, for example, to reveal the whereabouts of a Jewish person to members of the SS, we have no option but to tell the truth and reveal the hiding place. Is this ethical? No. The ethical response is to exist for those who are oppressed or victims of evil. Ethics is about living in responsibility for and to other human beings. It is not about doing good, thus earning a place in heaven, which is actually one way of avoiding responsibility. If I know the rules and follow them, then I am not responsible; I make someone else responsible. This is far from an ethical life. An ethical life requires accountability; the more we choose to act responsibly, the more we become accountable. Living for others is a manifestation of relating to Christ as the Son of Man, rather than expecting Jesus to serve as a personal Superman. We choose to act responsibly, to come of age, thus, to conform to the reality of Christ the Son of Man, who chose to act responsibly for the world.

It has been said that a reformer tinkers with machinery to make it work as before, and a revolutionary insists that the entire structure must be changed. But only the radical, who is one with his/her roots, can dare to venture into uncharted territory. As Bonhoeffer wrote in *Letters and Papers from Prison*: "Faith alone can dare to doubt–to the death." I do not worship Jesus Christ Superman, but Jesus Christ Son of Man, who comes not to save me from the world, but to show me how to serve for the world.

God's Glory

Leviticus 9:22-23
October 23, 2011

Eloise M. Crenshaw, *Assistant Minister*
Metropolitan Community Church
ICCC Trustee since 2005

God's Glory is the manifestation of God's character, God's ultimate power, transcendence, and moral perfection. He is completely above man and his limitation, yet he reveals himself to us so that we can worship and follow him.

Do you need God's Glory? Do you want God's glory? Receiving God's Glory comes from following his instruction. God's glory came as blessings. Moses said: "The Lord has ordered you to do this, so that he may appear to you in all of his glory." Moses, Aaron, and the people then got to work and completed God's instruction. Soon after, the glory of God appeared. Often we look for God's glorious acts, his blessing, without concern for following God's instructions.

After a complete act of obedience, God displayed his power by consuming Aaron's offering. People fell to the ground in awe; but some wondered, does God really exist because they don't see his activity in the World? God exists through believers, by God working through them to change lives. Are you a life changer through God? How can you effectively motivate people to change and live for God? Are you saying less of me and more of you is what I really need? Are you asking God to show his glory? God, show me your power like you did in Leviticus.

In Psalm 115:1 the psalmist asks that God's name be glorified not ours. We don't deserve praise. The Lord alone deserves all of the praise because of his love and faithfulness. When you pray and God answers the prayer, make sure God is glorified and not yourself. Too often we ask God to glorify his name with ours.

In order to receive God's Glory you must be working on your sins! In Leviticus 9:2, Moses told Aaron find a young bull and a ram that have nothing wrong with them. Offer the bull to the Lord as a sacrifice for sin and the ram as a sacrifice to please him. Are you working on your sins? Aaron was asked to make sacrifices for himself and the people of Israel. Sin makes us unclean so that we cannot approach God any more than a beggar can dine at a King's Table. Our only hope is our faith, but sin makes you angry.

Do you want the spirit of the Lord?

We can only worship God in spirit and in truth. God's Glory will be manifested through his son Jesus Christ. In Luke 24:25 Jesus' suffering was the path to glory. The path begins in Genesis with Christ as the promised seed. In Isaiah's suffering servant, in Zechariah's pierced one, in Malachi's messenger of the covenant, Christ is the thread woven through all the scripture, the central theme that binds them together. Read Genesis 3:12, Psalms 26:69-110, Isaiah 53, Jeremiah 31, Zechariah 9, and Malachi 3.

God is glorified. God's glory is the revelation of his character and presence. The lives of Jesus' disciples reveal his character, and he is present to the world through them. Can the world see Christ in you? 1 Corinthian 10:31 advises, "Whether therefore ye eat, or drink, or what so ever ye do, do all to the Glory of God!"

According to II Corinthian 3:18, the more closely we follow him, the more we will be like him. I Peter 4:11 declares, "if any man speak, let him speak as the oracles of God; if any man minister, let him do it as of the ability which God giveth, that God in all things may be glorified through Jesus Christ to whom be praise and dominance for ever and ever Amen."

How is God glorified when we use our abilities? When we use our talents for God, people will see Jesus in us and praise God not for us, but for the help they received. Peter thought of words Christ said in Matthew 5:16: "Let your light shine before me that they may see your good works and glorify your father which is in heaven."

To God be the Glory for the things he has done!

Try Again!

John 21:1-13
A New Year's sermon

George Davis, *Volunteer Chaplain*
Georgia Fulton County Prison,
former pastor of St Paul in New York

As we enter upon this New Year, there will be a recalling of "the good, the bad and the ugly" (to borrow from Clint Eastwood) in the various endeavors of life. Not unusually, many of us will pause long enough to recall some of the occurrences in our own personal lives as well. Candor will compel us to admit to ourselves, even if we are too leery about making such admissions to others, that in some important sectors of our lives we have left undone things we hoped to have done and have done some things we shouldn't have done. Perhaps that improvement in our relationship with a family member or friend, which we promised, has not worked out as we had hoped; that better job for which we pushed went to someone else; that annoying habit that we vowed to overcome has proven to be more baffling than we expected.

Worst of all, some of us may have had to endure the loss of someone dear to us, a relative or friend or a mentor on whom we depended. Some favorite friends may have disappointed us or may have even passed on to the larger life. We know that the disciples felt such a disappointment and loss in what had happened to their dear friend and mentor Jesus. The feelings were expressed poignantly by the two disciples along the road to the village of Emmaus, on Resurrection Sunday afternoon. "Haven't you heard," they asked their accompanying stranger, "how on Friday our chief priests and rulers condemned Jesus to death and crucified him; when we trusted that it was he who would have redeemed his nation Israel."

43

George Davis - Try Again!

Pondering deeply for some comfort in coping with this tragic experience, Simon Peter said to six of his fellow disciples, "I'm going fishing, something I know how to do." Since they had no better suggestion, they chimed in, "We'll go with you." So immediately the six went off with Peter to a night on the lake where they fished all night "and caught nothing."

Parenthetically, great success seems seldom achieved by a retreat to old ways that have already proven unsatisfying. Remember, they had left fishing as a vocation to follow Jesus three years before.

Whatever may have been the level of their skills as fishermen, the Gospel reports, "they fished all night, but caught nothing"–nothing but failure here!

1. "Try again," Jesus said to them with a new approach, "Cast your nets on the right side of the boat."

This was a challenge to their faith. Knowing the disappointed and sad state of mind of these disciples, Jesus had come to visit with them to challenge them. First, he asked if they had had any success in all their efforts of the night before, "you have no fish, have you?" They must have cast weary eyes to each other in momentary bafflement about whether they should admit their long night of failure to this stranger. Yet, he appeared to be truly concerned and caring; so they answered, all for one and one for all, "No."

Here the Gospel says, almost as a side comment but a comment crucial to the drama of the story, "the disciples did not know that this apparent stranger was Jesus." But, it seems they trusted what he told them, sensing that it could somehow become a touchstone for them for the rest of their lives. He seemed so believable, so positively reassuring that they strangely found themselves trusting him.

I like the hymn that witnesses, "'Tis so sweet to trust in Jesus,/ Just to take him at his word;/ Just to rest upon his promise,/ Just to know 'Thus saith the Lord.'" Then the hymn writer gives me a chance to proclaim my own testimony: "I'm so glad I learned to trust him,/ Precious Jesus, Savior, Friend;/ And I know that he is with me,/ Will be with me to the end."

2. "Try again," Jesus says," you'll be successful."

He knew, but left unsaid until they experienced it, that they would have a chance to share their success with others. Following Jesus' new instruction "to let down their nets on the right side of the boat" and believing it just might work, their success proved to be overwhelming. Indeed, "they were unable to draw in all the multitude of fish" in their nets. *If you stay in touch with God in daily prayer, "the right side" of living will be revealed to you.*

The sensitive young disciple John first felt that there was some new dynamic force at work among them in the morning's fishing situation. After all, they must have fished over most of this section of the lake throughout the night before. So John said to Simon Peter, "I recognize the man who spoke with us. He is none other than our master, Jesus himself."

Simon Peter was often a loudmouth and sometimes a rebel, but one thing he was not; he was no dummy. Upon hearing what John said and sensing that he was correct, Peter jumped into the lake, wasting no time in getting to Jesus on the shore. He was so excited that he could not wait for the boats to dock or for all the others to get to the shore. Having experienced all that had happened to them, turning their night of failure into such an unbelievable morning of success, "nobody needed to ask who Jesus was, *knowing that it was the Lord.*"

Once again the same Lord Jesus calls us together in worship to have us understand anew that our loses and our nights of fruitless toil need never become the dominate theme of our lives. For the miracle of that morning was not attributable to some magic in the lake upon which they had fished so unsuccessfully all the night before. The miracle was in the divine presence and power of Jesus in coming to them when they sorely needed his presence to comfort them and to intervene in their failing situation.

Similarly the miracles we need will not come because of some magic in our circumstances or in our environs. They will occur when Jesus Christ comes into our situation if we dare believe in him and follow his lead.

With their new success and enthusiasm these disciples needed the help and fellowship of fellow fishermen from other boats in order to haul in all the multitude of fish in their nets. So they called to fellow fishermen not only to help but undoubtedly to share in the joy of their success.

3. "Try again," said Jesus. "Experience the miracle of your successes and celebrate."

What a marvelous Savior we have in Jesus! How wonderful he is in understanding our failures, in challenging us to new directions, in inspiring us to the faith by which we can follow through. Not only do these blessings come from Jesus, he gives us reasons to reach out to those about us, inviting them to share in all that he is for us.

These disciples were to return to their fishing labors on the same lake where they had fished unsuccessfully all the night before. We too will continue residing in the same places, working on the same jobs, dealing with the same people. But when Jesus comes into our lives by his spirit and if we follow his teaching, our results can change right where we are. The "right side" might sound like only a metaphor, but our faith and follow-through will make it real in our lives.

In our church several weeks ago the suggested Bible readings for the week included chapters eight and nine of Matthew's Gospel. Reading through these chapters, I was awed by how often Jesus asked with people in need of healing of body or mind if they believed him to be able to heal their infirmity. When they affirmed their faith in his ability and will, they were healed. That Jesus' spirit is with us and that we trust implicitly in his capacity to make a difference with us makes all the difference in our circumstances.

When all the fish had been dragged in, Jesus was there on the beach with a fire of coals ready for a cookout to share a meal and to celebrate their effort and success. "Come on, let's eat," he called out to them. No wonder I like a good cookout so much!

Perhaps someone here may have been a little tardy in recognizing the presence and power of God. That's the reason Christ seeks to reveal himself to you anew, so that you'll be able to know without a doubt "it is the Lord." That's why we pause to invite you to join us in our celebration of worship this day.

It is no secret what God can do,
What he's done for others, he'll do for you.
With arms wide open, he'll pardon you.
It is no secret what God can do.
AMEN.

The Banquet

Luke 14:15-24
November 20, 2011,
At Chapel in the Pines, Read Feather Lakes, Colorado

Clement De Wall, *Ordained Roman Catholic priest,*
Member of ICCC, available for services on request.

T he Scripture reading for today, the parable of the banquet from Luke, is one that at first glance seems self-explanatory. But there are several reasons why we may fail to understand the parable of the banquet.

One is that the message of Jesus is so remarkable, and so different from our human way of thinking, that we just cannot believe it. We fail to take him at his word.

Another is that we are so far removed from the time and culture in which Jesus lived. The customs of the Middle East had much different social norms than we have today, and we have to see life as the people saw it then, rather than try to interpret things according to our modern way of thinking.

A third reason is that we cannot be sure of the *original* setting of the parable. The evangelists were diligent in trying to preserve the words of Jesus, but they seem to have felt free to modify the settings in which Jesus spoke. For example, Matthew, in the Sermon on the Mount has Jesus preaching from a mountain, while Luke has Jesus teaching in the same words *on the plain*. In the case of this parable, Luke makes it part of a discussion between Jesus and a Pharisee. However, Jesus spent much more of his time teaching the common people than he spent in the homes of Pharisees. If Jesus had not attracted huge crowds of people, thousands even, then it is not likely that the Pharisees would have invited him in to hear what he had to say. It is also likely that Jesus used this parable on more than one occasion. And so, in order for you to feel the full impact of the parable of the banquet, I am going to risk changing the setting and place it in the countryside or in a small village in Judea; and I will begin by asking you to imagine that you are one of the Jewish peasant laborers or farmers about to hear Jesus for the first time.

Picture yourself, then, as a Jewish peasant. You would be living in a small town or nearby, and you had heard that Jesus was on his way. There was no dressing up, since you only had the work clothes you were wearing. Like most people throughout the Roman Empire, you are living on the edge. If crops are good, you will probably have a decent year. If not, your meals will be meager if not fewer. Pray that you do not get something as minor as a toothache, which could turn into an infection or abscess and which could take your life within weeks.

Not every year produces good crops. To your Roman masters it makes no difference. Rome will collect its ten percent or so whether or not you are left with enough to feed your family.

In the Roman Empire the death rate was high, especially among children, and life expectancy was low. You had lived a full life if you reached the age of forty or forty-five. Thirty per cent of children died by the age of six.

If you were a woman, life was especially harsh. Women were considered incomplete human beings and were not believed competent to testify in a trial. Death in childbirth was common. And to keep the population of the Roman Empire at a steady forty or forty-five million or so, the average woman had to bear at least five children. And if you were one of those average women with five children, three of them would never live to the age of sixteen.

Clement De Wall - The Banquet

So imagine that you are a Jewish peasant. The news has circulated that Jesus is coming, so you have gathered on a hillside or at the edge of the village. Jesus begins to speak. And the first thing you hear is something about a banquet.

A banquet? Yes, a banquet, a big, fancy meal. But remember, you are a peasant. What did you have to eat that day? Well, you would not have had breakfast. You would have had nothing to eat until midday. Then you would have had mostly some bread, made probably from millet, barley or wheat, and some wine. But your wine would be watered down to about three-fourths wine and one-fourth water.

In the evening you might have some vegetables, usually onions, maybe a vegetable or fruit that was in season, and if you lived near a lake or river, maybe some fish. But again, most of your meal would consist of bread. At least half your calories each day would come from bread. So if you ever prayed, "Give us this day our daily bread," you were praying for life itself.

As a Jewish peasant, you would certainly know what a banquet was, but you would never have been to one. Unlike today, when we look forward to big meals on Thanksgiving, Christmas, New Year's and on and on throughout the year, as a Jewish peasant your food would always be mostly bread and watered-down wine; and you knew it always would be. Your chances of ever going to a banquet were nil. You have better odds today of having lunch with the queen of England.

Jesus then describes those who get invited to the banquet. The first is a man who is on his way to see some land he has just purchased. To understand what is going on here, we have to put ourselves into the culture of the first century. At that time the upper class did not determine their wealth by how much money they had but by how much land they owned. The more land you had, the higher up on the social ladder you were. So what we have to realize about this first man is not that he bought land without seeing it. It made no difference where the property was located or what it looked like. For him, the only thing that mattered was that he had more property. And the more he had, the higher he could rank himself on the social ladder.

The second example in the story is a man who has purchased five yoke of oxen and is on his way to test them. As a peasant, you may not own your own oxen; but you would almost certainly have plowed the ground behind them. You would know that oxen have to be well matched so that the team pulls neither to the right nor to the left but always straight ahead. It would have been the height of stupidity to buy one team of oxen without ever testing them. But in this case it's five teams, which only a very rich landowner could afford. This man was extremely wealthy and either very stupid or very insulting to his host. Or perhaps he did not care how the oxen reacted because he wasn't the one who would be walking behind them anyway.

The third man is the one who says he has just gotten married. And here we really have to become familiar with the culture of Middle-Easterners in the first century. At that time, in any small town, everyone knew everyone else. Whenever there was going to be a celebration of any kind, it was always announced to everyone sometime in advance. Everyone knew about it, and no one, not even the very wealthy, would try to compete with it or pre-empt it. So in this parable it simply would not have happened that someone in the community would put on a banquet near the time when someone was getting married. Besides that, there was no such thing as a private or secret marriage. As you hear the parable, you would have known instantly that the man claiming he was just married was just using evasive language, really saying he preferred not to come because he had a live-in partner in the back room. In this case, his response would have been recognized as a veiled insult.

We now come to the main point of the parable. Up to this point, everything in the parable has just been window dressing. All the details in the story, the irrational excuses and insulting behavior of those invited, have been extreme, so that the reaction of the host will seem plausible and reasonable.

Keep imagining that you are a Jewish peasant listening to Jesus. He is telling you that the host of the banquet is so angry that he now issues a general invitation to anyone and everyone, telling his messengers to *force* them to come in. This is the whole point of the story. So what is this about: *force* them to come in?

The one putting on the banquet belongs to the wealthy two per cent of the population. There is no middle class; you belong to the other nine-eight per cent. In first century Palestine and elsewhere throughout the Roman Empire the wealthy two per cent never socialized with the underclass ninety-eight per cent.

You are a Jewish peasant. If any rich person in your village were putting on a big dinner and if he sent out messengers to tell *you* that you were invited, you would have only one reaction: this must be a mistake. The invitation could not possibly be for you. It is against all the social and cultural norms of the time for you to mix with the rich in the same social circles. You would not fit in. You would not know how to act. You had only the clothes you were wearing, and these would not be suitable for an upper class dinner. In the culture of the Middle East at this time, it was against all the rules and customs for the poor to be present in the homes of the wealthy. You knew there had to be a mistake, and the only way to convince you that you were really welcome would be to *force* you, to drag you kicking and screaming into the rich man's home.

And so the parable is not about people offering silly or insulting excuses, nor is it about people being rejected from the banquet. It is really about *you,* and about how you see yourself. It is to persuade you that in God's eyes you *do* deserve to come to the banquet. You don't have to be like anyone else. You deserve to come just as you are.

Like the Jewish peasants, you may be tempted to think, "But I won't belong." Remember, you call God your Father. That makes you a child, a daughter or a son, of God. You certainly do belong. You are already one of the family.

Like the Jewish peasants, you might say, "But I won't fit in." But if you are God's daughter or son, then so is everyone else. Of course you will fit in. All present will be your brothers and sisters.

And then there is the fear that, I am not worthy because of my past sins and offenses. If this is your concern, then remember the prayer, "Forgive us our debts [our trespasses] as we forgive our debtors." Take Jesus at his word. If you forgive, you are already forgiven. It may not be easy, but it is simple. So, whatever you have done, if you forgive, you are forgiven. Of course you are worthy.

The lesson of the parable is simple. *You are already worthy. You already fit in. You already belong.* You don't have to be like anybody else. God sees you and loves you and accepts you as you are right now. God does not see or judge according to human standards and neither should you.

Daring Hope

Isaiah 40:21-31, Hebrews 11:32-12:2
January 22, 2012

Carolyn Cook Dipboye, *Pastor*
Grace Covenant Church
Oak Ridge, Tennessee
Editor of Inclusive Pulpit

In his sermon "People Who Fly," Otis Moss III, pastor of Chicago's Trinity United Church of Christ, shares a story that apparently originated in West Africa and was passed down by word of mouth among the slaves in South Carolina's low country. As the story goes, a band of slaves was picking cotton one day under the blazing, hot sun. As was often the case, a young woman in the field tended her small son as she worked. Suddenly, overwhelmed by the heat, she fell unconscious to the ground. Fearful that if the slave drivers saw her, she would be severely punished, the little boy struggled unsuccessfully to awaken his mother and get her back on her feet. An old man called "Preacher" or "Prophet" by the slaves and "Old Devil" by the slave drivers, viewed the situation and came over to them. He leaned over the woman, whispering into her ear: "Cooleebah! Cooleebah!" The young woman immediately arose and taking her young son by the hand, began to fly. The slave drivers observed in astonishment what was happening and did not know what to do. Taking advantage of their confusion, the old man rushed around to all the other Africans and began to shout, "Cooleebah! Cooleebah!" They, too, took flight. Fearing for their lives at the hands of an angry slave owner, the slave drivers tore into the old man. "Bring them back!" they demanded. "Bring them back!" "I cannot bring them back," the old man replied. "The word is already in them and since the word is already in them, it cannot be taken from them" (*30 Good Minutes*, Chicago Sunday Evening Club, 2006).

What difference, Moss asks, does the church's message of hope make in the lives of people today? Does the word we preach give the broken and discouraged, the dispirited and disinherited of our day the power to rise up and take flight?

We are called to give voice to the spirit of hope. Rewind now two and a half centuries. Rewind to a moment in time when another people languished in a foreign land. Ripped up from their roots, they were in need of a word of hope; but they were suspicious of any such word directed their way. "By the rivers of Babylon," the psalmist recalls, "we sat down and wept. Our captors asked us for songs, and our tormentors asked for mirth, saying, 'Sing us one of the songs of Zion!' How could we sing the Lord's song in a foreign land?" (Psalm 137).

The prophet Isaiah comes alongside this desolate people with a message of comfort and strength. He identifies their despair: "Why do you say," he asks, "'my way is hidden from the LORD, and my right is disregarded by my God'?" "Think back," he urges them, "to the word that has been told to you from the beginning, from the very foundations of the earth. Think back to who God is and take courage!"

Had they forgotten? Or had they come to the point where they were no longer convinced that God could be trusted? Who was this God who had made such promises? Who was this God who let them fall into the hands of the Babylonian people and their gods? Perhaps this Yahweh, this God of their ancestors, was not up to the challenge. Perhaps this God was inferior.

"Look at the stars," Isaiah bids them–an interesting move in light of the fact that the stars represented Babylon's host of deities. "Look to the stars," he says, "and do not be shy. Look to the stars and remember who created them. Remember who calls them into place every night. Remember who knows their names and has power over them."

"So you are discouraged?" Isaiah asks. "You feel God has forgotten about you and is unaware of your suffering? Remember! Remember the word that has kept God's people from the beginning: The LORD is the everlasting God, the Creator of the ends of the earth. He does not faint or grow weary; his understanding is unsearchable. The LORD gives power to the faint, and strengthens the powerless. Even youths will faint and be weary, and the young will fall exhausted; but those who wait for the LORD shall renew their strength, they shall mount up with wings like eagles, they shall run and not be weary, they shall walk and not faint."

To be honest, it is more than possible that the psalmist's heartbreak alongside the waters of Babylon was not Isaiah's greatest challenge. Perhaps complacency had taken the place of despair; or more exactly, perhaps complacency was the most obvious manifestation of the people's despair. Having been fed from the day of their birth the milk of their parents' longing to return home, perhaps the emerging generation had given up hope. Perhaps the younger generation that had never even seen the homeland had grown weary of the pain, tears and longing that had so dominated their parents' lives. Perhaps they had decided to settle in where they were. Captivity, after all, isn't such a bad thing, is it? You can adjust to it. You can make a new home and tuck the old ways, the old hopes, the old God safely away on a shelf somewhere, can't you?

Prophets, in case you haven't noticed, often go against the current. As a matter of fact, you might say that being a prophet, being prophetic, is just that. It is about calling people's attention to the way things are and reminding them of the way things were meant to be. It is about having the courage to face the darkness others deny is there and becoming convinced, as Walter Brueggemann puts it, that "something is 'on the move' in that darkness". It is about being encountered by a God of surprising freedom and finding ourselves possessed of an energy that takes us beyond weary resignation to daring hope. It is about imagining and living toward a different kind of future where the "hopes and yearnings that have been denied so

56

long and expressed so deeply that we no longer know they are there" become the engine that drives our lives (Brueggemann, *Prophetic Imagination,* 23, 67).

We are called to embody hope by building a community of hope. Lest we confuse the hope to which we are called with bland, harmless optimism, we should remember the course traveled by the prophet whose courage we have celebrated this week. Martin Luther King could not turn his eyes from the plight of his people caught in the terrible grip of racism, but still he dared to imagine and live toward a different kind of future. This prophet, remembered for his "I Have a Dream" speech, delivered his speech only after immersing himself in the hard struggle to confront the injustices under which his people labored. He had confronted the Bull Connors of things as they were before ascending the steps of the Lincoln Memorial. He would go from there to comfort the mothers of the children massacred in the bombing of Fourth Avenue Baptist Church, and he would walk the perilous path of Bloody Sunday. He would go through the dark night of the soul as he sat at his kitchen table contemplating death threats against him and his family, and he would see the inside of numerous jail cells. Yet his dream of a beloved community where all of God's children would be free would continue to live. It was a dream and it continues to be a dream; but it is God's dream. It is what community lived in light of God's Kingdom looks like. As with the Israelites long ago, it is a dream we cannot afford to abandon in discouragement.

If we sometimes feel overwhelmed at the task before us, if we feel tempted to give in to those inner and outer voices that counsel us to simply close ourselves off from the pain that is out there and focus on our own well-being, we should hear the counsel of Isaiah: "Those who wait on the Lord," those who give themselves to God's mission of peace and justice, those who throw themselves into the hard struggle, "shall renew their strength." If we feel overwhelmed with the mountain of despair that rises before us, if we feel somehow God has forgotten us and all is lost, we should remember with the writer of Hebrews the countless faithful who have gone before us. We should remember those "who through faith conquered kingdoms, administered justice, obtained promises, shut the mouths of lions, quenched raging fire, escaped the edge of the sword, won strength out of weakness." We should be reminded of those for whom faithfulness meant enduring "mocking and flogging, and even chains and imprisonment. They were stoned to death, they were sawn in two [by tradition, Isaiah], they were killed by the sword; they went about in skins of sheep and goats, destitute, persecuted, tormented--of whom the world was not worthy" (11:32-38).

So, if you feel overwhelmed by the distance still to be covered in resolving the inequities of racism, if you feel overwhelmed at the terrible scourge of hunger in our community, nation and world, if you long for the day when justice and peace will flow down like a mighty stream, if you long for a more hopeful day, a more beloved community in which all of God's children are cherished simply because they are God's children, then join the struggle of today and yesterday and every day. Don't expect the results of your efforts to be instantaneous but know that you are joining a long line of God's faithful and take heart. God is with us in the struggle, for the dream is God's dream. Where else could we be but here? Where else could we place our hope but here? And what more do we need than the assurance that God goes before us and with us and God is for us?

Thanks be to God!

Portrait of a Demagogue

Acts 12:1-23
August 21, 2011

Larry Dipboye, *Pastor*
Grace Covenant Church
Oak Ridge, Tennessee
Editor of Inclusive Pulpit

From Greek origin, the word *demagogue* simply means a leader of the people; but even in ancient Greece it was a pejorative term applied to leaders who play on popular ignorance and prejudice to enhance their power. A demagogue then as now was primarily a politician. The only difference between a politician and a demagogue was how far one would go to gain power and sustain control.

I recall a conversation the week after President Kennedy's assassination. I was a seminary student in Fort Worth, Texas, working for the TCU Library. A university history professor was involved in our casual conversation about the future of our nation. I expressed my reservation about the leadership of Lyndon Johnson. When pressed to state my misgivings, I said, "he is such a - a - a politician!" The history professor spoke up in defense of the new president, "Who else would you want to be a political leader but a politician?"

I knew and I think that the professor knew where I was coming from. Johnson had a reputation in Texas for walking on the political shady side. Had I been a bit more sophisticated, I might have accused Johnson of being a demagogue; but I really was expressing the common wisdom that all politicians are shady and will do or say anything to enhance their power. I think that my scholarly mentor was expressing a genuine concern that we not paint all politicians with the same broad brush.

Consider the distinctive character of a demagogue. Adolf Hitler is the prime historical example. He rose to power out of the ashes of World War I, blaming Jews and the non-Aryan world for the economic plight of Germany. He provided the rationale and rhetoric for a doctrine of German Aryan superiority. He convinced Germans that they were destined for world domination. He played to ethnic prejudice and a sense of national persecution that marched the German nation into the most geographically extensive war in history. He even drew the established Church into his political structure, and some German theologians stooped to provide religious justification for Nazi policies against the Jews. The Jews became scapegoats for all German problems. Germans were poor because Jews were rich. Although the Jewish Holocaust was mostly concealed from the public eye, the ground was prepared by feeding the hatred and bigotry that seems always to be present among a people. Guards and soldiers in the Jewish concentration camps were justified in dehumanizing, torturing, and killing Jews by the well-honed political doctrines of the Nazi government; and Hitler became for all time the personification of a *demagogue*.

Enter Herod, also known as Agrippa. Luke digresses to view the larger world into which the church was moving with the Christian gospel. Throughout Acts, Christians seem to spend a lot of time incarcerated, first in Jewish jails and later in Roman prisons. In his story of the birth and expansion of the early church in Acts, Luke identifies three major obstacles to the progressive movement of the gospel into the world–Jewish leaders, defective Christians, and Roman authorities.

From the beginning, religious opposition came from the Jewish establishment. Although Luke repeatedly accuses "the Jews" of persecuting the church, his focus is not on the Jewish religion or the Jewish people, which includes the followers of Jesus. Hostility toward the church came from the Jewish leadership attempting to protect their turf from a new Jewish sect. The story of Paul begins with his vigilance in persecution of Christians. He did not abandon his Jewish roots to become a Christian. Like Luke, Paul became convinced that Christ was the fulfillment of Jewish prophesy and that Christians were the true people of God.

A confessional note emerges in the exposure of defective Christians. The prime example is in Acts five, the story of Ananias and Sapphira who cheated in their sharing of wealth with the church and then covered their dishonesty with lies. Luke offers no brief for Christian insiders. In fact, corruption from within the church seems to hold more of a threat to the progressive movement of the gospel into the world than the opposition of sworn enemies.

The final and perhaps the greatest obstacle to the church came from Roman rule. To some extent, this was secular opposition with a political concern on the part of Rome to maintain popular control; but Rome did not distinguish religious from political concerns and did not allow totally independent status for any religion. All religion had to serve the purposes and needs of the Empire and the Emperor. Any religion that attempted to stand alone or apart from Roman authority was a threat to political control and had to be put down.

Divine justice determines the fate of a demagogue. Herod thus appears as a shrewd politician playing Jews against Christians in order to enhance his own authority. He comes from a long line of Roman puppet rulers of the Jews. Herod the Great, responsible for the new temple in Jerusalem and identified by Matthew with the slaughter of the innocents at the birth of Jesus, was the father of Herod Antipas, who ordered the execution of John the Baptist, and the grandfather of Herod Agrippa, who killed the Apostle James and ordered the imprisonment and execution of the Apostle Peter. A friend of the Emperor Caligula, Herod Agrippa maneuvered through the family pecking order and the Roman political system to become King of the

Jews in control of the largest Jewish territory since the time of his grandfather.

Luke cites a political motive for the arrest of Peter. The demagogue had gained political points by the execution of James, so he decided to play the hate-Christians game a little further by making a public example of Peter during Passover. But Peter is walked out of prison by an angel of God leaving the Roman guards to pay the penalty of death that had been given to Peter. After Peter's rescue and safe passage, Luke returns to tell the rest of Herod's story. This is one of the few places in the New Testament where corroborating documentation exists from another source.

Josephus left a detailed account of Herod's climb to the top which concluded with deposing his uncle Antipas and being granted his grandfather's title and territory by his friend Caligula. According to Josephus, Herod received a warning of his death by an owl and died five days later of pains in his abdomen and chest. Some speculate that he may have died of the same ailment of his grandfather, an intestinal gangrenous infection. So Luke's account of Herod's being eaten by worms seems to be an elaboration of public information; however, Luke tells the death of Herod as the judgment of God on one who would usurp the authority of God in the political arena. According to Luke, Herod the demagogue died because he allowed himself to be praised as a god by the people of Tyre and Sidon.

William Willimon offers a tongue in cheek interpretation: "God is not nice to those who try to be God. Hitler perishes huddled in a bunker in Berlin. Mussolini is [hanged] upside down. Thus ever to tyrants. Next to this ugly scene of Herod being devoured by worms, Luke laconically remarks, 'But the word of God grew and multiplied'" (*Interpretation, Acts*, p. 114).

The Christian gospel exists in political climates. Like it or not, Christians have always lived in a political world and must always press the demands of the gospel within a political context. Because

Christianity always transcends national loyalties and institutions, Christians have historically had to work with every political system in the human experience. To use H. Richard Niebuhr's categories, sometimes Christ is against the culture or above the culture, but always working to transform the culture.

Grace Covenant support of religious liberty through the separation of church and state is no secret in this congregation, but our view of separation does not justify silence before political powers. Just last week the former Director of our International Council of Community Churches Michael Livingston was arrested in the U.S. Capitol along with several other religious leaders for protesting the dimensions of the debate over the national debt that ignores the plight of the poor. The protest was not aimed at one party, at one president, or one house of Congress. The protest called for consideration of the people who live in poverty in this country. Sometimes that kind of stand puts Christians over and against a politician or a party stance, but the one thing we cannot abide as Christians is silence and passivity before injustice.

As I read Luke's account of the church moving out into the Roman Empire in Acts, I have a sense of "I wish it were so," when I read of the overpowering movement of the Holy Spirit and the miraculous rescues from prison. Historically Christians have more often experienced the suffering and death of James rather than the miraculous rescue of Peter, but even Luke does not assume that God is going to take care of the evil of this world without any involvement from Christians.

To no one's surprise, I like the dimensions of political involvement we describe in our church covenant:
We support a free church in a free state, advocating religious liberty through the separation of church and state and meticulously seeking to avoid using or being used by government authorities.
Yes!

63

Ready or Not,
Here He Comes!

Joshua 24: 1, 14-25: Joshua challenges the Hebrew people to choose to serve only the Lord.

1 Thessalonians 4:13-18: Paul says we should not grieve as those who have no hope, for our hope is in the Lord.

Matthew 25: 1-13: Jesus tells a story about ten bridesmaids, half of whom were ready for the bridegroom's arrival and half of whom were not..

Twenty-first Sunday after Pentecost, November 6, 2011

Paul R. Drake, *Pastor*
The Community Church of Little Neck
President of ICCC.
Sermon received January 31 before his death on April12, 2012
2005 Dr. Charles A. Trentham Homiletics Award

I've always had a fondness for this story, known variously as the Wise and Foolish Maidens (or Virgins), the Ten Bridesmaids, or, my personal favorite, the Delinquent Bridegroom. I like the last one because it sounds like it could be the title for a Perry Mason book—"The Case of the Delinquent Bridegroom." Part of the reason I am so fond of this story is that for once wisdom pays. So often in the New Testament wisdom gets a bad rap. Think about the number of places where Paul reminds the church that not many of them were wise or talks about how God's foolishness is wiser than human wisdom, etc. But here it's the foolish bridesmaids who are left out of the party. Having been at the top of my class in school, I appreciated that the smart kids came out on top, for once.

The real point of the story, of course, has nothing to do with being smart or foolish, but has everything to do with being ready. One of my favorite fictional characters, Spenser the private detective created by the late Robert Parker, often says that in his business, "readiness is all," which is a quotation from *Hamlet*, Act V, Scene II, just before Hamlet and Laertes begin their duel in which both are slain: "If it be now, 'tis not to come; if it be not to come, it will be now; if it be not now, yet it will come: the readiness is all." And in this instance, readiness really *is* all. The five girls who thought ahead and brought extra oil with them go in with the bridegroom to the wedding party; the five who foolishly did not come prepared get back too late and are left outside the banquet hall.

I took this sermon title from my childhood memories of playing hide-and-go-seek with the neighborhood kids. If you were "It," after counting down from 100 or whatever number was agreed beforehand, you were always supposed to shout out loud, "Ready or not, here I come!" That was the final warning to everybody; if they hadn't picked their hiding place, they had better move fast to get out of sight. And this story is a warning, too–a warning to those who are not ready for the coming of the Son of Man (Child of Humanity) as Jesus refers to himself in a number of places in the Gospel.

It seems to me that the church today has two main ways of dealing with the Second Coming, which is the more popular name for the coming of the Son of Man (Child of Humanity) or Jesus' return. One group is obsessed with knowing when it will take place to the point of predicting and re-predicting the date when it will happen, even though Jesus repeatedly warns us that no one knows the day and the hour except God. This is the group that spawned the *Left Behind* saga, going into agonizing detail about what it will be like for those who are not ready when Jesus returns. The other group, among whom we probably mostly count ourselves, tends to be totally unconcerned about the Second Coming to the point of living as though that day and hour will never come and therefore we don't need to be ready for it.

Both of these approaches miss the mark, it seems to me. Since we don't know the time when the Master will return, we must be ready every day. This means living as Jesus calls us to live at all times. If we do that, we don't need to know when he is returning. Whenever he comes, he will find us carrying out his mission here on earth. But if we don't believe he's ever returning or don't believe there will be a final judgment at all, then we have little incentive to live as he calls us to live.

A middle ground is called for here–one where we take Jesus' statements about his return seriously, without becoming obsessive about the details. This fits with the overall approach I recommend to the Bible that I was sharing with one of our new friends in answer to a question last week. We should take the Bible seriously but not literally, which is the subtitle to Marcus Borg's book, *Reading the Bible Again for the First Time*. I suggest that in much the same way we take the references to the Second Coming seriously but not literally.

We should take it seriously in the sense that, if we believe in God or in a Supreme Being of any kind, each of us will ultimately have to answer for the way we have lived our lives and account for the choices we have made. This will be the case whether or not there is an actual day at the end of the world when a Last Judgment takes place exactly as depicted in the Bible. But we should not become so wrapped up in understanding when and how it will all take place to the point that we parse every word and syllable of these stories in an attempt to gain some secret knowledge that will give us an advantage over the rest of the world. If we get too caught up in understanding the words, we won't have the time or energy to actually fulfill our mission as the body of Christ, which is, as Jesus says in the judgment scene itself, to feed the hungry, clothe the naked, welcome the stranger, visit those who are sick and in prison—in short, to care for "the least of these." And if we are doing that, it won't matter when Jesus returns, since whenever it happens, he will find us going about the mission to which he has called us.

I believe that one day, there will be a time when each of us hears the cry, "Ready or not, here he comes!" Speaking just for myself, living with what is probably terminal cancer, barring a miracle of some sort, I am coming to terms with the likelihood that that day will come sooner rather than later for me personally. Some of you are at an age when you may be realizing that same thing, while others are assuming you have plenty of time. But whenever that day comes, I want to be ready for it by living the way Jesus says we should every day, as much as possible. What about you?

Tell Us!

Matthew 22:15-22, *The Message*, translation by Eugene Peterson
October 16, 2011

Harry Foockle, *Pastor*
Antioch Community Church
Kansas City, Missouri
2009 Dr. Charles A. Trentham Homiletics Award

Tell Us! That's what they wanted. That's what we want. Tell Us!

Pastor Richard Fairchild in his Spirit Sermon tells us about a Sunday Magazine that created a "Faith in Life" award. Undoubtedly to increase readership as print media is a difficult "sell" today. They hoped the award would increase readership as well as recognize persons whose faith walk makes a difference in our world.

People were asked to nominate folks they thought best lived out their faith in their daily lives.

A large number of letters were received. Persons were nominated who had been faithful church attenders for years. Some had given large gifts of money to their church and to charities. They came with newspaper clippings telling the stories of their dedication.

The winner was announced. The letter of nomination was written in Crayola. No newspaper stories accompanied the letter. The letter of nomination read,

> Anthony is a plumber. He helped some people fix up a house
> for my friend's family because their house had burned down.
> He also visits my Grandmother in the nursing home and
> makes her happy with his stories and his harmonica playing.

Harry Foockle - Tell Us!

He is a lot like Jesus. I hope he wins. But if he doesn't it
won't matter. He will still be the same good old Anthony.
The letter was signed, "Love Anne."

Now, like I often tell you, put the story about Anthony the
Plumber, not Joe the Plumber, in your "putting" place. In a little while
we will understand why Anthony and today's story about Jesus are
important to each other and to us.

It had been several days since Jesus entered the City of Jerusalem
during Passover. Some folks had shouted him in. They put down palm
branches along the roadway. They shouted that he was coming in the
name of God. Anxious people strained to see this Jesus. When he
came into sight, surely a gasp must have gone up from the gathered
crowd. He was on a donkey with his feet dragging the ground, no
sword or shield, just a dusty garment draping his body. Some had said
he was the Messiah.

Messiah! Where was his horse? What about his sword and shield?
Was there no army with him? King David's seed? Surely not!

Jesus stopped in front of the Temple that day. He went in, and
seeing the money changers at work, he became upset. He told them to
get out of the Temple and take their tables with them. They say he
even turned some over spilling everything on the ground.

Oh no, it wasn't because they were money changers. The Temple
always had money changers. It was because the money changers were
cheating the people. They were over-charging and abusing their
power. Jesus let them know that they had no place in God's Temple.

He and his Disciples left the Temple that evening, went up into
the hills just outside of the city, and camped out overnight.

A couple of days pass. Jesus has been in the city teaching and
trying to get people to understand how they should live. The Pharisees

are upset at Jesus. He draws big crowds and says some outlandish things. If they don't put a stop to it, the Romans may get mad. The result could be the loss of their limited religious freedom and income. They plot a way to trap Jesus. Listen with me to the story from Matthew 22:15-22: "That's when the Pharisees plotted a way to trap him into saying something damaging. They sent their disciples, with a few of Herod's followers mixed in to ask."

Notice the Pharisees themselves did not go. They sent others to do their work. They even talked Herod into sending some of his followers. Herod was still the king, and he did not want someone who claimed to be a king to usurp his authority.

The story continues, "'Teacher, we know you have integrity, teach the way of God accurately, are indifferent to popular opinion, and don't pander to your students. So tell us honestly: Is it right to pay taxes to Caesar or not?' Jesus knew they were up to no good. He said, 'Why are you playing these games with me? Why are you trying to trap me? Do you have a coin? Let me see it.' They handed him a silver piece. 'This engraving, who does it look like, and whose name is on it?'"

Taxes had to be paid. It is no different today. We pay taxes. We know we have to. Do you remember that old saying, "Only two things in life are certain–death and taxes." Taxes are important and necessary. When we leave church this morning we will exit onto Antioch Street. It is there because of our taxes. If you drive too fast on Antioch, you may meet one of our finest dressed in blue driving a black ford sedan with red lights flashing, paid for by our taxes to protect us. A few blocks up the street heading north, lights across the middle of the street may suddenly flash red. Sirens will go off, and a huge truck with hook and ladder will leave the building on the way to a fire and/or accident, paid for by our taxes to save and keep us safe. Oh yes, taxes are important and necessary.

Taxes will have much to do with our next election in the United States. One side will want more taxes while the other will want less. Some will say we need more equity in our taxes. We will go to the polls and vote, and taxes will bear heavily when we mark our ballot.

Taxes were important to the people of Jesus' time. The Hebrews did not like paying taxes because they went to the Roman government leaving them little to live on. The coin that Jesus took and held up was more than just money. It carried the image of Caesar. Romans considered Caesar to be a god. The Commandment said, "Thou shall have no other god's before me." How difficult it must have been for them.

The story ends as he asks them about whose image was on the coin. "They said, 'Caesar.' Jesus replied, 'Then give to Caesar what is his, and give to God what is his.'" The Pharisees were speechless. They went off shaking their heads. Their trap had failed.

Now we are faced with the powerful question. We know we need to pay our taxes. Jesus said, "Give to Caesar what is his and to God what is his." So tell us, what is God's?

Here is what I believe. Everything we have belongs to God. It was God who has provided. I don't believe God wants us to be destitute. In terms of dollars, you might use the tithe for your giving; but the plain fact is that some folks in our economy cannot do that.

What is important for you to consider in your giving? First pray about it; and whatever amount you give, do it first. Don't give to God after your bills are all paid. Give to God first. Give to God out of your abundance not out of your lack. I believe you will be blessed. Here at the church we will soon be voting on our 2012 budget. We shall decide who and what amount of giving we plan for the coming year. Of course, we always keep in mind that the budget is a guideline, which, if necessary, can be changed during the year.

Harry Foockle - Tell Us!

One item we vote on is how much to give to the International Council of Community Churches (ICCC). We are charter members and have been faithful supporters of the ICCC. The question is why? ICCC is a historic and prophetic organization. In 1950 it became the largest merger of African American and white congregations in U.S. history. Think about that–1950!

Today we benefit in so many ways, and not only we but all who are connected with the ICCC. We have become partners with Ruth Applewhite and her work in Haiti. What blessings of giving! Each year we are blessed with a session of the ICCC Annual Conference. It is uplifting and spiritual. Bible studies abound, worship with profound messages of the Kingdom, and the absolute thrill of being a part of a group that rises above ethnic barriers to embrace one another.

As clergy I benefit from the association with other pastors in community churches. Clergy receive continuing education credits by attending Annual Conference. Agencies are present that can help us discover the needs of our communities and offer ways to meet them.

It is as Jesus said in Luke 6:38, "give, and it will be given to you; good measure, pressed down, shaken together, running over, will be put into your lap. For the measure you give will be the measure you get back."

But it's not just money, when we talk about giving to God. Remember Anthony the plumber and how he gave? He used his skill and helped others rebuild their home after a fire. He visited in a nursing home and shared his personality with those who are often forgotten. He gave his all, his everything.

In the name of Jesus, if you sing in the Praise Team give it your all. Be at the practice, study the music and show up to sing. Sing like it is the most important thing you can do in that moment. If you are to serve Holy Communion, come prepared and prayed up. You are sharing the gifts of the Lord Jesus our Christ. Serve like it is the greatest honor in the world.

Do you get the idea? God has gifted you. When you give to God what is his, give with everything you have. Share your gifts, and you will bless others in the name of God, and so shall you be blessed. It's what makes a Christian life.

"What if I give all?" is the title of a Ray Boltz song that sends us out to gift the world.

"Long ago a Father and a Son, saw the children lost in sin.
Can you see the tears in Father's eyes, as Jesus says to Him,
What if I give all I have, what will that gift do?
My Son, that gift will change the world, it will free the multitudes
We cannot close our eyes, and turn away,
when we hear His Spirit call,
We see the need, now let Him hear us say,
WHAT IF I GIVE ALL."

Thank you Anthony for telling us. Thank you Ray Boltz for telling us. Thank you Jesus for telling us.

Amen.

Lessons Learned in the Emerald Isle

Matthew 25:31-45

Herbert F. Freitag, *Pastor*
Chapel by the Sea, Clearwater Beach, Florida
1999, Dr. Charles A. Trentham Homiletics Award

In June, Lorraine and I went to Ireland for three weeks. This incredible country is about the size of Pennsylvania. It is green, rocky, mountainous; it is gorgeous. And the people are, as a whole, the friendliest I have ever met. Most of Ireland is rural, and you don't have to go very far beyond city limits to compete with cows and sheep and horses on the extremely narrow roads. Even the largest cities, with the possible exception of Dublin, are not nearly the size of Tampa. It rains with some frequency there, hence the reason for the "Emerald Isle" nickname; and the temperature is quite a bit cooler than here in Florida. The highs most of the days we were in Ireland rarely hit the sixties. Practically every town has its own ruined castle or abbey or monastery and golf course, pubs abound, the music is great, the food is wonderful, and chips (french fries) are served with just about everything including lasagna. Irish breakfasts are hearty with a complete disregard for cholesterol, evidenced by the fact that they consist of eggs, bacon, sausage, tomato (at least that's healthy), bread (wonderfully coarse and served with real butter), and something called "black pudding" the ingredients of which I did not want to pursue. Unfortunately we never saw any leprechauns; hence, the only "pot of gold" consisted of what we left, not what we found. But fortunately, we also did not see any banshees, the specters which are reputed to arrive when someone dies. And that at times seemed all too possible as we drove a stick-shift car on the left side of the road with the steering wheel on the right side of the auto. By the way, the pedals were also so close together that my big feet often hit the brake and the gas at the same time, so I was lucky the other foot was on the clutch and the car was thus in neutral.

It is said that travel is educational. I believe this to be true, from numerous perspectives. What one learns depends largely upon where one is doing that learning and how receptive one is to the lessons being offered. A great deal of what is to be learned in Ireland comes through that nation's history, an often glorious history with frequent bouts of cruel oppression and great poverty. Over and over as I reflected on what has happened throughout the centuries in and to Ireland and its people, I considered how the human actions and attitudes which produced such pain and suffering are, in reality, pretty universal; and I couldn't help but recall the biblical passages which I selected as this morning's scripture lesson.

Now, before I get into the "meat" of this sermon, let me make an observation regarding conditions which impacted on and greatly exacerbated Ireland's historical woes. Through most of that history, Ireland consisted of a collection of clans which were constantly fighting each other for power, for land, for cattle and sheep and horses and slaves, and for wealth in whatever form it took. The nation is "awash" in ruined tower castles and ring forts which were constructed to keep in what one clan possessed and to keep out those clans which wished to take it. It was Irish family against Irish family, and sometimes they hired or invited foreign armies to help them win their battles against their neighbors. Sometimes an outside conqueror got a foothold by invitation and then used it to advance the outside agenda.

This was certainly true regarding the arrival of the Vikings, the Northmen, the Normans, and others, although in most cases they simply invaded in small or large numbers and did what they did, pillage, kill, rob, enslave, and take whatever territory they were subsequently strong enough to keep. The Irish clans were too busy hating and fighting each other to unite in the common cause of repelling foreign invaders. One, Brian Boru, tried and almost succeeded in the eleventh century; but he died just before he could accomplish his goal of unification. I liken the situation to what occurred on the American continent as the white man defeated Indian tribe after Indian tribe. The tribes, like the Irish clans, were too busy fighting each other to present a unified front against their common enemy. So the human failings of the Irish themselves contributed to their frequent defeat and subsequent subjugation. This helps to explain but not excuse what they consequently endured.

One of Ireland's primary tourist attractions is Bunratty Castle not far from Limerick. It is a wonderfully restored fortress where, after climbing narrow spiral staircases and marveling at "great halls," visitors can attend a medieval banquet so that through period food and entertainment, they can imaginatively go back many centuries and get a taste of what life was like, at least for the nobility in a bygone time. On the grounds of Bunratty Castle is a folk park which recreates a fairly typical Irish village of the 1880's, kind of like a small Williamsburg. And in the Bunratty schoolhouse is stationed an elderly man playing the part of the schoolmaster. After regaling us with information of what it was like then for boys and girls, most of them poor, trying to get an education, he began to share some of his own story.

This man, probably in his late sixties, came from a family of nine children; and they did not have much just like the majority of their neighbors. He gave us an idea of what it was like for him and his siblings to grow up in poverty; but, similar to the revelations of American comedian Sam Levinson, he said that they were not unhappy because they did not know anything else. What really got to us, though, was when he talked about the wonder of Christmas as seen through his childhood eyes.

During the summer in Ireland, it is light from about 5:30 A.M. until about 10:30 P.M. But in the winter it is dark by 4:30. What he remembers about the Christmases he experienced then are not the presents he received, because he really didn't receive any presents. If the kids in his family got a candy bar for Christmas, it was a big deal and an exception. No, what he remembers, and what was so special were the lights, the lights from the candles which every woman in every home put in all the windows only at Christmastime to light the neighborhood and dispel the darkness. As he talked, we could see that he was doing more than remembering; he was experiencing again what he had experienced as a child; he was feeling again what he had felt as a child. And he was sharing with us the magic of those long ago moments.

Candles in windows! Remembering candles in windows still brightens his memories. That got me to thinking about how much we have and how often we are dissatisfied because it is not more. Would you as a child have been not only content but thrilled with candles in windows at Christmastime? And what about your children and grandchildren? How much do we need to be happy? And for how many of us is whatever we have never enough? Even the poorest of us here this morning have so much more than most of the people in the rest of the world. Where, then, do we find wonder; where, then, do we find magic? Candles in windows.

One of the most interesting places we visited in Ireland was Cobh (pronounced "cove"). It is and was a seaport village southeast of Cork and once called Queenstown. It was the last European departure point for the "unsinkable" Titanic as it set sail on its tragic maiden voyage to the United States. It was the town located nearest to the spot where the Lusitania was sunk by a German U-boat early in World War I and, hence, to which the survivors were brought after only about a third of the passengers were rescued. Memorials to both tragedies are in Cobh.

But of most historic interest is perhaps the number of immigrants who left Ireland from Cobh for new lives in new places, particularly during and after the Great Famine of the mid 1800's and for many years after that as well. The Great Famine was initially caused by a devastating potato blight that hit Ireland – an incomprehensible tragedy because the Irish people, most of whom were impoverished, depended on the potato as their main or only source of sustenance.

Before the famine the Irish had for centuries been oppressed by Great Britain. British aristocrats and businessmen owned most of the land and collected exorbitant rent as absentee landlords. Plots of ground were subdivided into smaller and smaller parcels until those living on them could barely survive. When the blight struck and their only food source was destroyed, they had nowhere to turn. During the Great Famine over one million people died and over one million people left, thereby decreasing Ireland's population by some twenty-five per cent. And millions more emigrated in subsequent years. Even after the famine was over, recovery was so slow that there were few alternatives.

The potato blight resulting in the Great Famine was bad enough, in and of itself. But the conditions which led to the blight's devastating effects were unconscionable, and the fact that during the famine when so many were dying landowners were exporting food in great quantity and letting those people starve to death is incomprehensible. How greedy can one get? How rich must one be? Does this provide lessons for us today when people of average or no means are pummeled by businesses and governments which use budget balancing as an excuse to reverse the Robin Hood psychology and take from the poor to give to the rich? Just like what happened in Ireland, it seems like we're dividing the pie into smaller and smaller pieces for some and larger and larger pieces for others. But now when the pieces get too small for some, they have no place else to go.

We spent three days in Dublin and during our vacation I was reading a book by Llywelyn Morgan entitled *1916*. It tells about the Easter Rising of that year in which native-born Irish rebels tried to throw off British rule. This was not the first such rebellion; and while it did not result in the number of deaths that previous ones had, it was successful in that it led to independence within a period of less than a decade. Instigated and planned by a coalition of labor leaders and scholarly intellectuals, it brought men and women from many walks of life to the fight for freedom; and when the defeated leaders were executed rather brutally, this resulted in an outcry which ultimately helped secure nationhood for most of the Irish island. It was interesting to walk the same streets and see the same sights as the historical figures in the book, and to speculate on what the Irish had endured for centuries before they were successful in this revolution.

Britain gained considerable control of Ireland beginning in the 1200's with the coming of the Normans, particularly during the reign of King John, the evil Prince John of the Robin Hood stories. He built massive castles all over the place, many of which are still standing with some in ruins. But it was under Oliver Cromwell in the 1600's that Ireland was totally subjugated and virtually destroyed. In his massive undertaking to wipe out Catholicism, this Puritan general killed hundreds of thousands, cut down the massive forests that once covered the land, and instituted harsh laws from which the Celtic Irish would not recover for centuries, indeed, against which the Easter Rising was reacting so many years later.

People were brought in from Scotland and England to populate the country and take the land, while the Irish whose country it was became little more than slaves. These, in fact, were considered barbarians and loafers of little intelligence; and the same kind of name-calling was sent in their direction that had been used to denigrate blacks in the United States in the days of slavery, this against a people whose cultural heritage included a high level of sophistication when their conquerors were still living in mud huts. In the final analysis, the thirst for freedom was too great for the rebels to hold down and the oppressors to stand against, much like what happened in our country before the Revolutionary War and in other places throughout history, including examples we could take from the Bible. Perhaps the poet and teacher Padraic Pearse spoke for people of all lands and all times when he said, at his trial:

I assume that I am speaking to Englishmen who value their own freedom... Believe that we too love freedom and desire it. If you strike us down now we shall rise again and renew the fight. You cannot conquer Ireland; you cannot extinguish the Irish passion for freedom. If our deed has not been sufficient to win freedom, then our children will win it by a better deed.

So many lessons learned regarding affluence and greed, brutality and violence, and all raise a question concerning what people do to people. Jesus in one of his most well-known parables spoke about a Judgment Day when the sheep and the goats would be separated. He was not giving literal information about heaven and hell. He was telling people how God wanted them to live and what would be pleasing to a God of love. How can one have a good relationship with the Divine and be a disciple of Jesus? Clothe the naked, feed the hungry, comfort the sick, visit the imprisoned! In other words, treat others as you want to be treated. Nothing is there about beliefs or dogmas or creeds. Think about it. And then do what you believe God wants you to do, and live like you believe God wants you to live!

Do You Know What Love Is?

1 John 4:11-12, Romans 12:9-18, 1 Corinthians 13:1-13

Carter S. Garner, *Pastor*
Park Road Community Church
Washington, D.C.

The Epistle of I John was written not to a particular church, but to diverse churches in order to confirm them in their steadfast adherence to the Lord Christ and to the sacred doctrines concerning his person and office. This letter also wants to urge them to adorn that doctrine of love to God and man and to each other as being descended from God.

The example of God should be our model. The objects of His divine love should be the objects of our love. How many times have we been selective in giving our love?

Matthew 5:43-46: "Ye have heard that it hath been said, Thou shalt love thy neighbour, and hate thine enemy. But I say unto you, Love your enemies, bless them that curse you, do good to them that hate you, and pray for them which despitefully use you, and persecute you; That ye may be the children of your Father which is in heaven: for he maketh his sun to rise on the evil and on the good, and sendeth rain on the just and on the unjust."

1 John 4:11-12: "Beloved, if God so loved us, we ought also to love one another. . . . If we love one another, God dwelleth in us."

In this world Satan's influence makes Christians falsely assured that we can be selective about whom we love. Often we love God but reject certain brothers and sisters. In order to be recognized as being of God, we have to learn to love in good and in difficult situations. (1 John 4:7-11)

I Corinthians 13 teaches that love is our capacity to embrace someone despite their faults and inadequacies. Real love is acted upon and acted out.

In John 13:34-35, Jesus commands us to love one another in the same way that he has loved us.

In our world today, we suffer from the lack of true love for one another. What is love? Do we really know? Love is probably the most misunderstood word used today. In the Bible, Samson and Delilah fell short in helping us to understand love. Shakespeare tried to show us. The 1960's love generation failed to show us. The list is endless. I believe that if we really understood love, crimes of hate and passion would be smaller, divorce rates would be lower, child abuse, drug use and random killings would not be rampant. Our elderly would hold places of esteem and not be pushed aside.

Let us examine some popular kinds of love in the world today:

First, there is erotic love, from the Greek word *eros* meaning passionate or affectionate love. This is a love with which many of us are very familiar. This is the love of our teen years. This is the love of people young in age and in spirit. This is the love which goes with lust and gets or has gotten many of us into trouble. We must be careful about this kind of love.

The second kind of love is *philos* which is Greek for friendship-brotherly, warm, caring relationships between friends and family. This is a brotherly love. Both parties benefit from this love. Mary and Martha had this love for Jesus. This is family love, parent love. This is the kind of love in which most of us participate. But does this answer the question, what is love?

As powerful as brotherly love is and as popular as erotic love is, there is still another kind of love much more loving with much more power. This love is known as *agape* love. This is the love Jesus had and taught. This is the love he would like the world to have. Agape love is divine in origin, total love. Agape is unconditional, without limitation.

My Bible tells me that God is the source of agape love. He made everything on earth and in heaven. His love brings peace and joy. His love flows from heart to heart and breast to breast. His love reaches into the entire world. Because of his love for the world, he gave his only begotten son so that whoever believes in him should not perish but have everlasting life. His love touches the young, the old, the weak, the strong, the great, the small, the rich, the poor, and all races, creeds, colors and nationalities. His love lifts us up when we're down, turns us around, and cheers us all the time. If we really want to love one another let us follow to the best of our ability God's example of love–agape, unconditional love.

Now we can answer the question. What is love? For GOD IS LOVE, and LOVE IS GOD.

Speaking With Authority

Mark 1:27: "The people were all so amazed that they asked each other, 'What is this?' A new teaching – and with authority!'"

Leroy McCreary, *Pastor*
People's Community Church
Berea, Ohio

L ast Monday morning at Berea High School (Berea, Ohio) I heard the principal over the intercom directing students as they got off the buses to head directly to the sports complex and pick up their class schedules for the second semester. Within fifteen minutes of the time I heard his announcement, students went into the sports complex and obtained their schedules. Clearly, the principal's voice to the students was one of authority, and they responded as such.

In the text, the voice of authority was Jesus. The people reached that conclusion after what they heard and saw in their synagogue. A man whom the people claimed had an unclean or evil spirit began behaving very strangely. Mark describes his behavior with these words: "What do you want with us, Jesus of Nazareth? Have you come to destroy us? I know who you are–the Holy One of God." I find it of compelling interest that this unclean spirit knew so much detail about Jesus and his mission. His words suggest that he knew Jesus had the power to destroy and that he was God's son, the Messiah.

It seems that almost immediately Jesus responded with these words: "Be quiet!" "Come out of him." Mark says the unclean spirit came out of him but only after he violently shook the man and made another loud noise.

Now, the people in the service that day were sure that Jesus was the voice of authority. They had ample evidence; they had seen Jesus go toe to toe with an evil spirit. They had seen Jesus exorcise the unclean spirit; they had seen him. So, for sure, Jesus was the voice of authority.

The people further made the point that Jesus was the voice of authority, because in their view his teaching was very different from the scribes, or teachers of the law as they are described in this version of the Scriptures. So how was his teaching different from the scribes? The scribes were primarily interpreters of the law. They didn't have anything new to teach. They were like one of the interpreters that accompanied former president Carter to Japan. President Carter appeared on the David Letterman show back in the 1990's and told the story about his giving a speech in Japan. He told the Japanese audience a joke. After the interpreter finished translating the joke the audience laughed and laughed. Carter was surprised and pleased. After his speech one of President Carter's friends who spoke Japanese approached him and told him why the Japanese laughed so loudly. The interpreter had said, "President Carter has told a very funny story. Everyone should laugh now."

So here is my point. The scribes were like President Carter's interpreter telling people how they should feel and respond rather than making clear what God had said. So they taught like the scribes and not with the voice of authority as they had witnessed Jesus doing with the man with the unclean spirit.

Mark doesn't inform us of the final destination of this unclean spirit that Jesus exorcised. Where did he go? Did he die a natural death? We just don't know. However, I suppose a case could be made today that he or his off-spring are still around. Our world seems to have more than its share of unclean spirits. I often wonder why there is so much evil in the world? Why is it that there is no day or season where there is no evil to report or talk about? Why is it that there is no place under the heavens where there is no evil? It may very well be that these spirits are still present and that they are still possessing people. I suppose there are many people inside and outside of the church that are possessed by something.

For example, what in the world possessed three young men in the Orange City School District (A local school district near Cleveland, Ohio) to incite panic that resulted in closing down the school for several days? These boys are sixteen, sixteen, and seventeen. Believe it or not, they came from good homes. They had never been in trouble. They were liked at their school and had good grades. What possessed them to do such a thing? Are we more possessed than we ever imagined? Are more and more people possessed by drugs, greed, and an insatiable appetite for sex than we could ever have imagined?

What we celebrate about this story is that our Lord continues to exorcise unclean spirits. That's what we believe. Even today in our forward thinking world I believe the Lord can and does exorcise unclean spirits in people who request him to do so. That's wonderful news, that's what gives us tremendous hope for living life, that's one other thing that keeps us clinging to Jesus, that's the evangel that empowers us to keep fighting evil wherever it is, and that's what we long to see happening in our churches throughout the country.

Thank God that Jesus has the power to drive the evil and unclean spirits out of anyone that is possessed. That's the point! You don't have to live with being possessed any more. Turn to Jesus who exorcised unclean spirits. He continues to do it; he had the power to say to the unclean spirits of that day: "Be quiet and come out of him." That's the blessed news for anyone today dealing with an unclean spirit or anyone who is possessed. That's the Lord we serve. Amen.

Hope Is Advent

Isaiah 7:10-14; Romans 1:1-7; Matt 1:18-24
Fourth Sunday of Advent

Elsie Hainz McGrath, *Roman Catholic Womenpriests*
The Federation of Christian Ministries in ICCC
One of three womenpriests at Threse of Divine Peace:
Inclusive Community
St. Louis, Missouri

Ahaz was king of Judah during the Syro-Ephraimitic War, c. 734 BCE. Judah was small and facing imminent defeat. Today, we heard God's prophet Isaiah deliver a message of hope to Ahaz. "If you do not take your stand on me you will not stand firm," God had said to Ahaz directly before today's reading. Ahaz was told to "pay attention… and… not be frightened." Then, as if to give him even more resolve, Ahaz was told to ask for a sign from God.

But Ahaz was afraid to do this. He was afraid of defeat. Perhaps he was afraid that God was not really with him, or that God was goading him into making a fool of himself at his enemies' expense. Or maybe, like many of us, Ahaz just plain didn't believe it was a good idea to ask God for signs or favors or special attentions. Isn't that being a bit presumptuous on our part? Why would we demand or even expect that God would favor us over anyone else?

Nevertheless, God gives a sign, by pointing out a young woman who is to bear a son. Every time I hear this story, I think: "Huh? We're talking life or death war here. What does a pregnant woman have to do with anything?"

But programmed as we have been to believe this basically has nothing to do with Ahaz or Judah or war anyway, because it is really a foretelling of Mary's motherhood-to-come, we push the question aside and think of Ahaz not a whit longer.

Except that this is a story about a *young woman* who is with child, NOT about a *virgin* who is with child. That mistranslation, possibly deliberate, has led to her more easily being equated with Mary.

And except that prophecy is, of course, NOT fortune-telling. Prophecy is telling it like it is, speaking truth to power. So the pregnant woman who was to name her child Emmanuel was actually living in 734 BCE. And she was a sign of hope, as the coming of new life is (or should be) a sign of hope. The name of the child – God is with is – was a further sign of hope.

Who was she? Honestly, we don't know. For *that* story's purposes, it didn't matter *who* she was, just *that* she was. It mattered that life was destined to go on. It mattered that God was with them.

But still Ahaz doubted. What happened to that first Emmanuel? If we continued reading the story Isaiah has given us, we would find that Ahaz's disbelief brought ruin upon the land of Judah. Without hope, there is no life.

What were signs of hope in Mary's day? We know the story well. But what do we *really* know of it?

We know that Mary and Joseph were betrothed. That is the only thing that our two nativity stories – from Matthew and from Luke – agree upon, aside from their agreement on Mary's pregnancy.

Betrothal was a public commitment ceremony, with witnesses. It *was* marriage, legally, which explains why the terms husband and wife are used in the gospel stories of the nativity of Jesus. To end betrothal, there had to be a legal divorce.

The betrothal period was usually a year long, during which the man built a house, or an addition to his father's house and furnished it for his bride. If the betrothed came up pregnant before the wedding – the point at which the marriage was consummated – divorce was a given, except in cases where the consummation had preceded the wedding and a "quickie" wedding was arranged to ward off scandal. Pregnant women who had not yet celebrated a wedding were often stoned to death.

Joseph found himself between a rock and a hard place. He was a good man, honest and hard-working, and in right relationship with God. He was in love with Mary. He prayed and agonized over the dilemma he was facing. His beloved was pregnant, and he was apparently certain he was not the father. The only way he could see to salvage an impossible situation was to divorce her quietly. Without the accusation of adultery, Mary could perhaps get out of town, maybe return to the home of Elizabeth and Zechariah and raise her son in safety.

Joseph wasn't resting easy with this decision, though. His nights were sleepless, his days filled with impossible dreams of a future that was not to be. Why had she done this thing? How could she have done this thing?

"In the night of death, hope sees a star, and listening love can hear the rustle of a wing," so said Robert Green Ingersoll.

In spite of her apparent infidelity, Joseph was not comfortable with his decision. He could not picture life without Mary. So he had a dream in which God spoke to him. Perhaps it was a real dream; perhaps it was an ah-ha moment during prayer or meditation. It doesn't matter *how* it happened, only *that* it happened. Joseph had a revelation, and he believed it fully, and he was faithful to it.

Quoth Jonas Salk: "Hope lies in dreams, in imagination, and in the courage of those who dare to make dreams into reality."

Joseph was a descendant of King David, and that is an important part of the Jesus story because it was *always* the father who established the bloodline, and the "real" or "valid" Messiah had to come from the line of David. This gets a little tricky, of course, with the theological construct of Jesus' conception: Joseph isn't *really* the father. Not to mention that the family tree Luke presents to readers is from the mother's side, and establishes that *her* bloodline is Davidic.

Does it matter? Not in the larger scheme of things, obviously. But it mattered to those first-century readers for whom the nativity stories were written. From us, therefore, it demands attention. What is the message we need to "get" in order to *live* out of these ancient scriptures in 2010, in 2011, and beyond?

We need to "get" that God is faithful. We need to "get" that Joseph believed. We need to "get" that Mary's child, who was a sign of hope in those days, remains a sign of hope – *even* for *our* future.

We, as a people, have spent these past years of our lives so assiduously working at the devaluing of life that even seeing a young woman who is with child is something of a shock these days. I hear myself saying things like, "I'm glad I'm not trying to raise kids in this day and age," as if it is so far removed from the times when I was doing just that. In a sense, it does seem to be that far removed. And often, hope seems to be a thing of the past too.

In our days, *is* new life a sign of hope – a sign of hope for *us*, for our *families*, for our *world*? Is it possible for new life to *really* change things – the hatred, the killing, the destruction of life?

Hope *is* Advent. Erich Fromm said: "To hope means to be ready at any moment for that which is not yet born, and yet not become desperate if there is no birth in our lifetime."

Every year we celebrate the holy season of Advent. We pray prayers of longing and waiting, and sing songs of hope and promise. We prepare for the coming of new life, and name that life:

O Wisdom, O Holy Word of God, come.

O Sacred Adonai of Ancient Israel, come.

O Flower of Jesse's Stem, come.

O Key of David, O Royal Power of Israel, come.

O Radiant Dawn, Splendor of Eternal Light, Sun of Justice, come.

O Ruler of All the Nations, come.

O Keystone of the Church, come.

O Emmanuel, Desire of the Nations, Savior of All People, come.

Don Quixote, hero of impossible dreams, said: "Sanity may be madness, but the maddest of all is to see life as it is and not as it should be."

Do we believe?

What Would Jesus Have Me Do?

Luke 10:25-37

R. Tim Meadows, *Associate Pastor,*
Tellico Village Community Church
Loudon, Tennessee

If you stretch the arc of history long enough, at least twice around my lifetime, it has been a phenomenon, spurring a best-selling book the first time and a whole line of bad jewelry and accessories the second time. It is the question: What Would Jesus Do? (WWJD) I understand that for many people this is a meaningful question that forces them to think seriously about life decisions, and I understand that many of you really like much of that bad jewelry and those accessories you purchased, but I always thought the problem was that this was the wrong question. A few years ago, I ran across someone who agreed with me who, more eloquently than I, stated the obvious problem. The late Peter Gomes was the long time chaplain at Harvard University. He says about this question, "The proper question is not 'What Would Jesus Do' but 'What Would Jesus Have Me Do?' Jesus asks us to live into our full humanity and to do what is possible; this is the challenge that makes life interesting. The question "What would Jesus Do?" is inappropriate because the life of Jesus is his life, not ours; and our lives are ours and not his. The better question is what should we do based on what we know about Jesus?

What Would Jesus Have Me Do? This is the question that our New Testament lesson for today seeks to answer. Confronted with a narrow legal question, seeking a narrow legal finding, Jesus instead tells the story about the expansive grace of a culturally despised fellow. With this story Jesus seeks to answer the question of what we should do based on our experience with him.

Jesus insists that above all we should love others and through the story indicates that the definition of love is doing what we can, when we can, for whomever we can. Love is not complex and not passive. Love is what Jesus would have me do.

With this story Jesus declares that the culturally despised are often heroes in the work of God's love. People we would least expect, the most societally marginalized, often evidence God's love the most because they either do not know or do not follow the rules of polite society. Finding a lesson in love from people on the margins of society is what Jesus would have me do.

With this story Jesus reminds us that the work of God is done by our hands and demands our best. Rather than simply offering intercession and awaiting the intervention of God, Jesus reminds us that our answers to prayer come when we allow God to guide our hands to do the work needed, when we give the best of ourselves in response to the needs of others. Offering myself sacrificially to those in need, that is what Jesus would have me do.

With this story Jesus concludes that the work of God is something we are all capable of doing and should do. Whether we find ourselves among the culturally despised or the socially elite, we receive this ultimate compliment and charge from Jesus. You can do the work of God in the world; and in doing so, you will secure life for yourself and for others. Doing God's work, that is what Jesus would have me do.

Many of you are familiar with the name Bill Hybels, teaching pastor and founder at Willow Creek Community Church in South Barrington, Illinois. The following story, inasmuch as I can faithfully remember, is one I heard him tell:

93

Meadows - What Would Jesus Have Me Do?

While on break from Willow each summer we attend an African-American church, where I am often astounded at how the simplicity of the pastor's preaching commands great power. One instance I can remember, he seemed to build an entire sermon on the Good Samaritan on the words *Go* and *Do*. After working the crowd to a fever pitch, as he wound up the sermon, he simply had to lift his arms and the crowd would shout, as he lifted one arm they shouted "Go!" As he lifted the other arm, they shouted, "Do!" "Go!" "Do!" "Go!" "Do!" This went on for some time and finally wound down.

Some weeks later after returning home, I dropped my wife off for a volunteer shift at a local nursing home. I noticed as she exited the car a well-dressed proper lady seated on a waiting bench, obviously anticipating someone to pick her up. When I returned to get my wife, the woman was still seated, patiently waiting after several hours and having obviously gone nowhere in the interim. Curious, I parked the car and went in to inquire about the lady. The receptionist said, "Oh, that's Muriel. She does that every day. She says her son is coming to pick her up for lunch, but as far as I know it has never happened. We are not even sure she has a son." As I walked out, suddenly I began to hear in my mind two fever pitched words over and over: Go! Do! Go! Do! I could not ignore them, and so we took Muriel to lunch and had a wonderful time.

"Go! Do! Go! Do!" Jesus said, and you shall live. May God give us the grace to hear these words and respond at each opportunity, for in that response there is life.

AMEN!

Passing Our Test

Exodus 15:22-26
Healing Service, January 29, 2012

Kenneth Nelson, *Pastor*
Seneca Community Church
Germantown, Maryland
Past-president of the ICCC Ministerium

W e have tests in our lives that we must pass to achieve life's goals and ambitions. We have school tests, job tests, and we have social tests. And for some of this morning, it was a test getting out of bed. But thank God you have made it today, and we rejoice.

After one of the greatest redemptive acts in the Bible, the Israelites came to a place of testing. After one of Moses' great intercessory prayers, the Israelites came to a place of testing. Come let us read this account:

> Then Moses led Israel from the Red Sea and they went into the Desert of Shur. For three days they traveled in the desert without finding water (Exodus 15:22).
>
> When they came to Marah, they could not drink its water because it was bitter. (That is why the place is called Marah.) (Exodus 15:23) So the people grumbled against Moses, saying, "What are we to drink?" (Exodus 15:24) Then Moses cried out to the LORD, and the LORD showed him a piece of wood. He threw it into the water, and the water became sweet. There the LORD made a decree and a law for them, and there he tested them. (Exodus 15:25) He said, "If you listen carefully to the voice of the LORD your God and do what is right in his eyes, if you pay attention to his commands and keep all his decrees, I will not bring on you

any of the diseases I brought on the Egyptians, for I am the LORD, who heals you." (Exodus 15:26, NIV)

Here in the Book of Exodus between the Crossing of the Red Sea and the Manna from Heaven, we see God about to do something different. After the showing of His mighty act of deliverance, we see the people of God tested. Why, Lord, did you test your people now? Well, isn't that like life? We have a great triumph and we have to come back to the reality of our achievement and refocus. But this is one of many tests before the Israelites would go into the promise land.

When we review this passage, we see the necessity of the test. After only three days, there were some complainers in the camp, real grumblers. Now as then, we always have some grumblers in the camp. We always have someone who is satisfied with neither God nor man, and they let everyone know it. That they have walked through the Red Sea does not matter. That they walked on dry land where water and mud was does not matter. And that God had worked several miracles does not matter. Their flesh needed attention: "what are we to drink?" And their thirst needed to be addressed.

Moses prepares to give one of his great intercessory prayers. One cannot help but think: Where is the faithfulness of these people? Didn't God just free them from another 400 years of slavery, and didn't God just bring them through the Red Sea? Are we all so forgetful about God's faithfulness in our lives? The demands of the flesh seem to keep us from having a great relationship with God. Our technology, our cars, and our appliances that make us comfortable make us uncomfortable with God. But "Moses cried out to the LORD," and the LORD answers his prayer and then offers conditions, tests for these grumbling people. God offers these tests to be sure that those who enter the promise land were to be those who were most worthy. He offers a test to them and to us to become more holy and to continue our relationship with God.

Kenneth Nelson - Passing Our Test

In fact, I believe that God offers us tests in the passage that will help our relationship with him. God offers the test of fellowship, the test of lifestyle, the test of understanding, the test of commitment, and the test of hope. Before we get into the passage, I want you to consider and ancient story of healing that shows these tests in action.

During the ministry of Augustine, a great theologian of early Christianity, a devout woman discovered that she had breast cancer. She went to her physician, and he told her the disease was incurable. The woman, crushed by the report, turned to God and in a dream received instructions about her healing. She was to go to a certain place, wait for a certain woman, and ask her to make the sign of the cross over the cancerous breast.

The woman did what she was told and was healed. When she told her doctor what had happened, he responded with a contemptuous tone: "I thought you would reveal some great discovery to me," he said. Then, seeing her horrified look, he backpedaled saying, "what great thing was it for Christ to heal a cancer? He raised a man who had been dead for four days."[1]

This story illustrates the tests of fellowship, lifestyle, understanding, commitment, and hope. Sometimes in our walk, we can be so caught in the everyday of life, that we don't see the potential for God to keep His faithfulness to us. We forget that God is always working for our benefit. From Genesis to Revelation we see God repeatedly keeping his promise for our well-being. Notice in this story the contrast between a life commitment to God and just going along for the ride.

I believe God wants us to learn about these tests of fellowship, lifestyle, understanding, commitment, and hope. Let's look closely:

---

[1] Bruce Shelley, "Miracles Ended Long Ago—Or did they?" *Christian History* (Summer 2000).

Kenneth Nelson - Passing Our Test

God offers you and me the test of fellowship: "He said, '... listen carefully to the voice of the LORD your God.'" God asks us today, as then, to listen to him for His voice. No doubt some people in the camp were listening to themselves more than to God. It probably would not be a stretch of the imagination for some in the camp to think that they were not Israelites but Egyptians pushed out of Egypt because of their association with the Hebrews. Their grumbles were only the beginning of a case for returning to bondage. God pauses here to emphasis that the first test we must pass is the test of fellowship. God wants us to listen to his voice, to be in relationship with Him, and not to be devoted to ourselves or our possessions. God says to listen to His voice in the Bible, listen to His voice in our prayers, and listen to his voice daily over the voices of our world and ourselves.

God offers you and me, the test of lifestyle: "do what is right in his eyes." God wants us to live according to his promises. There is a subtle message here from God. I have been faithful to you. I keep my promises, and I want you to learn to do the right thing now. I don't want you to say that this crossing thing is good and then demand "how about some water." But I want you to live in a way that will honor the faithfulness and the promises that God has made and is keeping every day.

God offers to you and me the test of understanding. "Pay attention to his commands." God wants us to read closely what he is saying to us in his Bible. Sometimes we are so quick to say that I know that passage or I know that song. We go about our business not expecting God to reward or help us because we are studying His word. God says pay attention to what I am doing and don't miss anything because it is part of my growth plan.

God offers to you and me the test of commitment. "Keep all his decrees." God expects us to be committed to his word and to do His word in our lives. As a young boy, I had a reputation of being with the wrong crowd. When I started to change my ways, my old reputation preceded me. In fact, my middle school principal made a very stern

98

promise to me in September of the new school year. He said, "If you come to my office again, I will expel you." For the next nine months, I ran from every trouble situation I faced. I knew he meant what he was saying, and I knew my family would reward my mischief in very stern ways. I had to keep my promise to be a good kid. I had to keep my slate clean because of the consequences of failure were too great and painful. This is what God is saying to us today. I have rewards and consequences for your action; but if you keep my decrees, you will be alright.

God offers you and me the test of hope: "I will not bring on you any of the diseases I brought on the Egyptians, for I am the LORD, who heals you." God knew these Hebrews would remember the plagues upon Egypt, and He reminds them that there will consequences for their inaction. Most of us might think that frog legs can be good thing to eat sometimes. The Egyptians thought frogs were a good sign of the harvest season to come until God made them so plentiful they became hideous to them. When we choose lifestyles that are not good for us, the consequences are disastrous. We cannot continue to go to our physicians and ignore their prescriptions or to refuse responsibility for our own healing. We cannot be in denial about what is good for us. We cannot act as if we don't have some part in our healing.

In this passage God reveals a new character trait about him. He is Jehovah-Rapha, The Lord that Heals. In the first mention of healing, God reveals that he not only is the God who opens seas or provides water, but he is the God who will heal our disease. Sometimes our New Testament focus on God prevents us from seeing just how wonderful this new revelation can be for us. God has been, and will be our Great Physician. When we come to the reality that we need healing, God is there to give us what we need.

Now that we know about the tests, the next question is what grade can we expect from God? I believe in the spiritual realm there are only three grade levels–A, B, and C. The C grade is for all of us, "For all have sinned, and come short of the glory of God" (Romans 3:23). You can get your C grade by knowing both that you have sinned and you have a Savior in Jesus Christ.

Some of the high achievers in our camp will not want a C grade. They want to get a B, but a B grade just represents that you are a work in progress. Paul put it this way: "being confident of this, that he who began a good work in you will carry it on to completion until the day of Christ Jesus" (Philippians 1:6). God is still working on us. That is why reading our Bibles, saying our prayers, and serving our God is so important. God is still shaping us for His glory. Most of us are working on the B grade, but we can't give up here.

The final grade, the A grade, cannot be given by man. The A grade can only be given by God. Only God can give you the A grade. Only God can say to you: "Well done, good and faithful servant! You have been faithful with a few things; I will put you in charge of many things. Come and share your master's happiness!"(Matthew 25:23).

This morning we encourage you to pass your test with the "Lord that heals you." Amen.

Why Did God Establish the Church?

Ephesians 4:1-6, 25-5:2

Susan Burgess Parrish, *Executive Director*
of Habitat for Humanity of Anderson County,
clergy member of Grace Covenant Church
Oak Ridge, Tennessee

As we gather for worship this morning, I would like to invite you to think along with me about *why* it was that God established the church. When we stop to think about it, we all know that the most important reason for all of us to gather together as a church is to praise and worship God, so that would be the number one reason. We also know from our walk with the early church in Acts that we are to take what we learn and share it with others. That focus of sharing the message of God would be the second reason for the church. But is there another purpose for the church? Today we want to stop and think about yet another reason for the church to exist. The church is for us, God's children. Why did God establish the church?

I subscribe to several magazines; and though I thoroughly enjoy them, I don't actually get to them in the timeframe that the writers would like. I may get to flip through one quickly when it arrives, but they are more likely to pile up on the table beside my bed or in a stack on the floor until I get some spare time to look through them. Well, it was sometime over the summer that I actually got to read the *Better Homes and Gardens* issue that came in April. In it was an article that sparked several lengthy conversations at our house because it dealt with friends and relationships. In reading it, I could not help but think about the church. I laid it on the table and have used it as a catalyst for today's sermon.

"Friends for Life" by Michele Meyer begins with a scenario of a young woman who approaches a milestone in her life and finds that she really doesn't have anyone with whom to share her life, then a commentary on the American lifestyle. The article views the results of sociological studies by Duke University in 1985, repeated in 2004, that found "Americans' social circles had shrunk by one-third in the interim." They found that "the average person has just two close confidants (down from three in 1985), who are far more likely to be family members than unrelated pals. And that applies to those of us who are confiding in anyone at all. Fully 25 percent of survey respondents in 2004 admitted they had no close relationships – inside their families or not."

This should be of no surprise with the rise of *MySpace*, *Facebook* and *Twitter*, to name a few. These are social networks that act as a substitute for real communication and interaction with real friends, not just online friends who are little more than acquaintances. While I was not surprised by what I was reading, I was saddened. Everyone is looking for a place where people know their name, people who know them and with whom they can have a close relationship. That is what church is supposed to be for its members, a place of belonging and sharing. That was what God created it to be.

We know this to be true of our fellowship here. It is something that we work at, though honestly, it is an easy task most of the time. Because of the deep relationships we have forged through shared experiences, we like being together and sharing our lives with each other. We can pretty easily come up with a list of positive results of having this relationship in our lives. We know that when troubles come our way, we have people on which we can lean. We know that others will not only care, they will pray and then put feet to their prayers by doing whatever is needed to show that care and concern in a tangible form. It can be people with whom to celebrate joyous occasions and know that they truly are happy for us. It can mean people visiting a hospital or sitting with a loved one while they await the outcome of surgery. It can be a driver when one is needed for transportation to medical facilities. It can be food prepared in times of grief or illness. It is friends with whom to share the grief when a loved one is lost or the shared grief we all have felt when one from our midst is taken. Like I said, it is pretty easy to come up with a list of good things that result from this kind of relationship.

The article also listed what can happen when one has true friends with whom to share their lives, maybe some things that we haven't included on our list. Dr. Stephen Ilardi, professor of clinical psychology at the University of Kansas in Lawrence, notes in his book, *The Depression Cure*, that it doesn't take long for camaraderie to work its magic: "Levels of the toxic stress hormone cortisol drop dramatically when we find ourselves in the company of friends and loved ones. . . . If you layer in the physical touch of a friend, you also experience increased activity of the feel-good chemicals dopamine and oxytocin." The potentially life-saving results continue because "persistently high levels of stress hormones promote high levels of inflammation, a prime culprit in diseases such as fibromyalgia and type-2 diabetes." Dr. John T. Cacioppo, director of the Center for Cognitive Neuroscience at the University of Chicago takes it even further with his research indicating that loneliness leads to high blood pressure as well as increases in cortisol and less restful sleep. Lonely people will adopt unhealthy habits such as avoiding exercise and poor eating habits.

These results are not just for the immediate moment. University of Pittsburg researchers exposed 276 volunteers to a cold virus. Several days later, subjects with ample friendships were 4 times less likely than socially isolated people to have developed symptoms. In a more recent study researchers gave a flu vaccine to volunteers and found that those with large social circles responded fifteen to twenty per cent better to the shot than isolated people and this effect was still evident four months later. In further studies, these results indicate that one doesn't have to be around their closest friends all the time to get the same effects. Knowing friends on whom you can lean even if they are only reachable by phone also can lower stress and improve quality of life.

So, what does all this have to do with the church? While I'm not saying that church membership will make you physically healthier, I guess one could surmise that there are positive health effects from one's involvement in a church *if* that church is one where they can express who they really are and totally be themselves. Many of us read a few years ago several books of the day on the "Toxic Church" or "When the Church Becomes Evil" about how detrimental a church can be when its focus changes from its real purpose. The church has indicted entire groups of people on the basis of their disagreement on a variety of issues. We can also quickly bring to mind the harmful effects when churches pronounce judgment on one of their own who differs from their expectations. Obviously not all churches produce the desired positive effects mentioned in the article.

During the Baptist Holy Wars of the 1980's and 1990's, I wanted to write a book entitled "Baptist Bruises" and recount the battered lives of those who dared to disagree with the conservative resurgence that was taking control. All the evil inflicted on saints of God was being done under the guise of the church. Again, this is *not* an example of what the church is supposed to be. Disagreements should never resort to personal attacks, especially when one is supposed to be wearing the mantle of God. In Acts and the early church, we have seen examples of all kinds of churches. Not all of the examples are positive. Even the New Testament distinguishes what the church *is* from what it *ought* to be.

Today's text calls us to love one another with mutual affection, showing zeal in honoring one another, while walking through all that life has in store; but that is not all we are to do for each other. We are also to be strong enough in our relationships of love to be able to hold each other accountable for the life that we say we are striving to live.

Proverbs 27:17 says, "As irons sharpens iron, so are we to sharpen the countenance of our friends." Our friendships ought to sharpen, enhance, encourage, promote growth, and challenge us to live even better lives. To do less is to miss the mark of what true friends are and surely what true churchmanship is to be. Accountability is behind our public ceremonies of ordination, marriage, commitment, etc. We are announcing to the congregation and to the world the commitment and making and literally using peer pressure as a means of motivating us to stay true to the commitment we are making, so as not to disappoint those whom we love and before whom we are making our commitment.

When Paul wrote to the church at Ephesus, he was writing to a group of people that were Gentile Christians. He celebrated the church and what it was to be to the people who were members as well as to the rest of the world around them. In our text, we heard grand instructions on how we are to live together and how we are to act as members of the body of Christ. Paul was very concerned for the new churches that were trying to live out their witness in this new manner– sometimes very different from the life they had lived prior to their coming into the church. For that reason Paul was very careful to instruct on how to live and work together; for he knew that both those who lived around them still worshipping the gods of Rome and those within the Jerusalem church, who still viewed Gentile churches as suspect, would be watching very closely. So it was not enough for them to have a close relationship within their congregation and take care of each other behind closed doors. It was equally if not more important that they live that life of love for each other out in front of the world so that all could see. In doing so, they were witnessing to the change that can come through a relationship with the true God and others will be enticed to want that, too.

The same should be true for us today. While having a strong bond among ourselves is important, it is not the end of our responsibility. We are to live that bond openly so as to open the doors for others to join in on what we have found. Engaging others, inviting others to join with us in this journey, giving them the opportunity to have these kinds of relationships is also our responsibility. It also means that living corporately is a task at which we must work. Decisions of the body are to be made for the common and greater good, not for our own personal preferences. Just because we personally may not like a decision does not mean that it may not be for the greater good of the body, and we have to be keeping watch constantly on ourselves to ensure that we are working for the greater good instead of for our own good.

We have a dear friend with whom we visit periodically. He lives alone and is somewhat isolated from his family by distance and time. He is retired, and his closest relative, his daughter, works a lot. He has mentioned feelings of loneliness and how he is searching for friends with whom he can share his life. We think one day he will come with us to our church as part of that search, but he reminds me of the lady in the article that started this whole train of thought. Being in relationship with people is at the base of our make-up. God did not make us to live alone. We are made to be in community with people. In the early days, people lived in community for protection from animals and dangers. Together, they could collectively fight off the bad things. So when Christ came into the world and established the church, he left them together as a group, so that they could continue to fight off the evil things of the world. Christ also realized that we would need the strength that comes from each other and that to accomplish all that was needed, we would need the gifts of each one and the abilities that they bring to be able to carry on the work left for us. That is why in John 14, he prayed for us the church to have the strength, power and grace to continue together and grow.

Please understand that I am not saying that we cannot hold deep and abiding relationships with others outside the local church. (My family is blessed this weekend to be visited by just such a friend.) What I am saying is that the church should be the best example of those relationships. At Grace Covenant we are blessed to have an abundance of them. Many people outside of the church, outside of this or any church hope and dream for the kind of relationship we have and sometimes take for granted. Think about it. There are so many lonely, isolated people in our world. For some, it may be a new experience as they are coming to grips with the departure of a loved one through death or moving or the self-imposed isolation from illness or retirement. Our friendships, the bonds of love found here, are what so many people are searching for. To be the church we are meant to be means that we don't keep this to ourselves but that we demonstrate it to others and invite them into our fellowship. While there are many ways to introduce our fellowship to others, we have to continue finding ways to do so.

So it all comes back full circle. While the church was established to worship and praise God, out of that worship comes the motivation to take the message out into the world as we work to bring in the Kingdom. As we do so together, we develop relationships that strengthen us as individuals and give us the energy and ability and apparently better health to continue the journey. With that in hand and with an attitude of gratitude for the blessings we have discovered, we are better able to worship and praise God, which in turn motivates us to even more opportunities of service, which makes us even stronger mentally and physically so that we can, well, you see the cycle here. God graciously gave us this thing called church. Apparently, we need it more than we may think. It is something that strengthens us, challenges us, encourages us, motivates us, helps us, assists us, holds us accountable, comforts us, forgives us, carries us, loves us. Thanks be to God for this incredible gift.

David's Plea for Forgiveness

Psalm 51:1-12

Julia Powe, *Coordinator,*
Women's Christian Fellowship, ICCC
Pastoral Associate, St. John Independent Methodist Church
Bessemer, Alabama

Psalm 51 speaks of David's sins, guilt and fears. Nathan the prophet came to David after David had gone in to Bathsheba and after David's committing adultery with Bathsheba. The results of this sin ended with the murder of her husband, Uriah. This was a "planned" sin; it did not happen unexpectedly. David saw Bathsheba bathing and acted upon the desires of his flesh. II Samuel 11:2-3 states the reason why there was a need for David to repent. After seeing Bathsheba, David asked who she was. He was told that she was the wife of Uriah the Hittite. When told that she was another man's wife, this should have closed any further inquiry from David, but it didn't. David sent messengers to go and bring Bathsheba to him. The Bible says that "she came in unto David and he lay with her."

Bathsheba conceived and sent word to the king that she was with child. David had many wives and concubines but he wanted more; he wanted Uriah's wife. David *planned* his sin, *plotted* to carry out his sin, and then tried to *conceal* his sin. Let us remember that we are not above temptation. When we commit sin, we too must confess our sin and ask for God's forgiveness.

David prayed for God to "Have mercy upon me, O God, according to thy lovingkindness: according unto the multitude of thy tender mercies blot out my transgressions." He asked God to forgive him even though he felt unworthy of God's forgiveness. He knew that

108

God is a merciful God and full of compassion. He also knew that God is a forgiving God.

David asked God to have mercy on him; without God's mercy we would all be under the penalty of death. David appealed for God to do three things: He asked God to "blot out his transgressions," meaning to forget or erase this sin according to Hebrews 8:12: "For I will be merciful to their unrighteousness, and their sins and their iniquities will I remember no more." He then asked God to "wash him of his iniquity." Finally he wanted God to "cleanse him from his sin."

When we sin, our relationship with God is stained and we must seek forgiveness to wash away the stain. Stain can result in the feeling of guilt, sadness and, yes, sometimes anger. God wants us to return to Him. Guilt can be a good thing. Guilt tells us that something is wrong, not physically but spiritually we have come under attack. If there were no guilt, there would be no warning sign telling us that our relationship with God is headed in the wrong direction.

First of all David acknowledged his sin with his mind by taking responsibility for what he had done. Proverbs 28:13 says, "He who covers his sins will not prosper, but whoever confesses and forsakes them will have mercy." We can only be helped when we confess that it's "not my mother, not my father, not my sister and not my brother, but it's me oh Lord, standing in the need of prayer."

David also acknowledged his sin with his spirit. Verse four reads, "Against thee, thee only, have I sinned, and done this evil in thy sight." Sin hurts our spiritual relationship with God. David knew that he must first come before God. This had to be done in order for God to reshape David's life. He knew that God was a righteous God and that everything that he (David) had done was by his own free will. He accepted the blame for his thoughts and his actions. David admits that "he was shaped in iniquity." He sees himself; he comes face to face with himself. Coming to that point is the only way change can begin.

As long as we have the attitude that we are OK, there is no room for God to work in our lives.

David says, "in sin did my mother conceive me." This settles it for the Christian. If the Bible says we were "shaped in iniquity" and "conceived in sin," then it has to be so. There are many interpretations of this verse, but Christians believe what the Bible says. Yes, we were born in sin, so we must be born again. We must be baptized with the Holy Ghost and with fire.

God wants nothing less than complete honesty from us. Who we are on the inside is to be in agreement with who we are on the outside. When we speak of "a sincere heart," we are not only speaking of a person with a perfect heart or a holy heart, but we are speaking of a heart which says, "this is I, nothing more and nothing less."

David wanted to be purified. He wanted this dreadful sin disease removed because he knew that he could not live in sin and feel the Savior's love. He knew that he had to get right with God and do it now. He wanted to be pronounced clean by God.

"Wash me, and I shall be whiter than snow." David compared his sins with a person with a dreadful disease. He felt stained by the blood of Uriah. He knew that if God washed him that he would be whiter than snow. He asked God to clean him thoroughly, knowing that only the cleansing *power* of God can make him clean and pure. Although his sins have covered him and stained him, a cleansing from God could make him whiter than snow.

"Make me to hear joy and gladness." David's ear had become heavy with sin, and so he prays, "Make me to hear." David's joy was lost. Most times, joy is felt and not heard. When God speaks peace into our lives after repentance, we have joy. We also become stronger because the "joy of the LORD is our strength."

David asked, "That the bones which thou hast broken may rejoice." David felt broken, he felt crushed, but he knew the One that could make him whole again. When we sin we break our relationship with God. David knew that although he had sinned, he could call upon the Lord to cast his sins away and to make him whole again. He knew that the joy of the Lord would revive his soul.

God hates sin, but He loves the sinner. God's forgiveness is for you and for me. By His grace, we are freed from the penalty of sin. We are covered by the blood of Christ.

As we study the sins of David, we cannot leave it there. This sin continues to happen even today. Not only are the unsaved guilty of adultery, fornication and other sins, but the saved sometimes fall in the clutches of Satan. Just because we are saved doesn't give us permission to go against the Word of God.

Yes, I understand how David felt, wanting God to hide his sins. He wanted God to place them in a place where He would not see them and to blot out any remembrance of them. When we do wrong, the Holy Spirit informs us that we have done things according to the flesh and not of the Spirit. We find ourselves saying, "I wish I had thought this out before I acted it out." The action taken wounds the spirit of the inward man because we acted on our own and denied Jesus the opportunity to work with us.

David asks God to "create in him a clean heart and to renew a right spirit within him." David wanted to again experience the joy of the Lord. He now knows how unclean his own heart is and asks God to clean it, because he couldn't clean it himself. David wants to be made right again.

David didn't want to be left out of favor with God. "Cast me not away from thy presence." He prays that he might not be thrown out of God's protection but that wherever he went, he might feel the presence of God with him. He asked God not to abandon him and not to take away the anointing of the Holy Spirit from him.

We are undone when God takes His Holy Spirit from us. David fervently asked: "LORD, whatever thou take from me, take not thy Holy Spirit from me." Yes, my brothers, yes, my sisters, David needed God's loving kindness and His tender mercies. He needed God to wash, cleanse and to purge him; but after all of this was done, he asked God not to take away His Holy Spirit. We need the Holy Spirit to lead, guide and help us to remember that God is with us, even when we feel that our backs are against the wall.

God loves for us to call upon Him in our time of trouble because He is our Present Help. He is there with us even when we think that we are walking alone. When friends and loved ones turn their backs on us, there is no need for us to walk through the valley alone; God is with us every step of the way. When your spouse won't act right, just keep walking and talking to your Present Help. When the children want to do their own thing, just put them in the hands of your Present Help.

David knew that he had a Present Help, One who will forgive him for his sins. God not only forgave David, God will forgive us also. But we must go to Him in sincerity and in truth. God is not looking for excuses from us when we do wrong. He wants us to come to Him acknowledging our wrong and repenting of our sins.

David wanted his joy to be restored. When we sin, we can't feel the joy that we once had with God. The Christian's joy comes in believing, but the Lord Himself is our joy and our salvation. Sin will make us sad and we must do what David did and ask God to restore our joy.

David asked God to, "uphold him with thy free spirit." David is asking God to make him willing to follow Him. We know our weaknesses; we cannot control them on our own. Our prayer like

112

David's be, "I need Your help, I need Your encouragement, and I need You, because I am weak, but You are strong."

When we allow God to cleanse us, great things happen. Our guilt is removed, our condemnation is taken away, and our sins are buried in the grave. God removes the penalty of our sin, restores our joy and receives us back into fellowship with Himself. Don't you want that for yourself? You can have it right now. So where do you stand today? Are you drowning in guilt or shame? Have peace and joy forgotten your address? If so, you need to return to the Father who is waiting with opened arms to receive you.

Amen, amen, amen.

Life's Parachutes

Chappy's On Eagle's Wings

Ron Ringo, Ph.d., *Certified Trauma Specialist*
U.S. Navy/Marine Retired Chaplain, Endorsed by ICCC
San Diego, California

P ondering lately on the blessings in my life, I started wondering why we often don't see the little things all around us, or those who make them happen. If you were to take just a moment to reflect on the many people who impact your life on a daily basis, I know you would be amazed. Go ahead. Take a few minutes, then come back to the article.

Ever since I was a young Marine in the 1970's, I had always wanted to go to jump school. Many said I was crazy; but in my fortieth year, I finally got the opportunity to attend the Army Airborne School at Fort Benning, Georgia. The first two weeks beat up my body mercilessly. It was reminiscent of my Marine boot-camp and infantry school days. But, at forty, my physical body wasn't doing what my twentyish mindset thought it should. I quickly realized that I would need a lot of help to make it through training. So I asked a few Navy Seals to surround me on the runs to keep me moving at the right speed. And a fellow old fogy, a flight surgeon, would go with me to the O-Club; and we'd motivate each other to stretch and soak in the hot tub. The instructors taught us all they could to make us safe, and the parachute riggers gave us safe chutes so we'd live to jump another day.

Most all aspects of our life, if we really think about it, are filled with similar people giving similar aid. A story you may have heard, expresses this point in a very meaningful way. It is entitled, "Packing Your Parachute."

Charles Plumb, a U.S. Naval Academy graduate, was a jet fighter pilot in Vietnam. After seventy-five combat missions his plane was destroyed by a surface-to-air missile. Plumb ejected and parachuted into enemy hands. He was captured and spent six years in a Vietnamese prisoner of war camp. He survived that ordeal and now lectures about the lessons learned from that experience.

One day, when Plumb and his wife were sitting in a restaurant, a man at another table came up and said, "You're Plumb! You flew jet fighters in Vietnam from the aircraft carrier Kitty Hawk. You were shot down!" "How in the world did you know that?" asked Plumb. "I packed your parachute," the man replied.

Plumb gasped in surprise and gratitude. The man pumped his hand and said, "I guess it worked!" Plumb assured him, "It sure did! If your chute hadn't worked, I wouldn't be here today."

Plumb couldn't sleep that night, thinking about that man. Plumb says, "I kept wondering what he might have looked like in a Navy uniform: a Dixie cup hat, a bib in the back, and bell bottom trousers. I wondered how many times I might have seen him and not even said good morning, how are you or anything because, you see, I was a fighter pilot, and he was just a sailor."

Plumb thought of the many hours the sailor had spent on a long wooden table in the bowels of the ship carefully weaving the shrouds and folding the silks of each chute, each time holding in his hands the fate of someone he didn't know.

Then Plumb asked his audience, "Who's packing your parachute?" Everyone has someone who provides what he or she needs to make it through the day. Plumb also points out that he needed many kinds of parachutes when his plane was shot down over enemy territory. He needed his physical parachute, his mental parachute, his emotional parachute, and *his spiritual parachute*. He called on all these supports before reaching safety. His experience reminds us all to prepare ourselves to weather whatever storms lie ahead. *Suggestion*: Recognize people who pack your parachute and strengthen yourself to prevail through tough times!

A couple of years ago, I met Plumb; and to this day he thinks of this experience and is appreciative for those who serve and bless the lives of others.

My own jump school experience was very humbling. It gave me a much greater appreciation for my family and friends and for life. I'll never forget going into that third and last week of jump school, "jump week," with five exciting jumps ahead of me. I stood up, hooked up, and shuffled out the door of a C-141 Jet, and then counted to four. My chute opened wide; and I thanked all responsible both silently and aloud that it did. But then, with forty seconds before hitting the ground, I rapidly found myself at the mercy of nature. All the training we did didn't prepare us for unfriendly thermals and the lack of real control we had over the antiquated old rope chutes we were using. So my chute went where the thermal wind wanted to take it.

I remember the surprise of waking up in the hospital sometime that night with broken ribs and a concussion. I again thanked everyone responsible for getting me there. But it was disheartening to find out that they couldn't let me finish my jumps at that time. I would have to return six months later after the ribs had healed, which I did.

After jump school, I found that I looked at life differently. I saw much the same attitude a few years ago when I rode home on the different ships returning from Iraq, providing Warrior Transition Training. Many expressed that they had gained a profound regard for their family, loved ones, life, and, yes, even Jacksonville, North

Carolina. Having seen what the people who don't have what we have endure in Iraq opened many eyes and hearts.

Let's not wait to have life threatening, life changing experiences before we start enjoying and being grateful for our blessings, grateful especially for the people who touch our lives in so many ways. Be kinder to the motorist next to you, the waitress who is doing her best with six tables alone, the child who is noisy because he is just a child, etc. Look around and see the good all about, then take the time to express appreciation to those who make it happen.

The Roman statesman Cicero said, "I never admired another's fortune so much that I became dissatisfied with my own." By happily focusing on what we have, we can have a more joyful life. That joy will always reach beyond ourselves and can bless so many others. May we try more consistently to have a *gratitude attitude* this week is my prayer.

As always, it is my hope that this message will help you this week to, "*mount up as on eagle's wings*," and renew a little of your strength to keep moving forward and find joy (Isaiah 40:31).

Until next time, may God bless you and may God continue to bless our great nation.

SEMPER FI

The Bible Says It's So

Matthew 18:20, Galatians 3: 28-29
A Thanksgiving ecumenical worship service at Big Macedonia
Baptist Church, in Supply, North Carolina

Fran Salone-Pelletier, *Lead Chaplain at Brunswick Novant Medical*
Center, Religious educator, retreat leader, and lecturer.
Author of Awakening to God: The Sunday Readings in our Lives,
A trilogy of Scriptural meditations (Cycles A, B, and C)
2011 Dr. Charles A. Trentham Homiletics Award

It is both encouraging and disheartening to hear what Jesus reminds us, "Where two or more are gathered in my name, there I am in the midst of them" (Matthew 18:20). There is great hope in those words. Numbers do not count. They are not crucial to our intent. Somebody, at least two somebodies, need to show up, desiring to gather in the name of the Christ, and he will be manifestly present.

It is also quite discouraging when those words are taken literally, and only two or a few more appear on the scene. Many are called. Few hear, heed, and accept the choice. Others remain among the "frozen chosen."

The Bible also recalls another profound truth for our pondering: "There is neither Jew nor Greek, slave nor free person, there is not male and female; for you are all one in Christ Jesus. And if you belong to Christ, then you are Abraham's descendants, heirs according to the promise" (Galatians 3: 28-29).

Both messages, both truths, carry with them a challenge that simultaneously causes us to glow with grace and cringe with cowardice. We love the idea of equality and intimacy, but we fear its consequences. We want the Trinity to remain a concept spelled with a

118

capital T, but we are frightened by its reality in the gathering of two or more persons with Christ amidst them. That trinity is fearsomely demanding. That trinity will not allow us to remain passive or lukewarm in our responses as people of God. That trinity is not about numbers. It is all about commitment, loyalty, courage, sacrifice, companionship, sharing, prayer, and intentional living. That trinity asks hard questions and will not leave us with easy answers. It will not settle for projects and plans, juries and judgments. It will not permit us to gain facts without growing in transformation or to pretend integration without authentic assimilation.

When I attended and participated in an ecumenical Thanksgiving service held at Big Macedonia Church, the power of a few like-minded people became wondrously evident. The church rocked with gospel music. White hands and black alike clapped their way through the hymns. Black faces and white ones were wreathed with smiles at the joy of just being together. With gracious prayerfulness, all joined hands in a union that can only be found in godliness and only employed in good will. In that place, at that time, all God's children had shoes and were ready for walking. In that place, there were no strangers. All were welcomed with handshakes and open hearts.

The evening was bright with the glory of God amid the representatives of five different denominations. These were folks who had arrived to pray with brothers and sisters, to hear God's word proclaimed and explained, to sing, and to enjoy each other's company and to voice gratitude. We celebrated with holy words and holy works, with food for the spirit and nourishment for the body. We discovered, once again, how much pleasure there is in being together without need for explanation or exploration. We knew that we were a beloved family in whom God was well pleased.

Some might count the numbers, note the quantity, and become discouraged that few were gathered. I choose to rejoice in the warm hospitality and common purpose of those who were there. I choose to delight in the sound of a choir whose voices were raised in heavenly praise and thanksgiving. I choose to be moved by the giftedness of the thirteen year old young man who caressed the keyboard with obvious ability and a desire to bring us closer to God with his music. I choose to be appreciative that sixty people left the warmth and comfort of their homes to come together in gratitude for all that God has given us. I choose to recognize that communal thankfulness and to know that it is not bound by race, color, or creed. I choose to believe that our gratefulness is deepened and intensified, made more clear and more real each time we push aside differences to find our human commonality.

The evening's program was simple and straightforward, reflective of the single-mindedness of the group. There was but one plan and one goal, grateful praise. The world around us might have been swirling with complexity and conflict. There may have been natural disasters that reminded us of the temporality of our existence. The darkness of the night recalled the need for us to be shining lights. The weariness of wars and their aftermath could easily have weighed us down. Life's heavy burdens could have been reason for despair. But in that place there was only faith and trust and radical hope. There was a spirit of holy thanksgiving and merciful compassion.

As was true in the Lucan gospel story proclaimed for us that evening, we had come as lepers, scabrous with sin and needing forgiveness. We showed our woundedness to the priestly community, asked for healing, and were made clean in the process. We saw the goodness of what happened and turned back to the God who made all of us in God's own image and likeness. We thanked God. We looked at each other with gratitude. Our faith had made us well. Our faith had changed us from ungrateful foreigners into graced friends.

And then, we got up and went our way, promising that we'd not forget the evening or our need for each other. We'd not forget to be thankful. And we'd tell the story until all the foreigners in our world become friends and all the lepers return to give thanks and all the churches come together as one family of God.

It will happen, because when two or more are gathered in God's name, God is there; and there is neither Jew nor Greek, slave nor free person, there is not male and female, black or white or brown or yellow, for we are all one. The Bible says it's so.

Do not be daunted by the enormity of the world's grief.

Do justly, now.

Love mercy, now.

Walk humbly, now.

You are not obligated to complete the work,

but neither are you free to abandon it.

The Talmud

Hidden Spiritual Graces

Acts 16:6-10
August 28, 2011

William F. Schnell, Senior Minister
The Church in Aurora, Aurora, Ohio
President of the Ohio Council of Churches,
serving on the Council's Faith, Justice and Mission Commission.
2008 Dr. Charles A. Trentham Homiletics Award

In my extended family, reference is often made to the "Bill Gene." That is the gene that results in Attention Deficit Hyperactive Disorder, commonly abbreviated as ADHD. Jim Bob got the Bill Gene in my family, Molly got it in Sister Sue's family, and Kory got it in Sister Betsy's family. Brother Jim got off scot-free with a calm and focused son, Brian. My brother stopped at a single child, in part I think, because he didn't want to push his luck in terms of getting a child with the Bill Gene. After all, Jim shared a bedroom with me throughout our childhood and adolescence and has more than paid his dues.

As you can see from the quote at the top of our bulletin, Oliver Sacks, Professor of Clinical Neurology at Albert Einstein College of Medicine, states that "Neurology's favorite word is 'deficit,' denoting an impairment or incapacity of neurological function." With that in mind, I must respectfully register my complaint with having the Bill Gene described as Attention Deficit. I rather think of it as Attention Different and not as an impairment or incapacity at all.

The world needs all kinds. It needs focused thinkers, but it also needs unfocused thinkers. Allow me to explain with the illustration of a light bulb. A spotlight is a highly focused beam of light and useful for highlighting actors on a stage or artwork on display. But you wouldn't want to use a spotlight to illuminate a football field or your driveway at night. No, for those applications you want a floodlight that disperses light over a large area.

Spotlight thinkers have a marvelous ability to zone in on a problem that requires a specific solution. However, that intensely focused attention may come at the expense of seeing the big picture. For that, you might want a floodlight thinker, who can see the big picture and make connections between elements within it. That broad but diffused form of attention may also come at the expense of focus; but, as was already said, the world needs all kind just like a manufacturing business needs both Research and Development types as well as Marketing types.

After I had been preaching for a while, my Mom confessed to a certain fear. She said, "I keep wondering when you are going to run out of stories." I tried to reassure her with a quote from Jimmy Durante: "I've got a million of 'em." I make connections between the timeless spiritual truths of scripture and my personal time and place all the time. Indeed, I have to work hard to balance sermons like this one with others of a more generic, less personal type because my floodlight attention is constantly seeing connections between the Bible's "then" and our "now" in the great grand scheme of things.

I owe it all to the Bill Gene. That is why I am grateful for my Attention Different Bill Gene. It is a spiritual grace as far as I am concerned. The title of our message is: "Hidden Spiritual Graces." I think a lot of things the world regards as deficits can actually prove to be hidden spiritual graces. Indeed if you believe that it takes one to know one, it seems pretty clear to me that St. Paul was an Attention Different sort of fellow as evidenced by his decision-making style in our text.

Our text is not like others in the Bible such as pithy proverbs or cryptic parables. No, our text deals with the mundane details of itinerary-making. Yet God in his wisdom has seen fit to include such seemingly inconsequential details in Holy Scripture so that, like other hidden spiritual graces, some real gems as may be uncovered as we dig into the text. As I read through our text, I want you to imagine how maddening it would be for any focused person with a plan and clear goals to follow Paul's lead anywhere.

"Paul and his companions traveled throughout the region of Phrygia and Galatia, having been kept by the Holy Spirit from preaching the word in the province of Asia" (verse 6). Now suppose your broker called you up and suggested you liquefy your well-diversified investment portfolio and put all the proceeds into a dot-com start-up because of a tip received from the Holy Spirit. What does that mean then or now? And why would the Holy Spirit want to keep the Word of God from being preached anywhere, especially while the Apostle is in the neighborhood? I guess it is a mystery.

Paul's decision-making style gets increasingly mysterious as our text continues. "When they came to the border of Mysia, they tried to enter Bithynia, but the Spirit of Jesus would not allow them to. So they passed by Mysia and went on down to Troas" (verses 7-8). Okay, if we were tempted to think that Paul and his companions were really not interested in preaching the Word of God in Asia, and the author of our text simply spiritualized the reporting of it, how do we understand that "they tried to enter Bithynia, but the Spirit of Jesus would not allow them to?" In other words, something is actually keeping Paul and his band from arriving at their intended destination.

This is a very squirrely route they are taking and not at all conducive to efficiency. Let us pray that Rev. Horak's tour of the Holy Land this winter is more organized. Imagine waking up in Tiberius and expecting to go to Jerusalem, but Rev. Horak greets you at breakfast with: "Change of plan, today we are going to Masada instead." Okay, it's a little out of the way but you can deal with it. But when at long last you arrive at the foot of Masada, Kevin announces, "The Spirit of Jesus is really not allowing us to take the cable car up today. Let's head over to Caesarea instead." I think you might get a little perturbed spending an entire day of your tour in a bus going nowhere.

Of course you know that an exceedingly well-organized, detail-oriented and focused guide like Rev. Horak would never subject a group to such disruptions. But an ADHD-type like St. Paul might and on nothing more than a whim. Our text continues: "During the night Paul had a vision of a man of Macedonia standing and begging him, 'Come over to Macedonia and help us.'" After Paul had seen the vision, we got ready at once to leave for Macedonia, concluding that God had called us to preach the gospel to them" (verse 10).

That little change of itinerary required passage on a ship westward across the Aegean Sea. But wouldn't you know that westward advance would leapfrog the Christian faith from Macedonia to Rome to England and eventually to America and the fair town of Aurora, Ohio. And while I would still rather follow Rev. Horak than St. Paul on a tour of the Holy Land, I've got to be grateful for the likes of St. Paul in expanding the reach of faith to me in his convoluted way. Like I said, it takes all kinds.

While we are talking about Rev. Horak, he has a reading "disorder" called dyslexia, which causes him to read words backward and which makes his advanced educational accomplishments all the more remarkable. But the marvelously organized way Rev. Horak compensates for that "disorder" has become a spiritual grace for him and for you and sometimes I think especially for an attention deficit sort of fellow like me. So there you have it: a professional church staff comprised of a deficit and a disorder. And don't let me get started on Toni Harris.

The Apostle Paul acknowledged a nagging personal weakness when he said: "there was given me a thorn in my flesh, a messenger of Satan, to torment me. Three times I pleaded with the Lord to take it away from me" (II Corinthians 12:7-8). And three times the Lord denied his request. Eventually Paul discovered a hidden spiritual grace in his thorny weakness. Unfortunately for folks who like "the untold story," Paul never reveals the exact nature of his thorny personal shortcoming, leaving people to guess or perhaps project their own personal deficits or disorders. Perhaps that is why I have suspected that Paul was ADHD. Others have suspected he was bipolar. Can you imagine anyone discovering a hidden spiritual grace in bipolar disorder?

Dr. Kay Redfield Jamison wrote not only the definitive psychiatric textbook on bipolar disorder, which is required reading for students of psychiatry; she also wrote an excellent book on the same subject for the general public entitled *An Unquiet Mind*. The latter is a compelling read from start to finish, made all the more compelling by the fact that the author is, herself, diagnosed with bipolar mood disorder. While Dr. Jaimison's disorder is not curable, it is treatable with medication and therapy, which largely reminds her about her need for medication when she is otherwise tempted to quit taking it.

At the end of the book, Dr. Jamison makes the startling admission that if bipolar disorder could be cured, she would rather forego the cure and remain as she is. Further, if she could really be anything at all she would choose to be slightly manic all the time. Why? Because of the flashes of authentic brilliance and creativity associated with that state of mind. Many of the original ideas which have made her writings so accepted by her chosen profession and the general public were first formulated in that state of mind. What many regard as a serious mental health disorder has proven to be a hidden spiritual grace. You can read more about that in her third book *Touched with Fire: Manic Depressive Illness and the Artistic Temperament*.

If you Google "famous people with bipolar" you might be surprised to discover who has either been clinically diagnosed with, or whose historical writings and other evidences strongly suggest, bipolar disorder. The list includes several American presidents including Abraham Lincoln and Prime Ministers such as Winston Churchill; musical geniuses from Beethoven to Mozart; entrepreneurs like Ted Turner; comedians, of course, like Jim Carey and Robin Williams; actors like Ben Stiller; astronaut Buzz Aldrin; author Mark Twain—you name it.

So, parents, the next time you are tempted to beat your square child into the round hole of normalcy when test results show he or she may be outside the norm for this or that category, I want you to remember two things. First, what you actually may have is an exceptional kid on your hands who defies the norm in a way that will one day prove to be gifted and talented. Second, there has never been nor will there ever be a completely normal person. That includes you.

If you aren't attention different or dyslexic or bipolar, then you are painfully shy or phobic in any number of ways, or you are an alcoholic or other kind of addict hopefully recovering. If you are completely normal in every way, then you've got to be the most mediocre and b-o-r-i-n-g person on the planet. But you are not, because being completely normal is a myth. God doesn't make completely normal people. He makes people with thorns in their sides and then challenges them to find the hidden spiritual graces in those thorny circumstances.

So congratulations on being human. Welcome to the club. Now that is settled, what are the special spiritual graces hidden in your abnormalities? Maybe by discovering them you will become the next Rev. Kevin Horak or Dr. Kay Redfield Jamison or Mozart or St. Paul. Or maybe you will just be a very special version of you. I guarantee you that the world could use an authentic you right now because, frankly, there is absolutely no one else who can fit the bill as well as you. That is why God made you and graced you just as you are. May we all discover a hidden spiritual grace as we come to Jesus and the table he has set for us today.

The High Cost of Red Stew
Matthew 13:1-9, 18-23

Martin C. Singley, III, *Senior Pastor*
Tellico Village Community Church
Loudon, Tennessee
1998 and 2010 Dr. Charles A. Trentham Homiletics Award

There's a cute little saying about the human brain that goes something like this: "The brain is an amazing organ. It starts working the moment you are born … and doesn't stop until the minute you stand up to speak in public."

I like that! And that little saying about the brain has inspired me to think up a similar saying about human life: "Life is an amazing, joyful and powerful gift! It starts the moment you are born and doesn't stop until the minute you start eating red stew."

That's a reference, of course, to our first reading from the book of Genesis. It's the story of Esau and Jacob, the twin boys born to Isaac and Rebekkah. At birth, Esau exited the womb first with his younger brother Jacob just seconds behind and holding onto the ankle of his older brother as if trying to win the race into their mother's arms, or more accurately, into their father's will. You see, in those days the firstborn son was entitled to inherit the majority of his father's estate, which, in the case of Isaac, was quite substantial. This was called "the birthright." So Jacob tried but failed to win the birthright from his brother Esau.

Now Esau, which means "hairy man," was the apple of his father's eye. He was a man's man, a hunter, fisherman, an outdoorsman just like his dad. The two of them used to love to shop at the Bass Pro Shop, and to sit in front of the TV on Sunday afternoon watching NFL football and discussing the importance of protecting the Second Amendment right to own and bear arms. Esau was a GUY!

Jacob liked hanging around with his mom and the neighbor ladies, not that there's anything wrong with that. In fact, the great benefit was that Jacob learned to cook! And he was good at it!

One day in the middle of hunting season, Jacob cooked up a big pot of what the Bible literally calls "red stuff." The translators of many Bibles apparently decided that "red stuff" was not all that appealing, so they changed the words to "red stew." And there was Jacob, stirring up this red stew when his brother Esau came in from hunting.

"I'm starving!" Esau declared. "Give me some of that red stew to eat!" "Sure," said Jacob, "but it'll cost you." "I don't care WHAT it costs," answered Esau. "I'm so hungry I'll die if I don't get something to eat this very moment." Then Jacob told his older brother, the future heir of their father's estate, what the price of the red stew would be. "Sell me your birthright," Jacob said.

And drooling over the delicious aroma of that red stew, Esau said, "Well, if I die of starvation that inheritance won't do me any good anyway. So, okay, it's yours!" And Esau sold the birthright to his brother for a bowl of red stew.

I wonder if we could possibly add up the ultimate price of that bowl of red stew. I would say it *pretty much cost Esau his life,* his future. You see, the Bible shows us that life is not just about being alive. Life is meant to be lived, and the life God created us for is a life with three basic components – a past, a present, and a future. And these three components of life give us the best possible life when they are held in balance. The past gives us the experience and knowledge we need to live in the present. In the present, we enjoy life and make decisions and take actions that create the future. And the future is that yet unseen component of life that is God's ultimate gift to us!

As Paul writes in 1 Corinthians 2:9, "Eye has not seen, nor ear heard, nor heart even imagined the things God has in store for those who love him." So God created us to be creatures who receive the gift of the past to guide and inform us; the gift of the present to enjoy the moment and step forward into the future; and a future that is overflowing with wonderful surprises, experiences, discoveries and gifts we cannot even imagine today, but are hidden in God's storehouse awaiting our stepping through its doors.

As I was watching the news coverage the other day of the last space shuttle mission, I was feeling a little sad because I've always wanted to ride on the shuttle. That fantastic contraption has fascinated me from the time years and years ago when they tested its flight characteristics by launching it piggyback-style from a big Boeing 747. Do you remember? And then the first launch from Cape Canaveral in 1981, thirty years and 135 missions ago. There were tragedies along the way and triumphs of science and technology. And as I watched the coverage this past Friday of the last launch of Atlantis, the last of the shuttles, I found myself feeling great joy for having been able to witness and experience all this.

And then I remembered something. It was back in the 1970's. Sandy and I were enjoying lunch with some friends at the Depot Street Tavern in Hillsboro, New Hampshire. At the table next to us was a group of young men who looked like engineers. I could tell by the pocket protectors and the fifteen Cross pens precisely lined up inside them. And I could tell they were engineers of some sort because they were talking about some very strange things that just sounded like the geeky things engineers would talk about. I had no idea what they meant when they said words like "launch angle" and "booster separation" and "G-forces at transonic speeds." What in the world was a command capsule, or an external fuel tank, or any of the other things they were discussing that day? It wasn't until almost a decade later that I heard many of those same words again when the space shuttle Columbia roared off the pad on STS-1, the first space shuttle mission. And that day it clicked for me. Those young guys had been talking about things they were probably working on way back in the 1970's that ultimately became reality in the 1980's and brought great meaning to all our lives right to this very day.

The ultimate destination of life is the future. That's why God made little babies with an inner urge to get up and crawl, then to stand up and walk, and then to follow dreams, and to step into an always-inviting future.

The ultimate destination of your life is the future! And the decisions we make in the present, the actions we take in this moment now, determine what the future will bring.

I was listening a while ago to an interview with Ivan Lendl who is considered to be one of the best tennis players of all time. Lendl no longer plays tennis but has become a pretty good amateur golfer. And his daughters are all about golf. Two of them play golf for the University of Florida, and a third has signed a national letter of intent with the University of Alabama. The person interviewing Ivan pointed out the irony that the children of a star tennis player had become golfers. He responded that when the girls were little, he and his wife Samantha decided they wanted to give them a sport they could enjoy all their lives. Competitive tennis at the highest levels has a comparatively short lifespan. So they taught their girls golf. The decisions they made in the present made all the difference to their kids in the future.

Sandy and I are proud of the fact that when our grandson Ryan was born, his parents Pete and Melissa decided to give him the gift of reading. He's been reading since he was a tiny tot. And Ryan loves to read. Now at *nine* years old, we can see the impact of the decision his parents made way back when he was an infant. Reading has given Ryan a wonderful imagination and a rather sophisticated understanding of the larger world in which he lives and the gift of language. Oh, can that boy talk! And negotiate! A while back, Ryan misbehaved and his father told him to go to his room. Ryan said, "Well, dad, I suppose I could go to my room, or perhaps I could just go downstairs and watch TV quietly."

The decisions we make today have an impact upon the future. Learning to live toward the future is one of the best things you can do for yourself and others. It's how God made us to be! But sometimes, we get hung up in the present. Sometimes we let go of the future for the sake of slurping down the red stew of today. And that's when life as God intends it comes to an end. Sometimes people die long before they are dead.

I once knew a woman named Carol. She was a member of a church I served, and it didn't take long after meeting Carol that I learned what a mistake it was to ever ask Carol how she was. She'd tell you. And it was never good. Carol had a way of pointing out all that was wrong with the church, her husband, her neighbors, the country. You name it; Carol complained about it. And everybody knew this about Carol. In fact, if someone in passing just happened to say, "Hey Carol, how are you?" you could almost see them trying to push the words back into their mouths!

Complaining about things made Carol feel good. It was like eating red stew. It fulfilled some present need in her life. But it drove people away. For the sake of indulging the need of the present, Carol lost the ability to form friendships into the future. Her husband eventually left. Her friends backed away. And when she died, she died pretty much alone.

Red stew comes at a very high price. It costs you relationships. It costs you happiness. It costs you the future. Sometimes in significant moments of transition, when we are stricken with a serious illness, when we make a terrible mistake, when we accomplish a great goal, or even when we achieve some milestone like retirement, we can become so focused on where we are right now, what our wants are right now, what we think we need right now that we lose sight of where we are going tomorrow. And when that happens, we begin to die spiritually. God did not make babies with the idea they would remain in diapers forever. Kids were not created to ride only tricycles. The human brain was not made to take in a certain amount of information and then just stop. People were not fashioned to reach a point in life where all that is left is to play bad golf and drink boxed wine.

That's why faith is so important. Faith, the Bible says, is confidence in what we hope for and the assurance about what we don't yet see. Faith is living today for the future God has in store. If you want to see what faith looks like, look at people who are forward thinking about all that God can bring about tomorrow through the decisions and actions they make and take today.

In our second reading today, we heard once again the parable of the sower. The image Jesus wants us to imagine is that of God going out among people and like a farmer spreading seeds of new life and growth. But human hearts are like different kinds of soil. Some peoples' hearts, like Carol's, are hard and nothing new can grow. Other hearts are tangled up with all sorts of thorns and bristles the concerns of today; and even if the seed starts growing, it eventually gets choked out.

But other people have hearts that are like good soil ready and waiting and willing to grow *new* things that will bring about the future and make life exciting and good. My friend Don Langille had one of those good-soil hearts. How sad I was when Don got cancer, bone cancer. By the time they found it, it was too late. Don was going to die. Once, when I was visiting with Don, I was sharing with him how sad I was about the situation he was in. He got upset with me. "Marty," he said, "you're talking to me as if I'm a cancer patient, as if this cancer is who I am, but it's not. I'm a human being who happens

133

to have cancer, and I have to deal with that. But this cancer does not define who and what I am."

Wow!

If anyone was entitled to anchor himself in the present, slurping up a bowl of red stew seasoned with lots of self-pity, it was Don. No one could possibly blame him for becoming solely focused on his present health dilemma. But he would have none of that. Don was not going to lose the future to the present of his terminal illness.

Some weeks later, Don came to me and said, "I got an idea!" "Oh? What's your idea?" "You know how we always collect money for turkeys at Thanksgiving time?" "Yeah." "Well I have an idea how we can maybe double or even triple the number of turkeys we give to people in need." "Tell me more." "What if we treated the appeal like a big turkey hunt? We can say, 'It's turkey hunting season at Greendale Peoples' Church!' I'll dress up like a hunter. I've got this Archie Bunker kind of outfit, and we'll ask people to buy turkey hunting licenses that will let me go and bag a bird and all the fixin's in their name! What do you think?"

"I think it's a great idea. Let's give it a try!" And that next November, Don's Great Turkey Hunt provided more turkeys for more people than ever before. When I moved down here, I brought Don's idea with me; and everybody knows how Dr. Deadeye Puckett has made our turkey hunt just as successful. Today, back at Greendale People's Church, it's now called the Don Langille Memorial Turkey Hunt. Don passed away shortly after the first one. But right up to very last day of his life on earth, DonLangille was giving life to God's future. His was a heart of good soil, and it still brings forth a good harvest even to this very day. Thousands of people have been blessed by what Don did back then as a person who happened to have cancer.

So where are *you* these days? Are you living only for the present? Or are you living toward the future? Today, God sets before us a menu and on it are only two items: red stew or our future inheritance as the children of God. Which one will it be for you?

On the Kingdom of Heaven

Matthew 25:1-13
Homily for the 32nd Sunday in Ordinary Time, Cycle A
November 6, 2011

Fr. Ron Stephens, *Pastor*
St. Andrew's Parish Warrenton, Virginia
(http://cacina-sta.webs.com/)

This Sunday's Gospel is yet another parable about the kingdom of heaven. What is the kingdom of heaven like? The difference is that this time Jesus is describing not so much the kingdom that we can experience here and now but is referring either to our own deaths or the last times. Jesus is the bridegroom who is coming. We don't know where or when, but we need to get ready for him. The wise virgins had all the things they needed to meet the bridegroom and escort him into the hall. They had their oil lamps. The foolish virgins weren't quite as prepared. They too were waiting; they knew the bridegroom could be coming but for some reason or other they had forgotten to bring the extra oil for their lamps. The bridegroom was very long in coming and all of them slept. When they thought they heard him coming, they awoke and grabbed their lamps; but the oil had been used up in the foolish virgins' lamps. They asked if they could share the others' oil, but they were refused. While they went to get some more, the bridegroom came, and the foolish virgins were locked out of the wedding.

The first idea I want to talk about today is preparation. When we really want something, we prepare for it. We make sure we do everything necessary to make it happen. Think of the care you have put into studying for an exam, packing for a trip, dressing for a special occasion or arranging a party for someone you love.

Preparation can also make something real for us that seems far off. First year students in college often waste a lot of time and don't do well, because they can't see ahead enough for the final goal of graduation. They don't begin early to prepare themselves. But once the preparations, the tests, the plans for the future make graduation real for them, they realize it is something they really want, and they prepare even more.

What does it mean to prepare? Do we prepare? How do we make things ready before we act? How do we prepare for a party, a wedding, intimacy, shopping, prayer?

The fact that none of us want to think about our death is another problem. It is hard to prepare for something without thinking about it and planning for it. Even old age is something difficult to prepare for because it seems so far away, and the feelings of our own immortality often get in the way.

When I went to Canada last summer for the twenty-fifth reunion of the founding of a school in which I was Principal for many years, I was amazed at how old everybody was, while I am sure they were saying the same thing about me.

St. Thomas Aquinas described wisdom as the habit of looking at everything in the light of our last end. The wise or sensible person is the one who evaluates everything, every option, every decision and choice in the light of what life is all about, the ultimate purpose of our existence. And this goal is our union with God and with the rest of the human race forever in heaven.

At the moment of death, described in today's Gospel as the moment when the bridegroom arrives to celebrate the wedding, this final goal, this ultimate purpose of our lives, will be very important to us. But right now we think of it very little. Like graduation, heaven is an abstraction which remains a remote possibility. And it will remain remote as long as we are not actually preparing for it. But most of us

137

do not make much preparation for heaven. We tend to think there will always be time to think about that later. Then suddenly we find ourselves at the end of our lives, having made little or no effort to "know, love and serve" God. And the only explanation we give for placing business, pleasure or the development of body and mind ahead of the development of our spiritual lives will be, "It just seemed more important at the time!"

I certainly am not intending to put a guilt trip on anyone, but I want to show you that preparing for our end can be a positive and freeing thing. We often associate Jesus with the word *peace* because Jesus said very clearly that he came to bring peace.

Maybe a personal experience will help to understand this. Every year I always have my Christmas shopping done by the end of June. Originally, this was because my last car trip to Canada was around then, and it was my last chance to bring things into Canada without spending a fortune to mail them. I got into the habit of shopping early and continue doing it to this very day, even though I now most often drive to Canada at Christmas. I discovered that because of this early preparation, I didn't feel worried or pushed or hectic around Christmas. I was very peaceful, especially in relation to the people around me. My preparation had brought me an inner peace, a freedom that others didn't seem to have. Similarly, thinking about our end early in life and doing things that will get us ready to meet our Maker we will bring on a real sense of peace.

The second idea I want to leave you with is that *the parable about the kingdom of heaven is one of a wedding feast*. It is the wedding of heaven and earth that we will sing about in our final hymn today: "Come to the feast of heaven and earth, come to the table of plenty!" God wants to marry us. We are part of the cosmic wedding which was begun in the incarnation when God and man are wedded in Jesus Christ. But what has always bothered me about this reading is that all of these virgins were waiting for the bridegroom. They had prepared at least a little. The foolish virgins were there waiting, but they ended

138

up being locked out of heaven and were refused help even by the wise virgins. The foolish virgins weren't even that bad. So it has always seemed to me like a hard Gospel until I came to realize that if the ones with the oil shared their oil, no one would have had enough.

Consider the importance of self-care. On airplanes they always warn us to put the oxygen mask on yourself first before you attempt to assist another.

Also consider that no one else can provide something for which you alone are responsible. The fire of God comes from within, and no one can give it to us. We must take responsibility for the power of God within and not expect that someone can give us God. We can be pointed in the right direction, but each person must choose to embrace God or not. Each person must fill his or her own oil; no one else can do it for us.

God saves us, but we have to want to be saved. Baptism permeates us, but we have to want to be permeated. God loves us, but we have to want to be loved.

We can find ourselves outside the wedding feast, not because God wanted us outside, but rather because we refused to be prepared. The choices in life are always up to us. We can get the impression that we are locked out forever, but why? God is over and again at every moment inviting us no matter how many times we say no or we are not prepared. God still invites us. As we will sing in another hymn today, "We belong to you, O Lord our God. We belong to you,"

The final message comes from Jesus, "Stay awake!" One of our Catholic Apostolic priests saw this as Jesus' teaching on prayer. Prayer ultimately is learning how to stay awake. Prayer is paying attention. Unfortunately, we have often been taught prayers, taught to recite prayers by rote, but real prayer is not about reciting or memory. Prayer is about staying awake and paying attention. It may be at midnight, it may be when we are home, in a hospital or a prison, at work, in school, or on the Metro or wherever we are, God is coming to us. The wedding is happening; and if we are not paying attention, we will miss the marriage of a life time.

So what is the final message: *prepare,* which we can especially do in the Advent Season; *pray,* in order to stay awake; *pause,* long enough to do good things with our lives for others, and in doing so you will achieve the *peace* that Jesus so often offered us: My peace I give. My peace I leave you!

This then, my friends is the Good News that we celebrate today!

Poetry

God Is on Our Side

Bill Bruggen
Member of Tellico Village Community Church

"Join up today!" the captain called, "to fight the savage band.
They're laying waste to hearth and home and pillaging our land.
You must protect our country now!" the loyal captain cried.
"It is your bounden duty son, and God is on our side."

"The enemy are devils son, with horns and breathing flame.
They have no moral values, only wish to kill and maim.
But you must never fear son the courageous captain cried.
"The Lord will always guide you boy, for He is on our side!"

I joined the loyal ranks that day and learned to fire a gun.
I learned to follow orders–and that I must never run.
We learned to march, and practiced how to kill the deadly foe.
We couldn't wait to join the fight; we couldn't wait to go.

Just before the battle started the captain came around.
"The devils will attack us soon, but you must hold your ground.
Though you feel hell's breath upon you
          and you see old Satan's gun,
The Lord will always guard you boys, so never cut and run.

The battle sounds grew louder; we could hear the cannon's thud.
The steel death rained 'round us as we cowered in the mud.
And then we heard the Devil's shriek advancing through the trees.
An icy fear enveloped me and I got up to flee.

I stood. And right before me was a boy about my size.
He had fair skin and hair of gold, and fear shone in his eyes.

143

He was no fiery monster; he was not the Devil's son.
Like me he was a young farm boy–not yet turned twenty-one.
We stared at one another, this scared young Reb and I.
And we could feel the mirrored fear; we both began to cry.
Then from the right there came a shot and I could feel the pain.
A bullet struck his boyish cheek and lodged into his brain.

"No! No!" I cried in anguish as I rushed to stop his fall.
"You've shot a boy you fool, he's no Devil after all."
A puzzled look came to his eyes; his skin turned deathly pale.
I bent to hear his final words; his breath began to fail.

I wanted to do Your business, Lord,
     But my life was cut short by Fate.
I wanted to do Your work, Lord, So please open up the gate.

God's Trick

Bill Bruggen

I would surely laugh out loud,
So funny it would be,
If our loving God in Heaven
Has tricked both you and me.

And those lordly prophets too–
Those wisest men of old,
And the pulpit pounding preachers
So self-assured and bold.

If we could climb the ladder,
Peek over heaven's rim,
And to our surprise discover
A Her and not a Him.

A Church Is Not

Bill Bruggen

A church is not a hallowed pile
Of stone or wood or brick.
A church is people Heaven sent
To serve the poor and sick.

A church is not the windows tall
Of leaded glass embossed.
A church is gentle eyes that seek
The destitute and lost.

A church is not the buttressed walls
That shield the chosen blest.
A church is arms spread wide in peace
To offer food and rest.

A church is not a vaulted roof
With lofty bells that toll.
A church is minds in steadfast toil
To save the wayward soul.

A church is not a pulpit stout
That preaches doom and fear.
A church is voices raised on high
To sing God's praises clear.

A church is not a sacred cross
Upon an altar wall.
A church is hearts that overflow,
With tender love for all.

The Sermon

Reaction after listening to a sermon on radio
Sunday, April 20, 2008

Carl F. Burke passed from this life on August 9, 2011
Pastor Emeritus, Tellico Village Community Church
Loudon, Tennessee

Nearly every congregation
Gives unstilted admonition
To a well prepared oration
By the minister of God.

For the people love a sermon,
Whether Latin, French, or German,
If there is sense or logic to it.
Otherwise they'd rather boo it,
But in church they must not do it,
So they sit. . .
While the man of God is blowing
Holy Taurus ever throwing,
Evidently never knowing when to quit.

Some there are, and it's no wonder,
Seek escape in peaceful slumber,
But by far the greater number merely frown,
While they hear the talk distressing,
their inmost soul expressing,
"O for Pete's sake, give the Benediction
And sit down."

Welcome Baby Jesus

December, 2011

Marlene Wanamaker
Tellico Village Community Church,
Loudon, Tennessee

Once again it's Christmas
And we welcome the baby so dear
We pause again to remember
The Savior of the world is here.

We remember the angels singing
On a quiet starlit night
And think again of the shepherds
Hurrying to see the heavenly sight.

They found him in a stable
In the town of Bethlehem
And fell on their knees to worship him
Here was the King of Men.

After all these centuries later
We still seek the baby boy
And we find him deep within our hearts
And we are filled with joy.

May the baby born in Bethlehem
Who came to save all men
Fill your hearts with love and peace
As we welcome him again.

Prayer

A Prayer for Christmas Eve

Christmas Eve 2011

Robert M. Puckett,
Tellico Village Community Church
Loudon, Tennessee
2007 Dr. Charles A. Trentham Homiletics Award

Once again we gather on Christmas Eve to celebrate the birth of our Lord Jesus Christ and to remember the angelic message of good news of great joy which was for all humankind. And the heavenly host joined in the chorus saying, "Glory to God in the highest, and on earth peace and good will to men."

That wonderful message has been remembered on Christmas Eve down through the centuries only to be soon forgotten, as humanity resumes their warring ways and fails to practice good will to one another.

Forgive us O God that we have all too often claimed that you are on our side and failed to recognize that you have revealed yourself in the life of Jesus as the God of love, who is on the side of all who suffer physical pain, mental anguish, economic loss and the tragic destruction of interminable warfare.

May we not forget that we are ALL created in your image and worthy of mutual respect and love.

May we have the wisdom on this Christmas Eve truly to hear the message of peace on earth and goodwill to ALL others.

May we have the courage to beat our swords into plowshares and study war no more. May there truly be peace on earth and let begin in each of us present here tonight.

We give thanks that our troops are returning home from Iraq and ask you to bless them as they are reunited with their families.

May we have the wisdom and courage to put an end to the war in Afghanistan in the New Year that is soon to dawn, and may the people of Iraq and Afghanistan learn to live at peace with one another and the rest of the world.

We pray for those who have lost loved ones and those who have suffered life crippling wounds on all sides. Enable then to find comfort and peace.

May your Holy Spirit encourage people the world over to be guided by the highest and best in their religious values, rather than the worst, so that good will to all may shape the peace we so desperately need.

People all over the world long for lasting peace, especially during this season. But millions continue to suffer the ravages of war, hunger, and neglect. Many pray for peace but fail to act peacefully with their ncighbors.

Let us turn to God in prayer with a renewed commitment to become instruments of peace.

Special Occasions

Charge to the Congregation,
Barberton First Presbyterian Church
Service of Pastoral Installation
For Dr. Richard Lapehn

Richard O. Griffith, Pastor
New Covenant Community Church
Akron, Ohio

Ephesians 4: I therefore…beg you to lead a life worthy of the calling to which you have been called, with all lowliness and meekness, with patience, forbearing one another in love, eager to maintain the unity of the Spirit in the bond of peace. There is one body and one Spirit, just as you were called to the one hope that belongs to your call, one Lord, one faith, one baptism, one God … of us all, who is above all and through all and in all.

Speaking the truth in love, we are to grow up in every way into him who is the head, into Christ, from whom the whole body, joined and knit together by every joint with which it is supplied, when each part is working properly, makes bodily growth and upbuilds itself in love.

Mark 4: A sower went out to sow. And as he sowed, some seed … fell on rocky ground, where it had not much soil, and immediately it sprang up (but) since it had no depth … when the sun rose it was scorched … (and) withered away. … Other seeds fell on good soil and brought forth grain, growing up and increasing and yielding thirtyfold and sixtyfold and hundredfold. … (Those) who have ears to hear let (them) hear.

We are here today to install, yes, but more important to celebrate the call of Dr. Richard Lapehn to the pastorate of Barberton: First Presbyterian Church – a church of great history and significance, served over the years by clergy of great intellect and integrity. And to this congregation, which has been blessed by their ministries, Rev. Lapehn now comes and becomes part of the "great cloud of witnesses" who have given their all to all of the people.

You are the soil upon which your new pastor has agreed to labor and will endeavor to cultivate. You are the people who are called to be the *good* soil, yielding unknown but infinite increase especially spiritually, being the Godly oasis in the midst of a parched land, as folks find nourishment to receive them into the fellowship of the faithful.

Rich will be sowing the seed of the Word and watering it with pastoral care and Godly love. But what kind of soil will he find? All kinds, really, from sandy and shallow to the rich deep loam we all wish we were. But nutritious soil wasn't always that way. It was fertilized most of the time, naturally. And as we also know, fertilizer is a byproduct, the consequence of other activities, whether from fallen leaves or something else. I believe that in the Church the fertilizer of faith that enriches every*one* and every*thing* is the byproduct of dealing with differences. And we also know, as does the arena of athletics, "no pain, no gain."

How can we deal with differences? We listen, not only with our heads but with our hearts; we impute sincerity and Godly goodwill with those with whom we apparently disagree; we realize that others have perspectives that can enrich our own; we strive for consensus not necessarily unanimity; we search for win/win not win/lose outcomes; we realize that when, for whatever reason, votes need to be taken, the result is the result, and it is time to endeavor to move on.

So, dear friends, speak the truth in love, grow in every way to him who is the head of the Church, to Christ, growing and upbuilding yourselves in and through love; and be the rich soil God is calling us all to be.

AMEN

The Path Unending

Malcolm G. Shotwell

An invitation to ponder how we face and celebrate life and death.

In Loving Memory of His Brother
J.Ralph Shotwell 1926 – 2010

Early one Sunday morning, a group of women went to a tomb to anoint, as was the custom, the body of one they had loved and lost. When they arrived they found the tomb open and empty, they were met with the words: "Why do you seek the living among the dead? He is not here. He has risen! Come, see the place where he lay and go quickly and tell his disciples that he has risen from the dead."

"Come, see...go...tell," This invitation and this command have echoed down through the centuries. In the presence of death, many have found hope and help from that first Easter morning encounter at the garden tomb. Last February, my elder brother Ralph went home to be with the Lord. As I stood with the family and dear friends at his grave, we acknowledged the final resting place for the physical remains of our loved one. But we also called to mind the belief that he was not there. His soul, his spirit–that which gave his body life–had moved on into his eternal home. In preparation for that day, my brother and his wife Virginia had planned and written "A Celebration of New Beginnings." Included in that celebration was this poem, "The Path Unending," which my brother wrote:

> The mountain is tall, the valley deep,
> And the path I climb is very steep.
> While at the bottom where anyone starts,
> I learned that life has many parts.

Though the physical I thought at first,
I learned my body from my spirit burst.
Ere by body was, my spirit said,
"Let the body be for what's ahead."
Much needed knowledge has fed my mind;
While wisdom has been my spirit's find.
The Spirit from which my spirit came
Can see to it I'm reborn again.
Nothing will prevent my ascending
The mountain and the path unending.

It is this "path unending" that I want to invite you to travel with me as we ponder how the Christian faces life and death. For my brother's memorial service, his wife Virginia invited me to be one of the two voices in a dialogue presentation that she and Ralph had written and to also lead the committal service. Three nights before the service, Ralph appeared to me in a dream. He told me to go to the family file in my office and I would find something he wanted me to share at the service.

Early the next morning I followed those instructions and found a four page brochure that Ralph had written. It contained the poem I just shared. I already knew that he had written that into the script we were to read. I looked again and noticed the title of his writing: "I Do Not Fear Death." That's what he wanted me to say. In life, my elder brother often tried to tell me what to say; and now in death, he was still doing it. All kidding aside, he was telling me from beyond the grave on that unending path that he was *not* afraid of death.

Beneath that affirmation Ralph quoted the Apostle Paul from I Corinthians 15:40: "There are heavenly bodies and earthy bodies; the beauty that belongs to heavenly bodies is different from the beauty that belongs to earthy bodies."

Among the books that my brother has written, there is one entitled *Ceilings and Floors*. It contains forty-eight meditations. The one

159

suggested for the time when we gathered for Ralph's memorial service included these words: "Fear Neither Life Nor Death":

Disaster after disaster fell upon the biblical character Job. While early in these trying times, he sought God intellectually, he later awakened to a higher consciousness and began to seek God through the heart thus gradually sensed the reality of God's presence and love, leading him to the proclamation: "I know that my redeemer lives!"

During one of my several serious illnesses, I benefited greatly as my wife Virginia read Job to me. She told me that in my stages of semi-consciousness, I could be heard quoting the twenty-third Psalm. This did not surprise me. Most often I have been able to hold firmly to my belief that God provides my every need, gives me strength, guides me in right paths, restores my spirit, gives me inner peace. Even when I am passing through such as "the valley of the shadow of death," God is with me. Indeed, I believe that I can never be separated from God's presence, goodness and love.

As in life, also in death there is much that is miraculous. St. Paul wrote: "what is mortal must be changed into what is immortal; what will die must be changed into what cannot die." While I will always have questions, I do not doubt that just as life in my mother's womb was preparing me for life in this world, life in it has been preparing me for a peaceful, joyful, love-filled life in the world beyond this one.

Let me speak here to some of you who may be thinking that death is not a subject you want to hear. It is a difficult, sobering subject. The fact is, death is not limited to one age, and it is inevitable for all of us. The mortality rate on earth is 100 per cent. Almost daily we read or hear on TV of dedicated service men and women losing their lives in service to our country.

As I write these words a neighboring town is bemoaning the death of a twenty-nine year-old staff sergeant who is on that unending path beyond the grave, as is my oldest daughter who went home to be with

160

the Lord when she was only seventeen. Death has no respect for age. It can come anytime. The question is not *when* but *how* we face death, regardless of our age.

When sorrow comes, as come it must;
In God we all must put our trust.
With all the wealth which we may own,
we cannot meet this test alone:
And only we will stand serene
Who have a faith on which to lean.

To illustrate his belief in a spiritual immortality, Ralph found meaning in a writing by Walter Dudley Cavert:

In the bottom of an old pond lived some grubs who could not understand why none of their group ever came back after crawling up the lily stems to the top of the water. They promised each other that the next one who was called to make the upward climb would return and tell what had happened. Soon one of them felt an urgent impulse to seek the surface. He rested himself on the top of a lily pad and went through a glorious transformation which made him a dragonfly with beautiful wings.

In vain he tried to keep his promise. Flying back and forth over the pond, he peered down at his friends below. Then he realized that even if they could see him they would not recognize such a radiant creature as one of their number.

Harry Emerson Fosdick speaks on this new dimension in his book *The Assurance of Immortality.* He wrote:

The Christian affirmation is not that we have souls, but that we are souls; that we substantially are spirit, as invisible as God.... The affirmation of the materialist is not that we have bodies, but that we are bodies; that flesh is the essence of us, and that all our intellectual and moral life, like the peal of a bell, is a transient result of physical vibration, and ceases when the cause is stopped.

Between these two affirmations the decision lies: either we are bodies that for a little time possess a spiritual aspect, or else we are spirits using an instrument of flesh.

If your scientific mind cannot grasp this spiritual dimension and you are having trouble accepting the belief in life beyond the grave, let me suggest you read *Life After Death–The Evidence* by Dinesh D'Souza. It is heavy reading and I must admit that I could not follow all his logic. It is provocative and combines philosophical arguments with physics and biology and contains an incisive analysis of how the world's major religions have viewed the afterlife and why we can expect that what Shakespeare called the "undiscovered country" will be discovered by us someday.

Jesus talked about that "someday" when he said: "Do not let your hearts be troubled. Believe in God, believe also in me. In my Father's house there are many dwelling places. If it were not so, would I have told you that I go to prepare a place for you? And if I go and prepare a place for you, I will come again and will take you to myself, so that where I am, there you will be also. And you know the way to the place where I am going" (John 14:1-4 NRSV).

Thomas, one of the twelve disciples, asked our question when he said: "Lord, we do not know where you are going. How can we know the way?" Jesus replied to Thomas (and to us, if we will listen and understand): "I am the way, and the truth, and the life. No one comes to the Father except through me" (John 14:5). A few chapters earlier in John 11:25, following the raising of Lazarus from the dead, Jesus said: "I am the resurrection and the life. He who believes in me, though he were dead, yet shall he live. And whosoever lives and believes in me shall never die." And then Jesus adds this question: "Do you believe this?"

This question needs to be asked of each of us, individually and personally, as we ponder The Path Unending.

I find help in words from the Apostle Paul (I Corinthians 15:12-20, 35-38, 42, 44, 54-58): But how, we ask, can we be steadfast, immovable and keep on working for the Lord with the fear of death hanging around? Simply, but profoundly, by accepting the invitation found in John 3:16: "For God so loved the world, that he gave his only Son, so that everyone who believes in him may not perish but may have eternal life" (NRSV).

The key words *love – gave – believe – eternal life* are essential ingredients for our journey on the path of life, if we do not want it to end. And the giver and receiver of these vital ingredients are God and the *believer*–that includes you and me.

One day in the waiting room of a prompt care facility in Springfield, I read these words on a poster: "The Healing Power of LOVE" My brother's wife Virginia focused on this message in a poem she authored and I read at Ralph's memorial service "What Is Love?

Love puts music in laughter, beauty in song,
warmth in a shoulder, gentle in strong.
Love is magic in memories, sunshine in skies,
gladness in giving, starlight in eyes.
Love is fun in together, sad in apart,
faith in tomorrow, joy in a heart.
Love takes lumps from the throat, tears from the eye,
aches from the loss, darks from the sky.
Love is a mystery, a message and a miracle
and the mastery of the magnitude of life.

As you and I travel toward that path unending, let's make sure our days are filled with love–love toward God, love toward others, and love for self. That's the healing power that will help us face life and death and life everlasting.

Rick Warren, the author of *The Purpose Driven Life* and *The Purpose Driven Church,* penned some more meaningful words: "In a

163

nutshell, life is preparation for eternity. We were not made to last forever, and God wants us to be with Him in Heaven. One day my heart is going to stop, and that will be the end of my body–but not the end of me. I may live sixty to one-hundred years on earth, but I am going to spend trillions of years in eternity. God wants us to practice on earth what we will do forever in eternity." Good words for us to heed on our path unending.

Ralph selected verses from hymns for his memorial service, "Great Is Thy Faithfulness."

Great is thy faithfulness, O God my Father.
There is no shadow of turning with thee.
Thou changest not, thy compassions they fail not.
As thou hast been, thou forever will be.

REFRAIN: Great is thy faithfulness! Great is thy faithfulness!
Morning by morning new mercies I see.
All I have needed thy hand hath provided.
Great is thy faithfulness unto me.

Summer and winter, springtime and harvest,
sun, moon and stars in their courses above
join with all nature in manifold witness
to thy great faithfulness, mercy and love.

"Spirit of God, Descend Upon my Heart"

Spirit of God, descend upon my heart;
wean it from earth through all its pulses move.
Stoop to my weakness, mighty as thou art,
And make me love thee as ought to love.

Teach me to feel that thou art always right;
teach me the struggles of the soul to bear,
to check the rising doubt, the rebel sigh.
Teach me the patience of unanswered prayer.

God's faithfulness and a prayer for His Spirit to come into our hearts, with these two traveling with us, the path through life and death and into eternity will take on added meaning and purpose.

In my last conversation with my brother he said: "Mac, I'm in the Lord's hands" and then he added as he often did "I love you."

A social worker at the hospice asked Ralph something about his faith; would it sustain him during his journey now? His reply was, "Now, more than ever, I know that God loves all of us and God cares for all of us." Then the social worker said something about how his faith would sustain him during his journey now. "The hospice would do nothing to hold him back" she added. Ralph then said emphatically: "Of course not. I'm going to be free."

It is easy now to see why Ralph picked those two hymns to be sung at his memorial service. God's faithfulness and God's Spirit were at work on his path unending.

Finally Ralph chose the hymn "O Love That Wilt Not Let Me Go"

O Love that wilt not let me go, I rest my weary soul in thee;
I give thee back the life I owe,
that in thine ocean depths its flow may richer, fuller be.

O Light that followeth all my way,
I yield my flickering torch to thee.
My heart restores its borrowed ray,
that in thy sunshine's blaze its day may brighter, fairer be.

O Joy that seeketh me through pain,
I cannot close my heart to thee.
I trace the rainbow in the rain,
and feel the promise is not in vain that morn shall tearless be.

165

Love, Light and Joy, three companions to have on our path unending. The unison benediction Ralph and Virginia chose for the climax of their "Celebration of New Beginnings" was from the prophet Isaiah:

> Those who hope in the Lord will renew their strength.
> They will walk and not be faint, run and not be weary.
> They will soar with wings like eagles. So be it. Amen.

May this be our prayer, too, on our Paths Unending.

Dr. Charles A. Trentham Homiletics Award

The Charles A. Trentham Homiletics Award is an annual award given for the best sermon reflecting the spirit and values of the community church movement submitted each year for publication in the *Inclusive Pulpit Journal*. It is conferred at the Annual Conference of the International Council of Community Churches. The deadline for submission of manuscripts for the year 2013 issue of the Journal is January 31, 2013. Selection of the recipient of this award will be made by the Community Press Editorial Board. Accompanying this award will be a $250 stipend.

Submission of sermons, prayers, poems, hymns, and liturgical readings for consideration should be carefully proofed and corrected, preferably as a computer Word document file.
E-mail: icccdc@sbcglobal.net.

Printed manuscripts should be mailed to
Inclusive Pulpit Journal
21116 Washington Parkway
Frankfort, Illinois 60423-3112

The Charles A Trentham Homiletics Award Winners

1996 - No Award Given

1997 - Rev. Virginia Leopold "The Never Ending Journey"

1998 - Rev. Martin Singley, III, "Living in an Open Circle"

1999 - Rev. Herbert Freitag "Children of the Same God"

2000 - Rev. David H. Blanchett "A Single Point of Difference"

2001 - Rev. Robert A Fread "One Baptism"

2002 - Rev. C. David Matthews "Tragedy and God"

2003 - Dr. C. George Fry "God is Good - Always"

2004 - Dr. Jeffrey R. Newhall "Receiving into Our Heart"

2005 - Rev. Paul Drake "Unity in Diversity"

2006 - Dr. Keith R. Haverkamp "How Big Is Your Table"

2007 - Dr. Robert M. Puckett "To Be a Man"

2008 - Dr. William F. Schnell "One Church"

2009 - Rev. Harry Foockle "Obama, the ICCC And Me"

2010 - Rev. Martin Singley, III, "Skeletons in the Closet"

2011 - Chaplain Fran Salone-Pelletier, "Devoted to Community"

Published by The Guilford Press
A Division of Guilford Publications, Inc.
72 Spring Street, New York, NY 10012

These papers were prepared with government financial support or by a government employee and are, therefore, in the public domain.

Printed in the United States of America
Last digit is print number: 9 8 7 6 5 4 3 2 1

ISBN 0-89862-383-9
Published simultaneously as Volume 19, Number 1
of *Suicide and Life-Threatening Behavior*, Spring 1989.

Strategies for Studying Suicide and Suicidal Behavior

Edited by
Irma S. Lann, MEd,
Eve K. Mościcki, ScD, MPH,
and Ronald Maris, PhD

The Guilford Press
New York   London

Notes on Contributors

Donald W. Black, MD, completed a fellowship in psychiatric epidemiology in 1976. He is now Assistant Professor of Psychiatry at the University of Iowa College of Medicine.

David A. Brent, MD, is Assistant Professor of Child Psychiatry at Western Psychiatric Institute and Clinic, Pittsburgh. He directs a clinic for suicidal adolescents, Services for Teens at Risk (STAR Center).

Lucy Davidson, MD, EdS, is Assistant Professor of Psychiatry at Emory University School of Medicine. Dr. Davidson was a member of the Secretary's Task Force on Youth Suicide, Department of Health and Human Services, for which she coauthored a paper with Dr. Gould on suicide contagion.

Eva Y. Deykin, MS, DPH, social worker and psychiatric epidemiologist, is Associate Professor and director of the doctoral program, Department of Maternal and Child Health, Harvard School of Public Health. Her research interests include mental disorders of children and adolescents with specific emphasis on depression and suicidal behavior. She is a recipient of the William T. Grant Faculty Scholars Award.

Felton Earls, MD, is the Blanche F. Ittleson Professor of Child Psychiatry and Director of the Division of Child Psychiatry at the Washington University School of Medicine, St. Louis. He has a long-term interest in the childhood antecedents of violent behavior.

Carol Z. Garrison, PhD, is Associate Professor of Epidemiology at the University of South Carolina. Her research has focused on the epidemiology of adolescent depression and suicide.

Madelyn S. Gould, PhD, MPH, is Assistant Professor of Psychiatry and Public Health (Epidemiology) at Columbia University College of Physicians and Surgeons, and is a Research Scientist at the New York State Psychiatric Institute. Dr. Gould is a recipient of a Faculty Scholars Award from the William T. Grant Foundation.

Irma S. Lann, MEd, is Head of the Affective and Anxiety Disorders Program in the Child and Adolescent Disorders Research Branch, Division of Clinical Research, National Institute of Mental Health. Research on youth suicide is one of her major program interests.

Eve K. Mościcki, ScD, MPH, is Assistant Chief of the Epidemiology and Psychopathology Research Branch, Division of Clinical Research, National Institute of Mental Health. She is also Head of the Suicide Consortium at the National Institute of Mental Health. One of her major research interests is the epidemiology of suicide and suicidal behaviors.

Cynthia R. Pfeffer, MD, is Associate Professor of Clinical Psychiatry, Cornell University Medical College, and Chief of the Child Psychiatry Inpatient Unit, New York Hospital–Westchester Division. She was president of the American Association of Suicidology in 1986–1987. She is the author of *The Suicidal Child* (Guilford Press, 1986). She was awarded the Erwin Stengel Award by the International Association for Suicide Prevention in 1987.

Patrick W. O'Carroll, MD, MPH, formerly an Epidemic Intelligence Officer in the Violence Epidemiology Branch of the Centers for Disease Control (CDC), is a medical epidemiologist with the Intentional Injuries Section of the Division of Injury Epidemiology and Control at CDC. He has the main responsibility for suicide prevention research at CDC and has also conducted research into the epidemiology and prevention of homicide and drowning.

Mary Jane Rotheram-Borus, PhD, is Associate Clinical Professor of Medical Psychology, Division of Child Psychiatry, Columbia University College of Physicians and Surgeons. Her research focuses on evaluation of suicide risk and cognitive behavioral interventions with runaway and homeless youths.

Barbara Stanley, PhD, is Associate Professor, Department of Psychology, John Jay College of Criminal Justice, City University of New York, and is also Associate Professor, Department of Psychiatry, Columbia University College of Physicians and Surgeons. Dr. Stanley is the recipient of several grants from the National Institute of Mental Health and private foundations for her work in the areas of suicide and ethical issues in psychiatric research.

Michael Stanley, PhD, is Associate Professor of Clinical Psychopharmacology, Departments of Psychiatry and Pharmacology, Columbia University College of Physicians and Surgeons, and is also Director of the Division of Neuroscience at New York State Psychiatric Institute. Dr. Stanley's research interests include biological research in suicide and suicidal behavior; neurochemistry of psychiatric and neurological illness; mechanisms of action of drugs used to treat mental illnesses; and ethical issues in psychiatric research.

Sylvan Wallenstein, PhD, is Associate Professor of Biostatistics at Columbia University School of Public Health. Dr. Wallenstein has been collaborating with Dr. Gould on a grant from the Centers for Disease Control that is examining clustering of suicide.

STRATEGIES FOR STUDYING SUICIDE
AND SUICIDAL BEHAVIOR

Foreword

Lewis L. Judd, MD
National Institute of Mental Health

Historically, the "convening power" of the Federal biomedical research establishment has proven to be among the more effective of the mechanisms utilized by programs either to stimulate needed research or to sharpen the focus of research pertinent to a given scientific or public health concern. The articulation of a research priority implicit in the calling by program staff of a workshop; the gathering of acknowledged experts to debate and discuss needs, gaps, gains, and opportunities; and the dissemination of proceedings tend often to be exceptionally generative. The intellectual foment evident in the give-and-take of an invited research workshop leads to enhanced professional and public awareness of an issue, and the feedback loop extends often to the IRGs and policy-making apparati responsible for ratings and, ultimately, funding decisions.

For these reasons, we are pleased to have the opportunity to publish, in this issue of *Suicide and Life-Threatening Behavior*, the papers presented at a workshop titled "Strategies for Studying Suicide and Suicidal Behavior," convened by the Division of Clinical Research, National Institute of Mental Health (NIMH). The NIMH has long maintained a productive commitment to the study of suicide. Many of the targeted initiatives pursued over the years are discussed in the introduction to this volume. Of equal significance is the NIMH's broad scientific program, which has made possible significant progress in the field's capacity to diagnose, treat, and in many instances prevent recurrences of the mood disorders so disproportionately represented in the life histories of individuals who complete suicide. These scientific gains have prompted the NIMH to initiate the Depression Awareness, Recognition, and Treatment (D/ART) program, a public and professional education campaign that is the first research-based prevention program ever directed toward a specific group of mental disorders.

Although the D/ART program promises to make substantial inroads in reducing the incidence of suicide, it is clear that diagnosable affective illness is not a sole and sufficient explanation for all suicidal behavior. Factors ranging from impulsivity to substance abuse to biochemical and genetic predisposition—and the intricate interaction of all of these putative precipitants—beg for empirical explication. Because incremental gains in knowledge in these and other areas often suggest new research needs and opportunities, it is essential that we identify innovative strategies for collecting, pooling, and analyzing epidemiologic and clinical research data. Thus, we present this report of the workshop as part of our systematic effort to stimulate, develop, and support a broad spectrum of basic and clinical research on suicide and suicidal behaviors.

Preface

Ronald W. Maris, PhD
University of South Carolina Center for the Study of Suicide

Special issues of this journal are devoted to in-depth analysis of one aspect of suicidal problems. *Suicide and Life-Threatening Behavior,* Volume 19, Number 1 reflects the serendipitous confluence of several new developments at the National Institute of Mental Health (NIMH) in the study and prevention of suicide. In addition to the NIMH workshop on strategies for studying suicide represented in the present issue, I refer to the report of the Health and Human Services Secretary's Task Force on Youth Suicide (Otis R. Bowen, MD, and Shervert H. Frazier, MD, 1988); and the creation of the Suicide Consortium at the NIMH.

Past special issues of the journal have considered ethics of the right to die (Volume 13, Number 4, 1983), psychobiology of suicide (Volume 16, Number 2, 1986), and prevention of suicide (Volume 18, Number 1, 1988). The present issue addresses problems in the scientific study of suicide. In spite of at least 100 years of research and thousands of articles and books on suicide, the basic knowledge of suicide has advanced surprisingly slowly. Even today there are no solid, comprehensive textbooks on suicidology comparable to those in psychiatry, psychology, economics, biology, sociology, and so on. What research findings we do have often tend to be clinically irrelevant. We still do a very poor job of predicting any individual's suicide before the fact. After the fact of suicide, we indignantly point to "clues to suicide." But, knowing just these antecedent clues and not the crucial suicidal outcome, we still get far too many false positives for suicide predictions to be very clinically useful.

Another serious problem is the lack of generalizability of our research results. Often our samples are born out of clinical convenience; basic research is an addendum to more pressing treatment concerns. Seldom are suicide research samples drawn properly, with sufficiently large numbers of subjects and controls. Usually we also have too narrow a focus in our dependent variables; for example, we study just adolescents, rather than suicide across the life span in normal as well as patient populations. In spite of the laudable Epidemiologic Catchment Area (ECA) program (see Mościcki, Chapter 11, this volume), a major first step in the right direction, we still lack national sample survey data on completed suicides. Of course, such studies are expensive, are time-consuming, tend to generate superficial data, and are difficult to conduct with accuracy after the fact of suicide.

Finally, there are subtle, poorly defined problems inhibiting the study of suicide. I refer here to the growing dilemma of doing needed basic suicide research versus protecting the rights of human subjects; to the tyranny of special disciplinary methods as the "only" or preferred way of doing suicide research; and to the lack of truly interdisciplinary, integrated suicide research.

Through the efforts of guest editors Irma Lann and Eve Mościcki, several new strategies for resolving these problems in the study of suicide are presented. These include the following:

- A more integrated biopsychosocial approach
- Use of standardized measurement instruments (e.g., the) Schedule for Affective Disorders and Schizophrenia, the Beck Depression Inventory, the Diagnostic Interview Schedule, etc.)
- Record linkages
- Study of nonclinical populations (e.g., schools, the ECA project, psychological autopsies of suicide completers, etc.)
- Improvement in size and comprehensiveness of samples
- Use of modern (especially multivariate) methodology (e.g., logit regression, log–linear methods, calculating power equations, improved sensitivity and specificity, better case–control studies, etc.)
- Examination of suicide across the life span, with a developmental focus
- More prospective and longitudinal studies
- More attention to groups at high risk for suicide (e.g., runaways, substance and alcohol abusers, AIDS patients, depressed individuals, prior suicide attempters, etc.).

I am delighted to be able to coedit this impressive volume. An experienced and highly competent group of contributors has been assembled. I think you will enjoy their stimulating papers. Of course, this special issue is just a start. Self-destruction is a recalcitrant, perennial problem that afflicts each generation anew. It deserves our brightest minds and best efforts.

Introduction

Irma S. Lann, MEd, and Eve K. Mościcki, ScD, MPH
Division of Clinical Research, National Institute of Mental Health

Durkheim defined suicide as "death resulting directly or indirectly from a positive or negative act of the victim himself, which he knows will produce this result" (Durkheim, 1897/1951). Deaths from self-inflicted injuries in the United States have increased steadily since the 1950s, making suicide the eighth leading cause of death in the 1980s (National Center for Health Statistics, 1987). As a cause of years of potential life lost, however, it ranks fourth (Centers for Disease Control, 1988). The rates of suicide increase in successive age groups from approximately 12 per 100,000 in the 15–24 cohort to 24 per 100,000 in those aged 75–84 (National Center for Health Statistics, 1987). It is the third leading cause of death among persons aged 15–24. The majority of completed suicides in all age groups are committed by white males; the majority of suicide attempts occur among white females.

Since Durkheim's seminal work in the late 19th century, and despite varying methodologies, certain risk factors have emerged that have consistently been associated with suicide and suicidal behaviors across a wide array of both clinical and epidemiologic studies. These include psychiatric disorder, sociodemographic risk factors, family history of suicide, biochemical risk factors, substance abuse, contagion, and firearms.

In the early 1970s, the field of suicide research was plagued by a lack of agreement on definitions of critical terms, inconsistent use of unstandardized measures, inadequate research designs and methods, and the absence of a solid empirical basis for early detection and prevention efforts. In the mid-1970s, an important book appeared in which leading investigators who had been brought together in conference by the National Institute of Mental Health (NIMH) attempted to remedy the situation. They critiqued existing research methods, and proposed various models for the measurement and prediction of suicide and suicidal behaviors (Beck, Resnik, & Lettieri, 1974).

Since that time there has been a new cycle of social crisis, led, in part, by media attention to the clustering of youth suicides and increased public awareness of the fact that the youth suicide rate has nearly tripled since the 1950s. With the aging of the population has come a greater appreciation of the high suicide rates in the elderly. The seriousness and saliency of the problem led to a Congressional mandate and earmarked monies for the study of suicide. In 1985, the Secretary of the Department of Health and Human Services created a Task Force on Youth Suicide and asked its members to synthesize available information and submit recommendations for action to both the public and private sectors. The results of those deliberations have recently been published (U.S. Department of Health and Human Services, 1988).

With so heavy a public demand for preventive intervention efforts and a consequent heightening of interest in research, it seemed timely to determine once again what progress was being made in this recalcitrant, complex, and extremely important area of research. In June 1987, NIMH's Division of Clinical Research convened a workshop titled "Strategies for Studying Suicide and Suicidal Behavior." This was one of a series of program development activities designed to assess the current state of knowledge, inform the field, and stimulate research. The purpose of the Workshop was to examine some of the more promising methods and approaches being used to study suicide and suicidal behavior, with particular emphasis on different settings and populations. Participants were asked to characterize the findings in their special area of research and to critically review the strengths and weaknesses associated with the approach. They were also asked to identify questions or problems that require further study. The papers from that workshop are presented in this special issue of *Suicide and Life-Threatening Behavior*.

The workshop opened with a consideration of what can be learned from completed suicides—an assessment of the utility of mortality statistics and autopsy data. It then moves to approaches for investigating suicidal behaviors among inpatients and outpatients seen in hospitals and emergency rooms. Next came an examination of research on populations in community settings such as health centers, runaway shelters, and schools. This was followed by a review of community survey studies of suicidal behavior in the general population. This order is preserved in the present special issue.

There were some important gaps in the workshop. Approaches to studying suicide and suicidal behavior in the elderly, minorities, and AIDS victims were not on the agenda. These are high-risk groups that warrant a special focus and considerable research attention.

Although the workshop contributions do not constitute a comprehensive review of progress in research, they highlight major developments. The advent of biological approaches is noteworthy, as is the potential increase in diagnostic and predictive power that is evident when biological and psychological approaches are combined. There have been important advances and refinements in measurement techniques, and substantial movement toward agreement on operational definitions of critical terms. Our understanding of correlates and risk factors of suicide and suicidal behavior has clearly grown, moving us closer to developing and testing sensitive, ethical, and clinically effective interventions.

Progress can also be gauged by what problems remain. As the papers point out, we have not resolved the persistent problems of appropriate sampling, appropriate control or comparison groups, and issues of validity in the measurement of suicidal behaviors. In discussions,[1] workshop participants identified several unmet needs. Among them was the need for prospective, collaborative, multisite studies, using standard operational definitions and assessments, and sharing a common protocol. There was also a call for more multidisciplinary cooperation that might bring together developmental, epidemiologic, clinical, and sociocultural perspectives.

We offer this volume in the hope that it will serve as a reference for investigators and promote good research. The content should also be of interest to clinicians, educators, and others concerned with suicide and suicidal behaviors.

References

Beck, A. T., Resnik, L. P., & Lettieri, D. J. (Eds.). *The prediction of suicide*. Bowie, Md.: Charles Press, 1974.

Centers for Disease Control. Changes in premature mortality—United States, 1979–1986. *Morbidity and Mortality Weekly Report*, 1988, *37*, 47–48.

Durkheim, E. *Suicide: A study in sociology* (G. Simpson, Ed.). Glencoe, Ill.: Free Press, 1951. (Originally published, 1897.)

National Center for Health Statistics. *Advance report of final mortality statistics, 1985* (Monthly Vital Statistics Report, Vol. 36, No. 15, Supp. DHHS Publication No. PHS 87-1120). Hyattsville, Md.: U.S. Public Health Service, 1987.

U.S. Department of Health and Human Services. *Report of the Secretary's Task Force on Youth Suicide: Vol. 1. Overview and recommendations*. Washington, D.C.: U.S. Government Printing Office, 1988.

---

[1] We appreciate the contribution of two participants who acted as discussants at the workshop: Mary Monk, PhD, Professor and Deputy Chairman, Department of Epidemiology, Johns Hopkins University School of Hygiene and Public Health, Baltimore, Maryland; and David Shaffer, MD, Irving Philips Professor of Child Psychiatry and Professor of Pediatrics, Columbia University College of Physicians and Surgeons, New York, New York.

1

A Consideration of the Validity and Reliability of Suicide Mortality Data

Patrick W. O'Carroll, MD, MPH
Centers for Disease Control

Since the 19th century, suicide mortality data have been used by so-ciologists and epidemiologists to assess the magnitude of the problem of suicide, to identify particular groups at high risk of suicide, and to generate and test hypotheses about the etiology of suicide (Durkheim, 1897/1951). Trends in the incidence of suicide have been used to evaluate the effectiveness of suicide prevention measures (Kreitman, 1976). Changes in the demographics of suicide mortality in the United States have recently inspired efforts that may have an enormous impact on the direction of health policy (U.S. Department of Health and Human Services, 1988). Suicide mortality statistics have even been used as a barometer of the general mental health of communities (Kraus & Tesser, 1971; Naroll, 1969). Yet there is an enormous body of literature that questions the validity and reliability, and thus the usefulness, of suicide mortality statistics. Certain investigators have suggested that the quality of official suicide statistics is so dubious that these data should not be used for research (Douglas, 1967) or even for purely descriptive purposes (Linden & Breed, 1976).

There are, of course, a number of compelling reasons to use suicide mortality data. These data have been collected over many years in most countries on earth, allowing temporal and international compar-isons. The demographic data collected on the decedents are useful for identifying risk groups at the descriptive level. Suicide mortality data in many countries are readily accessible on computer tape, and the information is coded according to a common international scheme. Nevertheless, there are a number of limitations to suicide mortality

Requests for reprints and any correspondence should be sent to Dr. Patrick W. O'Carroll, Centers for Disease Control, Mailstop F-36, 1600 Clifton Road NE, Atlanta, GA 30333.

data, not all of which are related to the question of their validity and reliability. For example, the number of variables available for investigation is quite limited, because the data are derived entirely from death certificates. Also, the national compilation of death certificate data in the United States usually takes several years, so the most recently available data may not be recent enough for many purposes.

But given the widespread use of suicide mortality statistics, questions concerning their validity and reliability are of central importance. I first briefly outline the problems associated with the definition and official certification of suicide, and then review the literature pertaining to the validity and reliability of suicide statistics. Finally, I consider the process of suicide certification as a "test" and estimate its sensitivity, specificity, and predictive value, using data from studies reviewed in this chapter.

Issues in the Definition and Certification of Suicide as a Mode of Death

As a concept, suicide is not difficult to define. The World Health Organization has proposed that a suicidal act may be defined as "self-injury with varying degrees of lethal intent" and that suicide may be defined as "a suicidal act with a fatal outcome" (World Health Organization, 1968). This seems clear enough. Unfortunately, such definitions are inherently difficult to use in practice—that is, in determining whether a *particular* death was a suicide—for several reasons. For one thing, any definition of suicide requires that the injuries causing the death be self-inflicted. Determining self-infliction is straightforward in most cases, but impossible in others.

A far more difficult requirement in determining suicide as the mode[1] of death is establishing the victim's intent to take his or her own life. The problems inherent in having coroners and medical examiners determine a decedent's suicidal intention have been reviewed elsewhere (Farberow, MacKinnon, & Nelson, 1977; Litman, 1968), but three major aspects are mentioned here. First, coroners and medical examiners are rarely adequately trained to evaluate psychological factors in death, and determining the victim's intention to die requires a psychological evaluation. Second, assessing a victim's intention requires information

---

[1] In certifying a particular death, the "mode" of death (also referred to as the "manner" of death) is distinguished by coroners and medical examiners from the biological "cause" of death. For example, if someone were to commit suicide by jumping from a high place, the biological cause of death would be the traumatic injuries resulting from the fall, but the mode of death would be suicide.

from family, friends, or others about the victim's personality and behavior. The amount and quality of such information varies widely from case to case. Finally, the amount and nature of information required by a *particular* coroner or medical examiner before he or she will certify a death as a suicide vary tremendously. Litman, Curphey, Shneidman, Farberow, and Tabachnik (1963) noted, for example, that authorities in one city would not certify a death as a suicide unless a suicide note was present.

Another complication regarding suicide is that the proper *legal* decision regarding the mode of death may be completely different from the *clinical* decision. The former must rely on what can be proved and is the basis of the official death certification, whereas the latter decision is a judgment based on available information and the balance of probabilities. These differing approaches to deciding modes of death have very real implications for the validity of official suicide rates (Clarke & Finnegan & Fahy, 1983; Warshauer & Monk, 1978); these implications are reviewed later.

A final consideration relates to the process by which modes of death are certified in the United States. Nelson, Farberow, and MacKinnon (1978) summarized this process as follows:

[E]ach State is responsible for its own vital registry system. In addition, each State has the option of selecting either a centralized system of coroners or some type of decentralized system allowing for varying degrees of autonomy for individual counties. Since each State has its own system, defining which cases come under the certifying authority of the coroner or medical examiner, the information required on the death certificate, the legal definition of suicide, the types of death subject to medicolegal review, etc., vary from State to State. Moreover, the qualifications of the coroner or official responsible for medicolegal certification varies greatly. This person may be a forensic pathologist, general practitioner, mortician, sheriff, lawyer, or a layman, who may be elected, appointed, or operating in some ex-officio capacity. (p. 77)

The decentralized nature of the vital registry system in the United States gives rise to legitimate concerns about the reliability of death certification from county to county and state to state.

In addition to errors in certification that result from varying state and local certification procedures and certifier training, errors can also occur when vital statistics data are transferred from the local to the state to the federal levels (Malla & Hoenig, 1983). A certain frequency of such errors is to be expected, however, and the errors would threaten the overall validity of suicide statistics only if they systematically occurred more frequently for suicide than for other modes of death. Another complication arises from the fact that nosologists actually record the vital statistics data from the death certificates filled out by coroners and medical examiners. If there are inconsistencies between the certified mode of death and other information on a death certificate, a nosologist will record the most appropriate external cause-of-death code, which may or may not be consistent with the certified mode of death. However, for the purposes of this chapter, I assume that the validity and reliability of suicide statistics are synonymous with the validity and reliability of the certification of suicide as a mode of death.

The Validity and Reliability of Suicide Mortality Statistics

The validity of a particular assessment or judgment is a measure of its accuracy or correctness. The concept of validity may be juxtaposed to that of reliability, which is a measure of precision or (conversely) variability. With regard to the certification of suicide as a mode of death, the validity of the decisions made is a measure of the degree to which true suicides are certified as suicides, and true nonsuicides are certified as other than suicides. On the other hand, the reliability of suicide certification is a measure of the variability of the certification process (and thus suicide statistics) among different jurisdictions or in a single jurisdiction over time. Suicide certification as a process can have poor validity and yet good reliability across jurisdictional boundaries: Theoretically, each jurisdiction might systematically misclassify the same deaths.

Are Suicide Mortality Statistics Valid?

Ideally, the validity of a particular test is measured against some "gold standard." For example, the validity of certifications of the biological cause of death can be assessed by the performance of autopsies (Kircher, Nelson, & Burdo, 1985). Unfortunately, no definitive standard exists by which the validity of suicide certification can be assessed, and thus investigators have used a number of other strategies to assess the validity of suicide statistics.

Legal and Administrative Changes in the Certification of Suicide.   If the process by which deaths are certified as suicides changes, and if these changes are such that certain deaths would be considered suicides under one set of rules but not under the other, then the certification of suicide may be said to be less valid under one set of rules than under the other. It may be unclear *which* set of rules leads to more valid judgments. Nevertheless, several investigators have exploited such procedural changes to see whether they shed light on the validity of suicide statistics.

Changes in the process of certifying suicide deaths occur at the international level with each revision of the *International Classification of Diseases* (ICD). With the introduction in 1958 of the seventh revision of ICD (ICD-7), deaths from self-inflicted injury were to be certified as suicides in the absence of a statement that the death was unintentional (Linden & Breed, 1976). With the introduction of the eighth revision of ICD in 1968 (ICD-8), an additional mode-of-death category—"circumstances undetermined"—was introduced. This shifted the burden of proof in the opposite direction: Self-inflicted deaths were *not* to be certified as suicides *unless* the certifier specified that the injuries were intentionally self-inflicted.

Despite these changing criteria, the changes in U.S. suicide rates attributable to ICD revisions were fairly modest. The introduction of ICD-7 resulted in an apparently artifactual increase of approximately 3% nationally in the number of deaths certified as suicides (National Center for Health Statistics, 1965), whereas the introduction of ICD-8 resulted in a decrease of 5–6% in the reported number of suicides (National Center for Health Statistics, 1968). These revisions may have had more profound effects in certain localities that are not reflected in the national estimates (Warshauer & Monk, 1978).

Jennings and Barraclough (1980) extended this approach to assessing the validity of suicide statistics by examining the rates of death certified as suicides and accidents[2] in England from 1900 to 1976 in light of various changes introduced during this period in the acts and rules governing death certification. They reasoned that if suicides were being erroneously certified as accidents, then the changes in suicide rates associated with the promulgation of new certification regulations should be mirrored by changes in the *opposite* direction in the rates of death certified as accidents. The researchers found, however, that none of the legal and administrative changes appeared to explain the fluctuations in the English suicide rate during the period studied.

Deaths of Undetermined Mode. If a true suicide is not certified as such, how else might it be certified? Under ICD-8 and ICD-9 (the present revision), the mode of death may be certified as undetermined. Several investigators have examined deaths of undetermined mode in conjunction with deaths certified as accidents and suicides. Holding and Barraclough (1975) noted a high prevalence of psychiatric morbidity in a sample of 110 undetermined deaths in a particular London district. They found

---

[2] The term "unintentional injury" is preferred by injury epidemiologists to the term "accident," because the latter seems to imply an inevitable, unforeseeable event rather than a preventable cause of morbidity and mortality. However, coroners and medical examiners use the term "accident" for the mode of death when death is due to unintentional injuries; thus, this term is used here.

that 73% of the decedents were diagnosed as mentally ill, 54% had been receiving medical care for psychological symptoms, 42% had a history of psychiatric care, and 24% had made previous suicide attempts. They concluded that many undetermined deaths were probably suicides. Warshauer and Monk (1978) noted that, under ICD-8, many deaths in New York City that were assigned as suicides within the medical examiner's office were ultimately certified as undetermined. These investigators suggest that, to the extent that true suicides are certified as undetermined, official suicide statistics are not entirely valid.

Only 2–5% of all deaths, however, are typically certified in the undetermined category (Murphy, 1979), and thus the potential impact of such certification errors is limited. Furthermore, Sainsbury and Jenkins (1982) found that combining suicides with undetermined and certain accidental deaths (by poisoning and drowning, especially) did not alter the trends or sex patterns of suicide appreciably. McClure (1984) noted that the increase in the suicide rate in England and Wales from 1975 to 1980 could not be accounted for by changes in the pattern of deaths certified as undetermined or accidents.

Differential Certification of Suicide.   Another method of assessing the validity of suicide mortality statistics is to conduct a comparison of suicide certification among different groups. If certification varies from group to group, then presumably the certification of suicide is not equally valid for all such groups. Andress (1977) noted that many Native Americans living in California are misidentified as Mexican-Americans at the time of death. Therefore, suicide rates (and death rates in general) tend to be underestimated for the former and overestimated for the latter. Warshauer and Monk (1978) demonstrated that in New York City, more black than white suicides (as assigned but not so legally certified by the medical examiner) were certified as undetermined. This resulted in an underestimation of the suicide rate of 42% for whites and 80% for blacks.

In addition to race and ethnicity, the process of suicide certification has been reported to vary by suicide method. Walsh, Walsh, and Whelan (1975) reviewed 5 years of coroners' inquest records in Ireland and, based on the clinical judgments of two psychiatrists, culled 210 suicides from these records. By reviewing discrepant cases—where the official mode-of-death determination had *not* been suicide—Walsh et al. determined that coroners were more likely to miss true suicides (i.e., to incorrectly certify true suicides as other than suicides) if the method of suicide had been drowning, jumping, shooting, or ingesting poison. Warshauer and Monk (1978) also found that the process of suicide certification varied by method. They reported, however, that coroners were more likely to miss true suicides when the method of death was jumping or "other"; coroners were more likely to correctly certify suicide as the mode of death when the methods were shooting, hanging, and (to a lesser extent) ingesting poison.

Researchers have also noted that the deaths of persons with known histories of mental illness are more likely to be certified as suicides (Monk, 1987; Walsh et al., 1975). It is difficult to determine, however, to what extent this suggests a problem with the validity of these certifications. Indeed, a history of mental illness may well be an appropriate factor to consider when suicide is suspected.

Incentives to Avoid Suicide Certification in Equivocal Cases. Many who question the validity of suicide statistics argue that at least some true suicides are incorrectly certified, sometimes deliberately, in response to a variety of factors that influence coroners and medical examiners to avoid certifying deaths as due to suicide. These factors may be sociocultural (Douglas, 1967), religious (McCarthy & Walsh, 1975), financial (Litman et al., 1963), or political. Although there is anecdotal evidence that such factors do indeed influence the decisions of coroners and medical examiners, the degree to which suicide statistics are invalidated by these influences is difficult to gauge.

Presumably, sociocultural and other such factors are potentially most influential for equivocal suicides and for those deaths that are certified as undetermined. Litman et al. (1963) noted that in Los Angeles approximately 10% of all deaths certified as suicide could be considered equivocal cases. Combining this figure with the percentage of deaths usually certified as undetermined would yield an estimated range of 12–15% of potential suicides for which the mode of death certification might have been influenced by social, religious, or other such factors. This percentage is almost certainly an underestimate. First, it includes only those equivocal cases that were ultimately certified as suicides. Yet many equivocal deaths are certified as accidents unless they can be proven to be suicides (Brooke & Atkinson, 1974). Furthermore, certain suicides may occur under circumstances that do not even arouse the certifier's suspicion of suicide. These apparently "unequivocal" deaths may be certified as accidents or even as natural deaths (Johnson, 1969).

Are Suicide Mortality Statistics Reliable?

The reliability of suicide statistics depends on the comparability of suicide certification across different jurisdictions or over time. A wealth of literature on the etiology and prevention of suicide uses temporal or geographic differences in suicide rates as its basis. The question of the reliability of suicide statistics is crucial to any estimate of the legitimacy of much of this literature.

Cross-National Reliability of Suicide Statistics. A number of investigators have concluded that cross-national comparisons of suicide rates may be inappropriate because of widely varying methods used in death certification from country to country (Farberow & Neuringer, 1971). In a review of countries reporting to the World Health Organization, Stengel and Farberow (1968) found extensive variation in suicide certification procedures. Atkinson, Kessel, and Dalgaard (1975) found striking differences, for example, in suicide ascertainment procedures between Denmark and England. Barraclough (1972) reviewed various factors that might lead to a differential assignment of equivocal cases in Scotland and England. Finally, Clarke-Finnegan and Fahy (1983) noted that suicide determinations in Ireland and England were based on very different types of information.

However, differences in the process of suicide certification do not necessarily imply differences in the outcome. In other words, different procedures may result in equally reliable suicide certifications. This issue was explored by Atkinson et al. (1975) through a blinded exchange of a sample of death records between Denmark and England. They demonstrated that the Danes consistently reported more suicides than the English when given the same case material. This finding was consistent with the differences already noted in the ascertainment procedures for suicide in Denmark and England. But Ross and Kreitman (1975) conducted a similar blind exchange of death records between England and Scotland, which also have procedural differences that might affect the certification of suicide. They found that procedural differences did *not* seem to have an effect on the reliability of suicide certification.

If we assume that there are differences in the reliability of suicide certification from country to country, is there evidence that these differences are so great that conclusions drawn from cross-national comparisons are invalid? Sainsbury and Barraclough (1968) noted that the rank order of suicide as a cause of death among immigrants to the United States was nearly identical to the rank order of suicide in their 11 countries of origin, suggesting that sociocultural influences on the certification of suicide were not so pervasive as to invalidate cross-country comparisons. On the other hand, Clarke-Finnegan and Fahy (1983) estimated that underreporting in Ireland was so extensive that it invalidated the apparent differences seen between English and Irish suicide rates.

Intranational Reliability of Suicide Statistics. As noted previously, both the procedures for death certification and the training of the certifiers vary greatly in the United States from county to county. In a sample of 202 counties in the western United States, Farberow et al. (1977) determined that county-specific procedures for certifying suicide and the attitudes and training of coroners explained intercounty variations in suicide rates almost as well as sociological community variables such as income and housing. Atkinson et al. (1975) demonstrated considerable variation in the proportion of deaths by poisoning certified as suicide among different districts in England and Wales.

On the other hand, Sainsbury (1983) compared coroners' districts in England and Wales where there had been a change in coroner to districts where there had not been a change. He concluded that the idiosyncrasies of particular coroners could not explain the differences reported between districts. Barraclough, Holding, and Fayers (1976) found that *within* a single coroner's district, there was no indication that particular coroner's officers or pathologists were responsible for a disproportionate number of suicide, undetermined, or accident determinations. Finally, Sainsbury and Jenkins (1982) noted that the scientific value of intranational comparisons was corroborated by the fact that conclusions inferred about suicide from a comparison of district-level suicide rates were corroborated by case–control studies of suicide at the individual level.

Temporal Reliability of Suicide Statistics. As noted previously, the changing criteria for certifying suicide from one revision of the ICD to another result in artifactual changes in the number of reported suicides. The apparent magnitude of such changes, again, does not appear to be very great at the national level. More local changes in death certification—for example, as a county moves from an appointed coroner system to a medical examiner system—may be more profound. Research into the implications of such local changes in death certification is contradictory (Sainsbury, 1983; Warshauer & Monk, 1978) and incomplete. Currently, the evidence suggesting artifactual variability in the quality of suicide statistics is more compelling for the geographic than for the temporal dimension.

The Certification of Suicide as a "Test"

Suicide certification may be thought of as a process in which a dichotomous decision is made: A particular death either is or is not a suicide. This process may be viewed as a "test," and the validity of the process may be estimated in terms of sensitivity, specificity, and predictive value.

The literature addressing the validity of suicide mortality statistics focuses almost entirely on one side of the question: the sensitivity of suicide certification, which is a measure of the degree to which true suicides are correctly identified as suicides in the certification process. The other side of the validity question—specificity, or the degree to which true nonsuicides are correctly certified as other than suicides— has been ignored because it is assumed that deaths from modes other than suicide are rarely if ever certified as suicides. I estimate both the sensitivity and the specificity of suicide certification, using data provided directly or indirectly in the published literature.

In the studies reviewed previously that actually demonstrated undercounting of suicide, the true suicide rate was estimated to range from 1.2 (Holding & Barraclough, 1975) to 3.8 (McCarthy & Walsh, 1975) times the officially reported rate. In most studies, the true rate was estimated at 1.4 to 1.8 times the reported rate (Warshauer & Monk, 1978). Calculating the inverse of these figures yields estimates of the sensitivity of suicide certification; these estimates range from 26% to 83%, with common estimates in the range of 56% to 71%.

Two of the reviewed studies provide sufficient information for a calculation of both the sensitivity and specificity of suicide certification. McCarthy and Walsh (1975) reviewed an unspecified number of coroners' inquest records from 1964 through 1968 in Dublin, from which they determined that, in their clinical judgment, 210 cases were suicides. In my analysis, these decisions are considered the "gold standard." McCarthy and Walsh noted that in no case did the coroners certify a death as a suicide when the authors themselves had determined that the mode of death was not suicide. In a companion paper by Walsh et al. (1975), it is noted that 58 of the 210 suicides they identified were certified as suicides by the coroners; by subtraction, 152 were not certified as suicides (Table 1.1). The calculated sensitivity of the certification

TABLE 1.1. A Calculation of the Sensitivity, Specificity, and Predictive Value of the Process of Determining Suicide as a Mode of Death: All Inquest Records, Dublin, Ireland, 1964–1968

Coroners' judgments ("test" data)	Mode of death, as judged by two psychiatrists ("gold standard")		Total
	Suicide	Not suicide	
Suicide	58	0	58
Not suicide	152	X	$152 + X$
Total	210	X	$210 + X$

Note. Data source: McCarthy & Walsh (1975).
Sensitivity = $58/(152 + 58)$ = 27.6%.
Specificity = $X/(0 + X)$ = 100.0%.
Predictive value $(+) = 58/(58 + 0)$ = 100.0%.
Predictive value $(-) = X/(152 + X)$.

process in this example is 27.6%. McCarthy and Walsh did not report the number of nonsuicides, but because we know there were no false positives—cases of nonsuicide that the coroner certified as suicide—the specificity may be inferred to be 100%.

These estimates must be considered suspect. In this example, the "gold standard" is the clinical judgment of two psychiatrists based solely on inquest records. They made no attempt to gather additional data on the cases through, for example, psychological autopsies. Thus, the coroners' judgment is simply compared with the judgment of the two investigators. Except for the considerations reviewed previously regarding factors that might influence coroners to undercertify suicide—for example, the additional burden of proof imposed with ICD-8—there is no *a priori* reason to accept the judgments of McCarthy and Walsh as the "gold standard."

Litman et al. (1963) employed somewhat more objective methods, and the data they presented provide a more legitimate basis for estimating the sensitivity and specificity of the process of suicide certification. They noted that approximately 10,000 cases were referred to the medical examiner in Los Angeles each year. Of these, approximately 1,000 were certified as suicides. Litman et al. further noted that approximately 100 cases a year were regarded by the medical examiner—but not necessarily certified—as equivocal suicides. The medical examiner for Los Angeles County referred 100 cases of equivocal suicide for further investigation and consultation to a death investigation team staffed by the Los Angeles Suicide Prevention Center. Before referral, each case was given a tentative certification by the medical examiner. After investigation, the original certification was changed in 19 cases. In this analysis, these final judgments are considered the "gold standard."

Litman et al.'s data permit the calculation of the sensitivity and specificity of suicide certification at two levels: certification for *equivocal* suicides, and certification for suicides in general. Of the 100 equivocal suicides, 55 were ultimately certified as suicides; the medical examiner's tentative certification was changed from accident to suicide in 11 cases, and from suicide to accident or natural death in eight cases (Table 1.2). The sensitivity of suicide certification in equivocal cases is thus 80.0%, and the specificity is 82.2%. For equivocal suicides, the predictive value of a positive suicide certification (i.e., the proportion of positive suicide certifications that were for true suicides) is 84.6%, and the predictive value of a certification of a nonsuicide mode of death is 77.1%.

If we assume that all suicides in Los Angeles County were identified by the medical examiner as either suicides or equivocal cases, then similar calculations may be made for suicides in general. Without consultation by the death investigation team, 1,000 deaths out of 10,000 referred to the medical examiner would have been certified as suicide

TABLE 1.2. A Calculation of the Sensitivity, Specificity, and
Predictive Value of the Process of Determining Suicide as a
Mode of Death: 100 Equivocal Cases Referred to Medical
Examiner, Los Angeles County, California

Medical examiner's tentative judgments ("test" data)	Mode of death, as judged by death investigation team ("gold standard")		Total
	Suicide	Not suicide	
Suicide	44	8	52
Not suicide	11	37	48
Total	55	45	100

Note. Data source: Litman, Curphey, Shneidman, Farberow, & Tabachnick (1963).
Sensitivity = 44/(11 + 44) = 80.0%.
Specificity = 37/(8 + 37) = 82.2%.
Predictive value (+) = 44/(8 + 44) = 84.6%.
Predictive value (−) = 37/(11 + 37) = 77.1%.

by the medical examiner, and 9,000 would have been certified as other
than suicide. According to Litman et al., of the 100 equivocal cases
that would have been assigned to one of these two categories, the
certification of suicide by the medical examiner would have been incorrect
in 8 cases, and the certification of a nonsuicide mode of death would
have been incorrect in 11 cases. In Table 1.3, the remaining cells in
the 2 × 2 table are calculated by subtraction. For unequivocal and
equivocal suicides combined, the sensitivity and specificity of suicide

TABLE 1.3. A Calculation of the Sensitivity, Specificity, and
Predictive Value of the Process of Determining Suicide as a
Mode of Death: 10,000 Total Cases Referred to Medical
Examiner, Los Angeles County, California

Medical examiner's tentative judgments ("test" data)	Mode of death, as judged by death investigation team ("gold standard")		Total
	Suicide	Not suicide	
Suicide	992	8	1,000
Not suicide	11	8,989	9,000
Total	1,003	8,997	10,000

Note. Data source: Litman et al. (1963).
Sensitivity = 992/(11 + 992) = 98.9%.
Specificity = 8,989/(8 + 8, 989) = 99.9%.
Predictive value (+) = 992/(8 + 992) = 99.2%.
Predictive value (−) = 8,989/(11 + 8, 989) = 99.9%.

certification are calculated to be 98.9% and 99.9%, respectively. The predictive value for both suicide and nonsuicide certifications exceeds 99%.

The data from both McCarthy and Walsh (1975) and Litman et al. (1963) yield similar, high estimates of specificity. In other words, the data suggest that, on the whole, true nonsuicides are rarely if ever certified as suicides. The data from the two investigations yield dramatically different estimates of sensitivity, however. Whereas the estimates based on McCarthy and Walsh's data may be too pessimistic, those based on Litman et al.'s data may be too optimistic. The latter calculations are based on the assumption that all true cases of suicide were either recognized outright or were suspected to be suicides. In fact, some suicides are certified as accidents or natural deaths because suicide is never suspected (Johnson, 1969). Furthermore, Litman et al.'s data were obtained from a jurisdiction with a relatively sophisticated medical examiner system in which, by Litman et al.'s own report, the medical examiner was sensitized to the need for consultation with psychologists and psychiatrists in assessing the suicidal intent of the decedent. One may assume that these conditions would have increased the validity of suicide certification. Unfortunately, such conditions do not exist in most U.S. jurisdictions.

Summary

The question of the validity and reliability of suicide statistics may be considered at three levels: (1) Are suicide deaths misidentified or differentially identified across jurisdictions or over time? (2) To what degree are suicide deaths misidentified? and (3) Is the degree to which suicides are misidentified sufficient to threaten the validity of research based on suicide statistics?

There is general agreement that suicides are likely to be undercounted, both for structural reasons (the burden-of-proof issue, the requirement that the coroner or medical examiner suspect the possibility of suicide) and for sociocultural reasons. There is also substantial anecdotal and empirical evidence suggesting that the mode of death for some true suicides is in fact certified as other than suicide. Overall, it does not seem that very many true nonsuicides are incorrectly certified as suicides.

There is not, however, much agreement as to the degree to which true suicides are undercounted. At least some of the inconsistencies in the findings of different investigators arise because the validity of suicide certification seems to vary from place to place. But the source of apparent conflicts in many of the findings is undoubtedly the lack of a "gold standard" against which the verdicts of any given death certification process can be measured. At best, we can estimate that the sensitivity with which coroners and medical examiners certify true suicides varies from approximately 55% to 99%.

A central question in estimating the sensitivity of suicide certification is this: What proportion of true suicides are either equivocal or likely to go unsuspected by the coroner or medical examiner? Very little has been done to investigate this issue. Yet the sensitivity of suicide certification clearly varies for equivocal versus unequivocal suicides. As shown in Table 1.2, specificity is also at issue when it comes to certifying equivocal cases.

The final question—whether the degree of undercounting of suicide deaths is so great that it threatens the validity of research based on official statistics—is at the crux of the general concern about suicide certification. There are examples of studies in which conclusions based on crude comparisons of reported suicide statistics appear to be invalid. For the most part, these are comparisons among nations with substantially differing death certification procedures. When official statistics are interpreted with a degree of caution and an understanding of the source and direction of biases likely to affect the published rates, however, it seems unlikely that major conclusions based on these statistics will be in error.

For example, certain patterns—for example, that male suicide rates are higher than female rates, or that widowed and divorced persons are at higher risk of suicide than married persons—are found so consistently that it is inconceivable that they could be due entirely to artifact (Centers for Disease Control, 1985). Also, some increase in suicide rates over time may be due to generally increasing willingness on the part of coroners and medical examiners to certify equivocal cases as suicides. But the tripling in suicide rates reported among persons 15–24 years of age in the United States from 1950 to 1980 could not possibly be explained merely by such changes in attitude (Centers for Disease Control, 1986). There simply are not that many equivocal cases.

Nevertheless, the extent to which suicide statistics are used by researchers and policy makers mandates that efforts be made to improve the validity and reliability of the certification of suicide. Toward this end, criteria were recently developed to assist coroners and medical examiners to more accurately determine suicide as a mode of death (Rosenberg, Davidson, Smith, et al., 1988). These criteria make explicit the questions that should be asked to determine whether a particular death was caused by self-inflicted injuries, and, if so, whether the decedent intended to take his or her life. The mode-of-death determination is still based on the judgment of the coroner or medical examiner, as it should be. But if these recommended criteria are used, these judgments will be based on a more uniform, appropriate, and complete body of information. This can only serve to increase both the validity and the reliability of suicide statistics.

References

Andress, V. R. Ethnic/racial misidentification in death: A problem which might distort suicide statistics. *Forensic Science*, 1977, *9*, 179–183.

Atkinson, M. W., Kessel, N., & Dalgaard, J. B. The comparability of suicide rates. *British Journal of Psychiatry*, 1975, *127*, 247–256.

Barraclough, B. M. Are the Scottish and English suicide rates really different? *British Journal of Psychiatry*, 1972, *120*, 267–273.

Barraclough, B. M., Holding, T., & Fayers, P. Influence of coroners' officers and pathologists on suicide verdicts. *British Journal of Psychiatry*, 1976, *128*, 471–474.

Brooke, E. M., & Atkinson, M. Ascertainment of deaths by suicide. In E. M. Brooke (Ed.), *Suicide and attempted suicide*. Geneva: World Health Organization, 1974.

Centers for Disease Control. *Suicide surveillance, 1970–1980*. Atlanta: Author, 1985.

Centers for Disease Control. *Youth suicide in the United States, 1970–1980*. Atlanta: Author, 1986.

Clarke-Finnegan, M., & Fahy, T. J. Suicide rates in Ireland. *Psychological Medicine*, 1983, *13*, 385–391.

Douglas, J. D. *The social meanings of suicide*. Princeton, N.J.: Princeton University Press, 1967.

Durkheim, E. *Suicide: A study in sociology* (G. Simpson, Ed.). Glencoe, Ill.: Free Press, 1951. (Originally published, 1897.)

Farberow, N. L., MacKinnon, D. R., & Nelson, F. L. Suicide: Who's counting? *Public Health Reports*, 1977, *92*, 223–232.

Farberow, N. L., & Neuringer, C. The social scientist as coroner's deputy. *Journal of Forensic Sciences*, 1971, *16*, 15–39.

Holding, T. A., & Barraclough, B. M. Psychiatric morbidity in a sample of a London coroner's open verdicts. *British Journal of Psychiatry*, 1975, *127*, 133–143.

Jennings, C., & Barraclough, B. Legal and administrative influences on the English suicide rate since 1900. *Psychological Medicine*, 1980, *10*, 407–418.

Johnson, H. R. M. The incidence of unnatural deaths which have been presumed to be natural in the coroner's autopsies. *Medicine, Science and the Law*, 1969, *9*, 102–106.

Kircher, T., Nelson, J., & Burdo, H. The autopsy as a measure of the accuracy of the death certificate. *New England Journal of Medicine*, 1985, *313*, 1263–1269.

Kraus, H. H., & Tesser, A. Social contexts of suicide. *Journal of Abnormal Psychology*, 1971, *78*, 222–228.

Kreitman, J. The coal gas story: United Kingdom suicide rates 1960–71. *British Journal of Preventive and Social Medicine*, 1976, *30*, 86–93.

Linden, & Breed, The demographic epidemiology of suicide. In E. Shneidman (Ed.), *Suicidology: Contemporary developments*. New York: Grune & Stratton, 1976.

Litman, R. E. Psychologic–psychiatric aspects in certifying modes of death. *Journal of Forensic Science*, 1968, *13*, 46–54.

Litman, R. E., Curphey, T., Shneidman, E. S., Farberow, N. L., & Tabachnick, N. Investigations of equivocal suicides. *Journal of the American Medical Association*, 1963, *184*, 924–929.

Malla, A., & Hoenig, J. Difference in suicide rates: An examination of under-reporting. *Canadian Journal of Psychiatry*, 1983, *28*, 291–293.

McCarthy, P. D., & Walsh, D. Suicide in Dublin: I. The underreporting of suicide and the consequences for national statistics. *British Journal of Psychiatry*, 1975, *126*, 301–308.

McClure, G. M. G. Trends in suicide for England and Wales, 1975–80. *British Journal of Psychiatry*, 1984, *144*, 119–126.

Monk, M. Epidemiology of suicide. *Epidemiologic Reviews*, 1987, *9*, 51–69.

Murphy, G. K. The "undetermined" ruling: A medicolegal dilemma. *Journal of Forensic Sciences*, 1979, *24*, 483–491.

Naroll, R. Cultural determinants and the concept of a sick society. In S. C. Plog & R. B. Edgerton (Eds.), *Changing perspectives in mental illness*. New York: Holt, Rinehart, & Winston, 1969.

National Center for Health Statistics. Comparability of mortality statistics for the sixth and seventh revisions of ICD: United States, 1958. *Vital Statistics Special Reports*, 1965, *51*, 4.

National Center for Health Statistics. Provisional estimates of selected comparability ratios based on dual coding of 1966 death certificates by the seventh and eighth revisions of the International Classification of Diseases. *Monthly Vital Statistics Report*, 1968, *17*, 8.

Nelson, F. L., Farberow, N. L., & MacKinnon, D. R. The certification of suicide in eleven Western states: An inquiry into the validity of reported suicide rates. *Suicide and Life-Threatening Behavior*, 1978, *8*, 75–88.

Rosenberg, M. L., Davidson, L. E., Smith, J. C., Berman, A. L., Buzbee, H., Gantner, G., Gay, G. A., Moore-Lewis, B., Mills, D. H., Murray, D., O'Carroll, P. W., & Jobes, D. Operational criteria for the determination of suicide. *Journal of Forensic Sciences*, 1988, *32*, 1445–1455.

Ross, O., & Kreitman, N. A further investigation of differences in the suicide rates of England and Wales and of Scotland. *British Journal of Psychiatry*, 1975, *127*, 575–582.

Sainsbury, P. Validity and reliability of trends in suicide statistics. *World Health Statistics Quarterly*, 1983, *36*, 339–348.

Sainsbury, P., & Barraclough, B. M. Differences between suicide rates. *Nature*, 1968, *220*, 1252.

Sainsbury, P., & Jenkins, S. J. The accuracy of officially reported suicide statistics for purposes of epidemiologic research. *Journal of Epidemiology and Community Health*, 1982, *36*, 43–48.

Stengel, E., & Farberow, N. L. Certification of suicide around the world. In N. L. Farberow (Ed.), *Proceedings of the Fourth International Conference for Suicide Prevention*. Los Angeles: Suicide Prevention Center, 1968.

U.S. Department of Health and Human Services. *Report of the Secretary's Task Force on Youth Suicide*. Washington, D.C.: U.S. Government Printing Office, in press, 1989.

Walsh, B., Walsh, D., & Whelan, B. Suicide in Dublin: II. The influence of some social and medical factors on coroners' verdicts. *British Journal of Psychiatry*, 1975, *126*, 309–312.

Warshauer, M. E., & Monk, M. Problems in suicide statistics for whites and blacks. *American Journal Public Health*, 1978, *68*, 383–388.

World Health Organization. *Prevention of suicide* (Public Health Paper No. 35). Geneva: Author, 1968.

2

Suicide Clusters: A Critical Review

Madelyn S. Gould, PhD, MPH
*Columbia University College of Physicians and Surgeons,
New York State Psychiatric Institute*
Sylvan Wallenstein, PhD
Columbia University School of Public Health
Lucy Davidson, MD, EdS
Emory University School of Medicine

A number of highly publicized suicide outbreaks in teenagers and young
adults has increased public concern about the role of contagion as a
risk factor for suicide (Blonston, 1985; Doan, 1984; Fox, Manitowabi,
& Ward, 1984; Gelman & Gangelhoff, 1983; McCain, 1984; Robbins &
Conroy, 1983; Taylor, 1984; Ward & Fox, 1977). A critical review of
reports and ongoing research on suicide "epidemics" or "cluster outbreaks" is the focus of this chapter.

Anecdotal Reports of Suicide Cluster Outbreaks

The terms "clusters," "contagion," and "imitation" are often used in-
terchangeably in the literature, leading to difficulties in communication
and understanding of the contribution of these factors to suicide (Biblarz,
1988). Suicides can cluster in time or space independently. However,
in this chapter, a suicide "cluster" refers to an excessive number of
suicides occurring in close temporal *and* geographic proximity because
this most closely approximates the concept of an "outbreak" in a particular community. Suicide "contagion" is the process by which one

This work was supported in part by National Institute of Mental Health Contract No.
278-85-0026; by Centers for Disease Control Contract No. 200-85-0834 (P); and by Faculty
Scholars Award No. 84-0954-84 from the William T. Grant Foundation. Portions of this
chapter were adapted from "Suicide Contagion among Adolescents" by M. S. Gould and
L. Davidson, in A. R. Stiffman & R. A. Feldman (Eds.), *Advances in Adolescent Mental
Health: Volume 3. Depression and Suicide.* Greenwich, Conn.: JAI Press, 1988.

suicide facilitates the occurrence of a subsequent suicide. Contagion assumes either direct or indirect awareness of the prior suicide. Various suicide contagion pathways may exist: direct contact or friendship with a victim, word-of-mouth knowledge, and indirect transmission through the media. "Imitation," the process by which one suicide becomes a compelling model for successive suicides, is one underlying theory to explain the occurrence of contagion.

If contagion does play a role in suicidal behavior, one would expect "outbreaks" of suicide. That is, an excessive number of suicides would occur in close temporal and geographic proximity. Evidence for suicide contagion has been reported in accounts of epidemic suicides from ancient times through the 20th century (Bakwin, 1957; Popow, 1911). Detailed accounts of epidemics or clusters of suicides have been presented by Coleman (1987) and Davidson and Gould (1988).

The anecdotal reports of cluster suicides have addressed diverse populations, including psychiatric inpatients (Anonymous, 1977; Crawford & Willis, 1966; Kahne, 1968; Kobler & Stotland, 1964; Sacks & Eth, 1981), high school and college students (Robbins & Conroy, 1983; Seiden, 1968), community samples (Ashton & Donnan, 1981; Nalin, 1973; Rubinstein, 1983; Walton, 1978), Native Americans (Ward & Fox, 1977), Marine troops (Hankoff, 1961), prison inmates (Niemi, 1978), and religious sects (Rovinsky, 1898). A number of studies highlight the choice of identical methods among suicides in a cluster (Ashton & Donnan, 1981; Crawford & Willis, 1966; Hankoff, 1961; Nalin, 1973; Rovinsky, 1898; Seiden, 1968; Walton, 1978). Contemporary researchers have also considered the impact of poor baseline emotional functioning on increasing susceptibility to suicide in a cluster (Ashton & Donnan, 1981; Niemi, 1978; Robbins & Conroy, 1983; Walton, 1978; Ward & Fox, 1977). However, the proportion of noncluster suicides with psychiatric problems (Robins, 1981) may not differ from proportions reported in case series of cluster suicides.

The mechanisms most often associated with epidemic suicides among susceptible individuals are imitation and identification (Bunch & Barraclough, 1971; Crawford & Willis, 1966; Niemi, 1978; Rosenbaum, 1983; Rubinstein, 1983; Sacks & Eth, 1981). Ward and Fox (1977) studied a suicide epidemic on a Native American reservation, during which eight adolescents and young adults died from among the 37 families in that community. The researchers examined the way in which one suicidal youth can serve as a role model to be imitated: "The stimulus of one suicide could suggest to others a similar mode of escaping an intolerable life situation." The model also may be an unintentional death, as in the series of antifreeze suicides reported by Walton (1978). Sacks and Eth (1981) explored the idea of pathological identification in a cluster of suicides among hospitalized patients. They felt that these pathological identifications are "fostered by the individual's past history that may contain many points of common experience."

Although imitation and identification may be powerful mechanisms, emphasizing these components exclusively, as in the term "copycat suicides," trivializes the many other factors contributing to suicide. Suicides remain multidetermined events even when they occur in clusters. Imitation alone cannot account for the susceptibility and stresses each decedent brings to that final pathway.

Some researchers have considered the social environment and the ways in which disruptions in that environment or negative social expectations within the milieu may foster epidemic suicides. Rubinstein (1983) viewed rapid sociocultural change as a precipitant for youth suicide, and cluster suicides in hospital settings have been attributed to social disruptions creating anomie or a sense of hopelessness (Anonymous, 1977; Kahne, 1968; Kobler & Stotland, 1964). Hankoff (1961) felt that the prospect of secondary gain was the major environmental influence for a cluster of suicide attempts among Marines. The environmental response to the first attempt provided significant secondary gains and became the harbinger of other attempts, which were finally averted by minimizing secondary gains.

These accounts of epidemic suicides indicate that temporal and geographic clustering of suicides does occur. Cluster suicides appear to be multidetermined, as are noncluster suicides, but imitation and identification are factors hypothesized to increase the likelihood of cluster suicides. Among susceptible individuals, the route of exposure to the model may be direct or indirect. Examples of direct exposures include close friendship with a suicide or observing a suicidal act. Indirect exposures include watching television news coverage of a prominent person's suicide or hearing about a suicide by word of mouth.

The nature of the existing research on suicide clusters limits conclusions that might be drawn. A critique of the research and areas recommended for further clarification are presented in the next sections.

Critique of Methods

Most of what is currently known about suicide clustering is based on anecdotal reports of case studies. There is no systematic surveillance or reporting system of suicide clusters. Therefore, the available case series have selection biases that affect their representativeness. Because these are descriptive studies, no comparison groups or statistical analyses have been included. Without reference to a comparison group, descriptions of the demographic and psychological characteristics of suicides that occur within the context of a cluster are speculative. What may appear to be a ubiquitous characteristic of cluster suicides may not differentiate them from noncluster suicides, and therefore may be of limited value in preventing this particular type of death. Furthermore, most of the studies describe suicides among adults, but recent reports of teen suicide clusters have led to concern that this phenomenon may be occurring now among young people. Youths may be differentially exposed and susceptible to the characteristics of suicide contagion presented in these case reports.

Until recently, there has been no systematic research on the extent to which cluster outbreaks occur. Sporadic reports of "outbreaks" are virtually impossible to interpret; even if the suicides are occurring essentially "at random," some clustering is bound to arise by chance alone, and if enough people are looking for it, some are bound to find it. What is necessary to determine is whether or not "outbreaks" are occurring to an extent greater than would be expected by chance variation. Such time–space clustering would be consistent with the mechanism of contagion.

The absence of a standard operational definition for the time and space parameters of a suicide cluster limits our ability to conduct research, compare results from the existing case studies, or develop surveillance procedures. Without a clear and replicable definition for suicide clusters, surveillance cannot be undertaken. A systematic surveillance procedure could determine what proportion of youth suicides appear to occur in clusters and how representative the findings from case series may be.

Studies in Progress

Ongoing studies are attempting to address the problems identified in the preceding section. The recent projects employ two diverse research strategies: "psychological autopsies" of several cluster outbreaks, and statistical analyses of time and space clustering of suicides.

Psychological Autopsies

Field studies applying a "psychological autopsy" protocol to several cluster outbreaks include comparison groups and detailed analyses of the relationships between the suicides in an attempt to identify possible mechanisms of suicide outbreaks. The Centers for Disease Control and the New York State Psychiatric Institute are conducting two such case studies (Davidson, personal communication, 1988; Shaffer & Gould, 1984). "The term 'psychological autopsy' was coined to describe a procedure that involves reconstruction of the life-style and circumstances of the victim, together with details of behaviors and events that led to the death of that individual" (Farberow & Neuringer, 1971; see Brent, Chapter 4, this volume). Data collection and analysis are still in progress for these studies; however, a preliminary examination of several suicide clusters reported to the Centers for Disease Control (e.g., Plano, Texas, 1983–1984; Westchester and Putnam Counties, New York, 1984; Clear Lake, Texas, 1984; Seattle, Washington, 1985; Wind River, Wyoming, 1985; Omaha, Nebraska, 1986), may highlight some mechanisms in the etiology of a cluster.

The studies on recent clusters indicate that it is not necessary for the decedents to have had direct contact with each other. In the outbreak in Westchester County, New York, indirect knowledge of the suicides appears to have been obtained through the news media. Other clusters have a combination of members from one social network and individuals unknown to each other directly. Among those who knew another decedent, the degree of acquaintance varied from closest friends to those in the same school or church who knew of each other but had little direct personal contact.

Methods may be similar for the majority of deaths within a cluster, indicating a possible underlying imitative mechanism. The clearest imitation of method was observed in Seattle's outbreak of expressway overpass jumpings—a method that had previously been extremely rare in that community. However, identical methods may not always reflect direct imitation of another decedent in the cluster. All of the suicides in the Wind River outbreak were by hanging; yet cultural factors may have predominated in that choice of method.

Time–Space Cluster Analysis

Another type of study uses epidemiological techniques to detect and statistically assess temporal and geographic clustering of suicides (Gould, Wallenstein, & Kleinman, 1987b). This research addresses basic questions such as these: (1) Are "outbreaks" of suicide "real" (in other words, are clusters occurring more frequently than by chance alone)? (2) Is clustering of suicides predominantly a phenomenon of youth? and (3) Is the proportion of cluster outbreaks changing over time?

Several epidemiological techniques have been developed to examine the occurrence and significance of time–space clusters of disease (e.g., Ederer, Myers, & Mantel, 1964; Knox, 1964; Mantel, 1967; see Mantel, 1967, and Smith, 1982, for reviews). Detailed presentations of the techniques are given here to familiarize researchers with the methods and to promote their application.

Time–space clustering methods are basically of two types: (1) those based on distances between pairs of observations (pair methods); and (2) those based on the maximum number of suicides within a "cell," defined by a combination of time and space units (cell methods).

Pair Methods. The pair methods consider all possible pairs of cases and the time and space distances between them. Thus, a pair method seeks to establish clustering by demonstrating a positive relationship between the time and space distances of a pair. The pair method that has been most extensively used is that devised by Knox (1964). Knox divides the data into a 2 × 2 table as shown in Table 2.1. An association indicates that cases close in time are also close in space. The Knox method can be employed for either continuous or discrete space units. The Knox statistic requires the specification of critical values for time and space to define "closeness." The test statistic involves a comparison of the observed number of cases close in time and space with the expected number. The expected number is simply the product of the number of pairs that are close in time, with the number of pairs close in space divided by the total number of pairs.

The Knox statistic can be evaluated using (1) the exact Poisson probability of the observed number of close–close pairs; or (2) a normal approximation using the Poisson variance as $Z = (O - E)/\sqrt{E}$; or (3)

TABLE 2.1. Summary Description of Knox Pair Method

	Time		
Space	Close	Far	Total
Close	a	b	a + b
Far	c	d	c + d
Total	a + c	b + d	a + b + c + d

Note. Compute [n(n − 1)]/2 pairs of N total cases. Dichotomize study area into "close" and "far." Dichotomize study period into "close" and "far." Measure the time interval between the members of all pairs. Measure the distance between the members of all pairs. Distribute all pairs into a fourfold table, as shown. Let O = a, the observed number of cases in the "close–close" cell. Let E = [(a + c) (a + b)]/(a + b + c + d). See text for details.

a normal approximation using the Barton–David (Mantel) formula for the variance as $Z = (O - E)/\sqrt{\text{variance}}$. The results of the first two methods differ only when the expected number of close–close pairs is less than 25.

Another pair method has been developed by Mantel (1967). Mantel's procedure is designed for the case where one has continuous data for both the time and space dimensions. It does not require critical values to define "closeness" in time or space. A regression approach is employed based on the statistic $M = \Sigma S_{ij} T_{ij}$ (where S_{ij} and T_{ij} represent the space and time distances, respectively, between the ith and jth individuals in the sample), and then all possible pairs are summed. Mantel suggests that S and T be of the form 1/(distance + constant), where the constant is inserted to prevent values of infinity and to "scale" values very close in time or space.

The simplest approach to test the significance of Mantel's statistic is to use the mean and variance of M under the null hypothesis of no clustering and then refer the statistic $(M - \text{mean})$/standard deviation to the tables of the normal distribution. (For a discussion of various aspects of Mantel's statistic, see Gould, Wallenstein, & Kleinman, 1987a.)

Cell Methods. Cell methods subdivide the area and period of study into time–space units, across which the cases are then distributed according to the time and place in which they arose. These methods seek to establish clustering by demonstrating an excess frequency of disease in certain times and places. The cell method that has been most extensively used is that devised by Ederer et al. (1964) (the EMM method). In this method, outlined in Table 2.2, the total time frame T (e.g., 4 years) is subdivided into L cells, each of length T/L. In the original formulation of the EMM method, each cell represented 1 year, although the employment of shorter time durations may be possible. The statistic is based on m_i, the maximum number of suicides in the ith cell. Under randomness, the expected number of suicides in an arbitrary cell is Ni/L, where N_i is the total number of suicides within the ith geographic region. The probability functions for the maximum, m_i, are based on summing the multinomial probabilities, and from these the $E(m_i)$, the expected value (or average) of the m_i, and the variance, $Var(m_i)$, are calculated. Observed values of m_i greater than the expected value indicate some evidence of time clustering within the ith region. A test statistic that summarizes the information concerning clustering over all geographical units is

$$Z = \Sigma (m_i - E(m_i))/\sqrt{\Sigma Var(m_i)}$$

TABLE 2.2. Summary Description of Ederer, Myers,
and Mantel (EMM) Cell Method

Space units	Time units			
(e.g., counties)	1981	1982	1983	1984
Autauga (Alabama)				
.				
.				
.				
Weston (Wyoming)				

Note. Divide study period into time units (e.g., calendar years). Divide study area into space units (e.g., counties). Distribute all cases into space–time cells. Cells with fewer than two cases are excluded from analysis. Expectations and variances for several different units of time have been tabulated by Ederer et al., 1964. See text for details.

The test statistic has a standardized normal distribution under the assumption of randomness. Thus, a value of 1.645 or greater indicates significant clustering at the .05 level.

A major limitation of the EMM method is that the time units are fixed, and thus the method may not detect clustering that overlaps two adjacent time periods. A "scan" statistic by Naus (1965) addresses this major limitation of the EMM method. The scan statistic employs a "moving window" of preselected length and finds the maximum number of cases revealed through the window as it scans or slides over the entire time period. The significance of the statistic within each geographic area is evaluated by determining the probability of observing the maximum number of cases (M) in the preselected length of time, under the hypothesis that the total number of events are randomly (uniformly) distributed over the entire time period. The scan statistic was originally designed to detect time clusters (Wallenstein, 1980), but has been extended so that it can be applied across discrete geographic areas (Gould et al., 1987a).

Application of Techniques. The epidemiological techniques to detect clusters have been applied to two population-based mortality data bases: (1) national mortality data obtained from the National Center for Health Statistics Mortality Detail Files for 1978 through 1984, and (2) state-level vital statistics obtained from one state within each of the nine regions of the United States (Gould et al., 1987b). The use of national data yields information on clusters occurring within county limits. The examination of data derived from state vital statistics enables the identification of clusters within smaller locales, such as towns. The analyses indicate that suicide clusters occur predominantly among teenagers and young adults; a cluster situation does not appear to accelerate suicidal behavior in individuals who would have killed themselves anyway as indicated by the lack of a "vacuities" in the number of suicides following the clusters. Rather, the cluster represents a significant excess of suicides; and cluster suicides account for approximately 1–5% of all teenage suicides. This estimate of clustering probably represents a lower bound due to the use of set definitions of a "cluster" and the sole employment of mortality data (to be discussed in the next section).

Limitations of Time–Space Cluster Analyses. Limitations of statistical time–space cluster analyses include the following:

1. The requirement of set time and space units. There appears to be variability in temporal and geographic patterns among clusters; yet the time–space cluster analytic methods require a predefined set of time and space units to characterize a cluster (e.g., suicides occuring within a county). Therefore, the methods may not detect all clustering that occurs.

2. The inability to identify the mechanisms underlying a cluster. For example, it is not possible to discern whether clusters are due to the influence of an initial suicide, acting as a model, or whether the presumed model merely happened to be the first individual who committed suicide in response to conditions that then led others to suicide. Field studies are better suited to identify the mechanisms of the clusters. A time–space cluster analysis can be employed to identify a representative sample of clusters for future complementary field investigations.

There are also limitations that are intrinsic not to the techniques, but to the available data:

1. A cluster can occur at a level that is not accessible via vital statistics data (e.g., schools). This problem can usually be circumvented either by the employment of a small space unit (e.g., a town) or by the employment of street addresses, which can yield continuous space distances between victims.

2. An underestimate of clustering may result from the sole employment of mortality data. Clusters of attempted suicides have been reported to occur (e.g., Hankoff, 1961); yet it is not possible to enumerate suicide attempts adequately, because no registry of attempts exists.

Mechanisms of Suicide Contagion

The mechanisms underlying the phenomenon of imitation or contagion have not been studied in the context of cluster suicides. In social learning theory, however, behavioral scientists have constructed a foundation on which many aspects of suicide contagion may build. According to this, most human behavior is learned observationally through modeling (Bandura, 1977). People can learn from example. Imitative learning is influenced by a number of factors, including the characteristics of the model and the consequences or rewards associated with the observed behavior (Bandura, 1977). Models who possess engaging qualities or who have high status are more likely to be imitated. Behaviors depicted as resulting in gains, including notoriety, are more effective in prompting imitation.

Consistent with these principles, Phillips and his colleagues (Bollen & Phillips, 1981, 1982; Phillips, 1974, 1979, 1980; Phillips & Carstensen, 1986) have reported that the magnitude of the increase in suicide behavior after prominent newspaper coverage is related to the "attractiveness" of the individual whose death is being reported and the amount of publicity given to the story. Likewise, Wasserman (1984) found that a significant rise in the national suicide rate occurred only after celebrity suicides were covered on the front page of the *New York Times*.

People cannot learn much by observation unless they attend to the modeled behavior (Bandura, 1977). A number of factors, some involving the *observers'* characteristics, regulate the amount of attention to an observed behavior. To date, the host characteristics that may yield a greater susceptibility to suicide imitation have not been studied. One host characteristic proposed by Sacks and Eth (1981) is a history of similar past experiences that lead to "pathological identification" with the victim.

In addition to imitative effects, the occurrence of suicides in the community or in the media may produce a familiarity with and acceptance of the *idea* of suicide. This mechanism was postulated by Rubinstein (1983) in his study of a suicide epidemic among Micronesian adolescents. Familiarity with suicide may eliminate the "taboo" of suicide, lower the threshold at which point the behavior is manifested, and introduce suicide as an acceptable alternative response or option to life stresses.

Conclusions

Anecdotal case reports and epidemiologic research suggest that significant time–space clustering of suicide does occur and appears to be primarily a phenomenon of youth. Field investigations are currently attempting to identify the underlying mechanisms of suicide clusters and the processes that initiate an outbreak.

Many unanswered questions remain that require research attention. These include the identification of the host characteristics that increase susceptibility to suicide contagion within the context of an "outbreak"; the extent to which cluster outbreaks may occur in certain age groups, geographic locations, or times; the duration of the "contagious" period; the characteristics of "model" suicides that are most influential in increasing the likelihoood of subsequent suicides; the combination of host susceptibility and contagion factors that is most lethal; and the sorts of prevention and intervention efforts that are most effective in averting cluster suicides. Field studies of representative samples of suicide outbreaks would be useful in answering these questions. In the interim, it is still necessary for guidelines to be provided and evaluated. Such a set of guidelines for communities' responses has recently been published by the Centers for Disease Control (Centers for Disease Control, 1988).

References

Anonymous, A suicide epidemic in a psychiatric hospital. *Diseases of the Nervous System*, 1977, *38*, 327–331.

Ashton, V. R., & Donnan, S. Suicide by burning as an epidemic phenomenon: An analysis of 82 deaths and inquests in England and Wales in 1978–79. *Psychological Medicine*, 1981, *11*, 735–739.

Bakwin, H. Suicide in children and adolescents. *Journal of Pediatrics*, 1957, *50*, 749–769.

Bandura, A. *Social learning theory*. Englewood Cliffs, N.J.: Prentice-Hall, 1977.

Biblarz, A. (Chair). *Minimizing the contagion phenomenon*. Panel conducted at the 21st annual meeting of the American Association of Suicidology, Washington, D.C., 1988.

Blonston, G. Suicides among Arapaho youths tied to "cultural identity crisis." *Hartford Courant*, October, 1977, pp. A14–A15.

Bollen, K. A., & Phillips, D. P. Suicidal motor vehicle fatalities in Detroit: A replication. *American Journal of Sociology*, 1981, *87*, 404–412.

Bollen, K. A., & Phillips, D. P. Imitative suicides: A national study of the effects of television news stories. *American Sociological Review*, 1982, *47*, 802–809.

Bunch, J., & Barraclough, B. L. The influence of parental death anniversaries upon suicide dates. *British Journal of Psychiatry*, 1971, *118*, 621–626.

Centers for Disease Control. CDC recommendations for a community plan for the prevention and containment of suicide clusters. *MMWR*, 1988, *37(5–6)*, 1–12.

Coleman, L. *Suicide clusters*. Boston: Faber & Faber, 1987.

Crawford, J. P., & Willis, J. R. Double suicide in psychiatric hospital patients. *British Journal of Psychiatry*, 1966, *112*, 1231–1235.

Davidson, L. Personal communication, 1988.

Davidson, L., & Gould, M. S. *Contagion as a risk factor for youth suicide*. IN USDHHS: Report of the Secretary's Task Force on Youth Suicide. Volume 2: Risk factors for youth suicide. Washington, DC: U.S. Government Printing Office, 1988.

Doan, M. As "cluster suicides" take toll of teenagers. *U.S. News and World Report*, November 12, 1984, p. 49.

Ederer, F., Myers, M. H., & Mantel, N. A statistical problem in space and time: Do leukemia cases come in clusters? *Biometrics*, 1964, *20*, 626–638.

Farberow, N. L., & Neuringer, C. The social scientist as coroner's deputy. *Journal of Forensic Sciences*, 1971, *16*, 15–39.

Fox, J., Manitowabi, D., & Ward, J. A. An Indian community with a high suicide rate— 5 years after. *Canadian Journal of Psychiatry*, 1984, *29*, 425–427.

Gelman, D., & Gangelhoff, B. K. Teen-age suicide in the Sunbelt. *Newsweek*, August 15, 1983, pp. 70–74.

Gould, M. S., Wallenstein, S., & Kleinman, M. *A study of time–space clustering of suicide* (Final Report, Centers for Disease Control Contract No. RFP 200-85-0834). New York: Columbia University/NY State Psychiatric Institute, 1987. (a)

Gould, M. S., Wallenstein, S., & Kleinman, M. *Time–space clustering of teenage suicide.* Paper presented at the 34th annual meeting of the American Academy of Child and Adolescent Psychiatry, Washington, D.C., October 1987. (b)

Hankoff, L. D. An epidemic of attempted suicide. *Comprehensive Psychiatry*, 1961, *2*, 294–298.

Kahne, M. J. Suicide among patients in mental hospitals. *Psychiatry*, 1968, *1*, 32–43.

Knox, G. The detection of space–time interactions. *Applied Statistics*, 1964, *3*, 25–29.

Kobler, A. L. L., & Stotland, E. *The end of hope: A social–clinical study of suicide.* London: The Free Press of Glencoe, 1964.

Mantel, N. The detection of disease clustering and a generalized regression approach. *Cancer Research*, 1967, *27*, 209–220.

McCain, M. Suicides at an early age. *Boston Globe*, March 1984, p. 12.

Nalin, D. R. Epidemic of suicide by malathion poisoning in Guyana. *Tropical and Geographical Medicine*, 1973, *25*, 8–14.

Naus, J. The distribution of the size of the maximum cluster of points on a line. *Journal of the American Statistical Association*, 1965, *60*, 532–538.

Niemi, T. The time–space distances of suicides committed in the lock-up in Finland in 1963–1967. *Israel Annals of Psychiatry and Related Disciplines*, 1978, *16*, 39–45.

Phillips, D. P. The influence of suggestion on suicide: Substantive and theoretical implications of the Werther effect. *American Sociological Review*, 1974, *39*, 340–354.

Phillips, D. P. Suicide, motor vehicle fatalities, and the mass media: Evidence toward a theory of suggestion. *American Journal of Sociology*, 1979, *84*, 1150–1174.

Phillips, D. P. Airplane accidents, murder, and the mass media: Towards a theory of imitation and suggestion. *Social Forces*, 1980, *58*, 1001–1004.

Phillips, D. P., & Carstensen, L. L. Clustering of teenage suicides after television news stories about suicide. *New England Journal of Medicine*, 1986, *315*, 685–689.

Popow, N. M. The present epidemic of school suicides in Russia. *Nevrol Nestnik* (Kazan), 1911, *18*, 312–355, 592–646.

Robins, E. *The final months.* New York: Oxford University Press, 1981.

Robbins, D., & Conroy, R. C. A cluster of adolescent suicide attempts: Is suicide contagious? *Journal of Adolescent Health Care*, 1983, *3*, 253–255.

Rovinsky, A. Epidemic suicides. *Boston Medical and Surgical Journal*, 1898, *138*, 238–239.

Rubinstein, D. H. Epidemic suicide among Micronesian adolescents. *Social Science and Medicine*, 1983, *17*, 657–665.

Sacks, M., & Eth, S. Pathological identification as a cause of suicide on an inpatient unit. *Hospital and Community Psychiatry*, 1981, *32*, 36–40.

Seiden, R. H. Suicidal behavior contagion on a college campus. In N. L. Farberow (Ed.), *Proceedings of the Fourth International Conference for Suicide Prevention.* Los Angeles: Suicide Prevention Center, 1968.

Shaffer, D., & Gould, M. S. *A study of completed and attempted suicide in adolescents* (NIMH Grant No. RO1 MH38198). New York: Columbia University/NY State Psychiatric Institute, 1984.

Smith, P. G. Spatial and temporal clustering. In D. Schottenfeld & J. F. Fraumeni (Eds.), *Cancer epidemiology and prevention.* Philadelphia: W. B. Saunders, 1982.

Taylor, P. Cluster phenomenon of young suicides raises contagion theory. *Washington Post*, March 11, 1984, pp. 15–16.

Wallenstein, S. A test for detection of clustering over time. *American Journal of Epidemiology*, 1980, *111*, 367–373.

Walton, E. W. An epidemic of antifreeze poisoning. *Medicine, Science and the Law*, 1978, *18*, 231–237.

Ward, J. A., & Fox, J. A suicide epidemic on an Indian reserve. *Canadian Psychiatric Association Journal*, 1977, *22*, 423–426.

Wasserman, I. H. Imitation and suicide: A reexamination of the Werther effect. *American Sociological Review*, 1984, *49*, 427–436.

3

Biochemical Studies in Suicide Victims: Current Findings and Future Implications

Michael Stanley, PhD
  Columbia University College of Physicians and Surgeons, New York State Psychiatric Institute
Barbara Stanley, PhD
  John Jay College of Criminal Justice, City University of New York, Columbia University College of Physicians and Surgeons

This chapter contains a review of some of the relevant neurochemical findings in postmortem suicide studies. As the results of these studies are described, we try to indicate their relative strengths and weaknesses, as well as to provide an overview regarding the advantages and shortcomings of a given technique or approach.

One important issue that should be addressed at the outset is the diagnostic heterogeneity of those individuals who commit suicide. Data indicate that approximately 50% of suicide victims are diagnosed as depressed; the remaining cases carry a variety of diagnoses, including schizophrenia, personality disorders, and alcoholism (Barraclough, Bunch, Nelson, & Sainsbury, 1974; Dorpat & Ripley, 1960; Robins, Murphy, Wilkinson, Gassner, & Kayes, 1959). Thus, it is of both theoretical and practical importance to note that suicide victims typically represent a diagnostically heterogeneous group of individuals. With regard to biochemical findings within this population, the diagnostic heterogeneity suggests that differences in neurochemistry may be more closely related to suicidal behavior than to any one diagnostic subgroup. Consequently suicide studies that restrict their enrollment to a single

Preparation of this chapter was supported in part by National Institute of Mental Health (NIMH) Contract No. 278-85-0026, NIMH Grant Nos. MH41847 and MH40210, The Lowenstein Foundation, and the Schizophrenia Research Program of the Scottish Rite.

diagnosis (e.g., depression) may provide atypical findings having little generalizability to the more diagnostically diverse groups of individuals who commit suicide.

Postmortem Studies of Brain Levels of Biogenic Amines and Their Metabolites

Ten studies have investigated the concentration of serotonin (5-HT), 5-hydroxyindoleacetic acid (5-HIAA), or both in several brain regions of suicide victims (Beskow, Gottfries, Roos, & Winblad, 1976; Bourne, Bunney, Colburn, Davis, Shaw, & Coppen, 1968; Cochrane, Robins, & Grote, 1976; Crow, Cross, Cooper, et al., 1984; Korpi, Kleinmen, Goodman, et al., 1983; Lloyd, Fraley, Deck, & Hornykiewicz, 1974; Owens, Cross, Crow, Deakin, Ferrier, Lofthouse, & Poulter, 1983; Pare, Yeung, Price, & Stacey, 1969; Shaw, Camps, & Eccleston, 1967; Stanley, McIntyre, & Gershon, 1983). In addition to measurements within the serotonergic system, a few studies also report findings for the noradrenergic and dopaminergic systems.

With regard to findings reported for the serotonergic system, six studies have reported significant decreases in the levels of 5-HT, 5-HIAA, or both. In general, decreases tend to be observed in the area of the brain stem (raphe nuclei) and in other subcortical nuclei (e.g., hypothalamus). Korpi et al. (1983) reported significant decreases in the hypothalamic concentration of 5-HT of suicide victims, compared with that of nonsuicide controls. They found that 5-HIAA levels were significantly lower in the nucleus accumbens of suicide victims than in that of controls.

In many of the studies listed above, factors such as death by overdose or carbon monoxide poisoning, extensive postmortem delay, and lack of age-matched control groups figure significantly in the interpretation of these findings. These variables may also account in part for the lack of uniformity of findings among the postmortem studies. In addition to these potential sources of error, the levels of monoamines and their metabolites are known to be influenced by factors such as diet, acute drug and alcohol use. Although it is possible to control for the acute influence of these factors in cerebrospinal fluid (CSF) studies, for obvious reasons this is not the case in postmortem assessments. In contrast to the findings for 5-HT and 5-HIAA, very little has been observed with dopamine (DA) and norepinephrine (NE) (cf. Mann & Stanley, 1986).

What other factors might exert an influence on these measures? An analysis of 50 cases with an age range of 16–79 years revealed no significant relationship between age and 5-HT or 5-HIAA (Stanley, 1985). Severson, Marwsson, and Osterburg (1985) have also published data on age effects and 5-HT and 5-HIAA levels. They, too, noted that age did not appear to influence 5-HT or 5-HIAA levels. They found that the ratio of 5-HIAA to 5-HT, an estimate of 5-HT turnover, was also uninfluenced by age.

Another area that also represents a potential problem in postmortem research is that of postmortem interval (PMI), the period between death and the time at which the brain tissue is removed and frozen. The human postmortem studies conducted by Stanley, Traskman-Bendz, and Dorovini-Zis (1985) assessed the influence of PMI on 5-HT and 5-HIAA levels. Their PMI was approximately 15 hours, with a range of 6–45 hours. They found that there was a significant positive correlation between frontal cortex 5-HT levels and PMI. No significant findings were noted for 5-HIAA levels with PMI. Severson et al. (1985) also found that PMI was related to significant changes in 5-HT levels. However, their findings were in the opposite direction from that which Stanley et al. (1985) observed—namely, Severson's group reported a significant decline in 5-HT with increasing PMI. One possible explanation for this discrepancy may be the difference in the length of PMI between the two studies. In Stanley et al.'s study, the PMI was approximately 15 hours, whereas in Severson et al.'s study PMI averaged 36 hours (in some cases it was greater than 72 hours). It may well be that although 5-HT levels appear to rise initially with a shorter PMI, they subsequently fall with a more extensive delay (more than 1½ days). In any case, previous research has shown that amines, such as DA and 5-HT, are more sensitive to PMI than are their acidic metabolites.

Another area of postmortem research that has resulted in variations both within and between studies is that of nonspecific or "regional" dissections. In animal studies, it had been the practice of Stanley and his colleagues and that of others to analyze samples taken from general areas (e.g., "frontal cortex"). It occurred to McIntyre and Stanley (1984) that this lack of precision in dissection might account for some of the variability observed from time to time.

In an attempt to investigate possible regional differences of 5-HT and 5-HIAA concentrations within the cortex, McIntyre and Stanley (1984) dissected homogeneous samples corresponding to frontal, temporal, and occipital cortex. In this experiment, the frontal cortex showed significantly higher concentrations of 5-HT and 5-HIAA than did temporal or occipital samples. In a second experiment, three progressive 1-mm slices of the frontal cortex were examined in a rostral-to-caudal fashion for regional concentration differences of 5-HT and 5-HIAA levels. Additional significant variation was noted within the frontal cortex with a rostral-to-caudal increase in 5-HIAA levels; 5-HT levels were consistent. Therefore, not only are differences found among the general areas of the cortex (i.e., frontal, temporal, and occipital), but significant differences can also be found within a cortical region.

As previously mentioned, amines and their metabolites can be changed by a number of acute influences. In an effort to minimize the impact of the aforementioned variables, Stanley, Virgilio, and Gershon (1982) decided to examine a system—receptor binding—that has been shown to be generally nonresponsive to these acute influences.

Binding studies have shown that changes in the number of sites (or their density) can be induced by either chronic exposure to a chemical agent (e.g., antidepressants) (Peroutka & Snyder, 1980) or deprivation of the particular amine by its removal (e.g., lesioning) (Brunello, Chuang, & Costa, 1982). Binding assays that appear to be associated with pre-synaptic (imipramine) and postsynaptic (spiroperidol) 5-HT neurons have been developed (Brunello et al., 1982; Langer, Briley, Raisman, et al., 1980). Imipramine binding sites have been characterized in platelets and various regions of the brain (Langer et al., 1980; Rainbow & Beigon, 1983). It has also been observed that the pharmacological profile of brain and platelet [^{3}H]imipramine binding sites is similar (Rehavi, Ittah, Price, et al., 1981).

The clinical significance of imipramine binding was provided by the studies of Langer and Raisman (1983), who reported decreases in the number of binding sites in the platelets of depressives. The combined association of imipramine binding with 5-HT function, as well as the significant reduction in binding density in depressives, suggested the possibility of alterations in imipramine binding in suicide victims. To test this hypothesis, Stanley et al. (1982) determined imipramine binding in the brains of suicide victims and controls. Because of the problems previous research groups had encountered conducting postmortem studies, Stanley et al. took particular care in selecting cases for this study. Thus, there were no significant differences between the two groups with respect to age, sex, and PMI. The suicide victims chosen for this study had died in a determined manner (e.g., gunshot wound, hanging, jumping from a height), and, as in the general practice of these researchers, the control group was chosen to match for sudden and violent deaths.

The findings indicated a significant reduction in the number of imipramine binding sites in frontal cortex of suicides when compared with normal controls with no difference in binding affinity (K_d). The results of this experiment seem to be consistent with the accumulating evidence suggesting the involvement of 5-HT in suicide. Specifically, reduced imipramine binding (associated with presynaptic terminals) may indicate reduced 5-HT release and may agree with reports of reduced postmortem levels of 5-HT and 5-HIAA in suicides, as well as reports of lower levels of 5-HIAA in the CSF of suicide attempters.

Since the completion of the Stanley et al. (1982) study, four other studies have measured imipramine binding either in suicide victims or in depressive persons who died from natural causes. Paul, Rehavi, Skolnick, and Goodwin (1984) measured imipramine binding in hypothalamic membranes from suicides and controls. Both groups were matched for age, gender, and PMI. Imipramine binding was significantly lower in the brains of the suicide victims than in those of controls. This group also measured desipramine binding in the same samples and noted no significant difference between the suicides and the control group. They interpreted this finding as arguing against the possibility that the reductions they had observed in imipramine binding could be attributed to a drug-induced effect. Perry, Marshall, Blessed, Tomlinson, and Perry (1983) measured imipramine binding in the cortex and hippocampus of depressed individuals dying from nonsuicidal causes. They reported a significant reduction in imipramine binding in the depressive group, relative to a nondepressed control group that had been matched for age, sex, and PMI. Crow et al. (1984) also reported significant decreases in imipramine binding in the cortex of suicide victims compared with controls.

In contrast to the findings cited above, the fourth study has reported an increase in imipramine binding in the brains of suicides compared with controls (Meyerson, Wennogle, Abel, Coupet, Lippa, Rauh, & Beer, 1982). Possible explanations offered to address this discrepant finding include single-point analysis instead of saturation isotherms and inadequate matching of factors such as age, gender, and PMI. In summary, five published postmortem studies have measured imipramine binding. Thus far, four of the five studies reported a decrease in imipramine binding, and one study found an increase.

With regard to factors that can influence this measure, Stanley (1985) and Severson et al. (1985) did note a significant positive correlation between imipramine binding and age (range 17–100 years). Severson et al.'s and Stanley's findings of a positive correlation between these variables are of interest, because the findings are in the opposite direction of those reported by Langer et al. (1980) for imipramine binding in the platelet. Langer et al. reported that platelet imipramine binding decreased as a function of age. These discrepant findings are of interest because imipramine binding in the platelet and the brain were formerly thought to be identical. Thus, findings such as these raise questions about the validity of peripheral measures as indices of central systems.

In addition to assessing postmortem presynaptic function of the 5-HT system in suicide, Stanley and Mann (1983) also measured postsynaptic 5-HT binding sites using [^{3}H]spiroperidol (5-HT$_2$). 5-HT$_2$ binding in animals has been shown to change in response to chronic antidepressant treatment and lesioning of 5-HT nuclei. In this study, suicide victims were compared with controls; as in previous studies, both groups were matched for age, sex, PMI, and suddenness of death. Also, care was taken to select subjects who had died by nonpharmacological means. The investigators found a significant increase in the number of 5-HT$_2$ binding sites in the frontal cortex of suicide victims, with no change in binding affinity.

Because many of the brains had also been used in the previous report on imipramine binding by Stanley et al. (1982), Stanley and Mann (1983) were interested in assessing the degree to which these measures of receptor function correlated. They found that the number of binding sites (B_{max}) for 5-HT$_2$ and imipramine was negatively correlated. This finding is of interest because it closely parallels the experimental observations noted in animal studies. Brunello et al. (1982) lesioned the raphe nucleus of rats using the 5-HT selective neurotoxin 5,7-dihydroxytryptamine. Two weeks following such lesions, 5-HT levels were significantly reduced. The same researchers found significant reductions in imipramine binding (associated with presynaptic serotonergic terminals), with significant increases in 5-HT$_2$ binding (postsynaptic). They suggested that the increase in 5-HT$_2$ binding might reflect a compensating increase in postsynaptic binding sites secondary to a loss of presynaptic input. To extrapolate these findings to human data in suicide victims, where Stanley's group observed an increase in postsynaptic binding sites as well as a decrease in presynaptic binding sites, it may be that the functional consequences of this receptor arrangement could result in an overall hypofunction of this system. Thus, reduced levels of 5-HIAA in the CSF of suicide attempters, as well as reduced levels of 5-HT and 5-HIAA in the brains of suicide victims, would be a logical consequence of hypofunctioning serotonergic systems.

Subsequent to the study done by Stanley's group, there have been four additional reports of 5-HT$_2$ binding in suicides. Owens et al. (1983) reported an increase in 5-HT$_2$ binding in nonmedicated suicide victims. Meltzer, Nash, Ohmori, Kregel, and Arora (1987) have also reported a significant increase in 5-HT$_2$ binding sites in the frontal cortex of suicide victims. Crow et al. (1984) found no change in 5-HT$_2$ binding between suicides and controls, and Cheetham, Cross, Crompton, Czudek, Katona, Parker, Reynolds, and Horton (1987) reported a significant increase in 5-HT$_2$ binding in suicides.

A significant age-related decrease in 5-HT$_2$ binding sites in frontal cortex ($r = -.42$, $n = 34$, $p < .01$) was observed in the study of Mann, Petito, Stanley, McBride, Chin, and Philogene (1985). This is, it will be recalled, in the opposite direction to the effect of age on imipramine binding.

In addition to examining serotonergic binding sites in suicide victims, Stanley also measured muscarinic binding in this group (Stanley, 1984). The rationale for this assessment was based in part on the several lines of cholinergic sensitivity with affective disorders and the high incidence of individuals diagnosed as having an affective disorder who subsequently commit suicide. In this study, muscarinic binding was estimated using the reversible antagonist 3-quinuclindyl benzilate (QNB). Samples of frontal cortex from 22 suicide and 22 controls matched for age, gender, PMI, and suddenness of death were used in this study. As before, care was taken to choose a majority of cases where the cause of death was nonpharmacological.

Scatchard analysis of the binding data indicated that there were no significant differences in the mean number of binding sites (B_{max}) between the two groups. B_{max} and K_d in either the suicide victims or the control subjects were not significantly related to factors such as age and PMI. However, when both groups were combined, B_{max} was significantly correlated with PMI ($r = .35$, $p < .02$).

Two other studies have estimated QNB binding in suicides and controls. Kaufman, Gillin, Hill, O'Laughlin, Phillips, Kleinmen, and Wyatt (1984) determined QNB binding in three brain regions (including frontal cortex) of suicide victims and found no differences between the groups for any of the regions studied. In contrast to our findings and those of Kaufman et al., Meyerson et al. (1982) reported a significant increase in QNB binding in the frontal cortex of a small group of suicides not adequately matched for factors such as age, sex, and PMI.

More recently, Mann, Stanley, McBride, and McEwen (1986) have measured beta-adrenergic receptors in suicide victims, in the hope that such studies might indicate the functional status of central catecholamine neurons in suicidal behavior. It has been suggested that down-regulation of beta-adrenergic receptors may be linked with the therapeutic effect of antidepressants, and that changes in these receptors may also relate to the neurochemical substrate of suicide and depression. Beta-adrenergic receptor binding was measured in the frontal cortex of suicide victims and controls using a single concentration of dihydroalphrenolol (DHA). There was a 73% increase in beta-adrenergic receptor binding in suicide victims compared with controls.

In addition to this study, Zanko and Beigon (1983) reported an increased number of binding sites (B_{max}), with no change in K_d in a small series of six suicide victims and matched controls. In contrast with the studies above, Meyerson et al. (1982) reported no alteration in DHA binding in suicide victims. Thus, two of three studies measuring beta-adrenergic receptors have reported an increase in binding in suicide victims. It should be noted that antemortem use of antidepressants would not explain the receptor alterations (increases) observed. Data from animal studies indicate that chronic antidepressant treatment causes a down-regulation of beta-adrenergic receptors. Findings in the suicide victims studied by Mann et al. (1986) indicated alterations in receptor binding in the opposite direction from that which would be expected if drug effects had been present. A statistically significant increase in cortical DHA binding with age was seen in the same study ($r = .60$, $n = 19$, $p < .01$). These directional differences in binding can be put to use by researchers as internal controls to indirectly monitor drug use in their samples.

One of our most recent findings in postmortem suicide research relates to corticotropin-releasing factor (CRF) binding in frontal cortex. CRF is a peptide containing 41 amino acids and is the hypothalamic releasing hormone that acts as the major physiological regulator of adrenocorticotropic hormone (ACTH). Two lines of evidence support the hypothesis that the hypercortisolemia observed in depressed patients is due to hypersecretion of CRF (at the level of the hypothalamus and possibly higher central nervous system areas). Two studies have reported that CSF concentrations of CRF are elevated in drug-free depressed patients, when compared to normal controls (Banki, Bissette, Arato, O'Connor, & Nemeroff, in press; Nemeroff, Widerlow, Bissette, Walleus, Karlsson, Eklund, Kilts, Loosen, & Vale, 1984). In addition, Gold, Chrousos, Kellner, Post, Roy, Augerinos, Schulte, Oldfield, and Loriaux (1984) and Holsboer, Muller, Doerrs, Sippwell, Stalla, Gerken, Steigert, Boll, and Benkert (1984) have demonstrated a blunted ACTH response to intravenously administered CRF in depressed patients when compared to normal controls—a finding consistent with down-regulation of CRF receptors in the adenohypophysis secondary to long-standing CRF hypersecretion.

Because of the findings described above and a growing behavioral literature (Kalin, Shelton, Kraemer, & McKinney, 1983; Thatcher-Britton, Lee, Vale, Rivier, & Koob, 1986) indicating that centrally administered CRF produces, in laboratory animals, a variety of effects (decreased sexual behavior, decreased appetite, altered locomotor activity) that are remarkably similar to the signs and symptoms of major depression, Owen, Stanley, Bissette, and Nemeroff (1986) measured the binding of radiolabeled CRF in the frontal cortex of suicide victims. It was thought that chronic CRF hypersecretion should result in a decrease (down-regulation) in the number of CRF binding sites. In the initial study, a significant decrease in approximately 12 suicides was observed, in comparison with 12 controls. The investigators subsequently increased the size in both groups to 27 suicides and 29 controls and replicated the preliminary finding (Owen et al., 1986).

The last area for review here is the application of postmortem findings. One of the potential criticisms of postmortem studies is that findings derived from them lack a proven clinical utility, as no means of monitoring the alterations reported is provided. Thus, the clinical significance of postmortem findings must be inferred. Therefore, it would be useful to develop a method with clinical application that could be used in postmortem studies.

In antemortem studies, biogenic amine metabolites in CSF are generally regarded as the best indicator of neuronal function in the brain. One way of testing the strength of this relationship is by simultaneously assessing the CSF and brain levels of the same metabolite in the same individual. Stanley et al. (1985) measured 5-HIAA and homovanillic acid (HVA) in the lumbar CSF and brains of the same individuals at autopsy. The postmortem lumbar punctures and samples of frontal cortex corresponding to Brodmann's area 8–9 were obtained from 48 individuals. The results of this study indicated the presence of a significant correlation between CSF and brain levels of 5-HIAA and HVA.

In addition to the principal aim of the project presented above (i.e., the assessment of the relationship between metabolite levels in CSF and brain), Stanley et al. (1985) were also interested in determining the degree to which postmortem CSF measures agreed with the CSF findings of antemortem studies. In this regard, some of the findings indicating similarities between these results and those obtained from living individuals were (1) a significant gradient in metabolite concentration in serial samples of CSF; (2) the mean CSF concentrations of 5-HIAA (34.4 ng/ml) and HVA (71.6 ng/ml); (3) an inverse correlation between body height and CSF levels of 5-HIAA; and (4) a significant correlation between the postmortem CSF concentrations of 5-HIAA and HVA ($r = .69, p < .001$).

Thus, the relationship between metabolite levels in the brain and CSF provides direct evidence for the validity of using these CSF measures as a index of brain metabolism in the living. Furthermore, this methodology could be used to examine the interrelationship between a biogenic amine or its metabolite and the status of the various receptors associated with the same neuronal system, as well as to provide a means for applying postmortem finding to the clinical setting.

In summary, the data presented in this review provide support for the utility of postmortem research. It is, however, important to pay careful attention to those variables that have been shown by Stanley and his colleagues among others to exert an influence on neurochemical measures. As complex as the neurochemistry of suicidal behavior may be, the behaviors that ultimately lead to suicide are equally complex. Despite this complexity, both components should nevertheless be an integral part of all suicide research.

Implications

The major neurochemical findings in suicide can be summarized as follows:

1. Dysfunction of the serotonergic system has been found in individuals who have committed suicide.
2. The association between serotonergic dysfunction and suicide appears to be present, irrespective of diagnosis.
3. The relationship between serotonergic dysfunction and suicide seems to remain consistent across the age span. However, studies targeting specific age groups at opposite ends of the spectrum, the young and the old, have yet to be conducted.

Based on these general findings, we can draw several implications about the biochemistry of suicidal behavior. First, biochemical vulnerability must be considered when examining risk factors for suicide. Conventional thinking in psychiatry about suicidal behavior usually portrays suicide as a product of mental illness, typically depression, and difficult life circumstances (e.g., severe loss or hardship). In light of recent research, biochemical abnormalities may have to be included in the equation in identifying suicide risk factors.

Second, although the diagnosis of depression is common in many individuals who commit suicide, several other diagnoses are represented in the suicide population. In addition, the finding of serotonergic dysfunction related to suicidal behavior occurs across diagnostic categories. Taken together, these findings can lead us to speculate that individuals who commit suicide may have two distinct conditions: one that consists of their primary psychiatric diagnosis (e.g., major depressive disorder, schizophrenic disorder), and a second disturbance related to serotonergic dysfunction that manifests itself in the form of suicidal behavior.

This "two-condition" theory draws on several sources of data for support: (1) the biochemical findings reviewed in this chapter; (2) the increased familial incidence of suicide; and (3) the incidence of suicide across diagnoses, coupled with a lack of suicidal behavior in many individuals with diagnoses that carry an increased risk for suicide. This theory suggests that suicide derives in part from a combination of a psychiatric condition (e.g., major depressive disorder) and a dysfunction of the serotonergic system. Much research is required to determine whether this formulation is valid. One approach would be to attempt to alter one psychiatric condition biochemically while not changing the other. For example, in suicidal schizophrenics, this theory would postulate that altering serotonergic functioning should diminish the suicidal behavior but should not improve the psychosis. Likewise, neuroleptics may be effective in resolving the psychosis, but may not have a major impact on suicidality. Ultimately, this type of research may lead to a new treatment strategy for suicidal patients. This approach may involve the administration of two separate medications: one for the primary psychiatric condition, and one that targets the suicidal behavior more specifically.

References

Banki, C. M., Bisset, G., Arato, M., O'Connor, L., & Nemeroff, C. B. CSF corticotropin-like immunoreactivity in depression and schizophrenia. *American Journal of Psychiatry*, in press.

Barraclough, B., Bunch, J., Nelson, B., & Sainsbury, P. A hundred cases of suicide: Clinical aspects. *British Journal of Psychiatry*, 1974, *125*, 355–373.

Beskow, J., Gottfries, C. G., Roos, B. E., & Winblad, B. Determination of monoamine and monoamine metabolites in the human brain: Post mortem studies in a group of suicides and in a control group. *Acta Psychiatrica Scandinavica*, 1976, *53*, 7–20.

Bourne, H. R., Bunney, W. E., Jr., Colburn, R. W., Davis, J. M., Shaw, D. M., & Coppen, A. J. Noradrenaline, 5-hydroxytryptamine, and 5-hydroxyindoleacetic acid in the hindbrains of suicidal patients. *Lancet*, 1968, *ii*, 805–808.

Brunello, N., Chuang, D. M., & Costa, E. Different synaptic location of mianserin and imipramine binding sites. *Science*, 1982, *215*, 1112–1115.

Cheetham, S. C., Cross, J. A., Crompton, M. R., Czudek, C., Katona, C. L. E., Parker, S. J., Reynolds, G. P., & Horton, R. W. Serotonin and GABA function in depressed and suicide victims. In *International Conference on New Directions in Affective Disorders: Book of abstracts*. 1987.

Cochrane, E., Robins, E., & Grote, S. Regional serotonin levels in brain: A comparison of depressive suicides and alcoholic suicides with controls. *Biological Psychiatry*, 1976, *11*, 283–294.

Crow, T. J., Cross, A. J., Cooper, S. J., et al. Neurotransmitter receptors and monamine metabolites in the brains of patients with Alzheimer-type dementia and depression in suicides. *Neuropharmacology*, 1984, *23*, 1561–1569.

Dorpat, T. L., & Ripley, H. S. A study of suicide in the Seattle area. *Comprehensive Psychiatry*, 1960, *1*, 349–359.

Gold, P. W., Chrousos, G., Kellner, C., Post, R., Roy, A., Augerinos, P., Schulte, H., Oldfield, E., & Loriaux, L. Psychiatric implications of basic and clinical studies with corticotropin-releasing factor. *American Journal of Psychiatry*, 1984, *141*, 619.

Holsboer, F., Muller, O. A., Doerrs, H. G., Sippwell, W. G., Stalla, G. K., Gerken, A., Steigert, A., Boll, E., & Benkert, O. ACTH and multisteroid responses to corticotropin-releasing factor in depressive illness; Relationship to multisteroid responses after ACTH stimulation and dexamethasone suppression. *Psychoneuroendocrinology*, 1984, *9*, 147–160.

Kalin, N. H., Shelton, S. E., Kraemer, G. W., & McKinney, W. T. Corticotropin-releasing factor administered intraventricularly to rhesus monkeys. *Peptides*, 1983, *4*, 217–220.

Kaufman, C. A., Gillin, J. C., Hill, B., O'Laughlin, T., Phillips, I., Kleinmen, J. E., & Wyatt, R. J. Muscarinic binding in suicides. *Psychiatry Research* 1984, *12*, 47–55.

Korpi, E. R., Kleinmen, J. E., Goodman, S. J., et al. *Serotonin and 5-hydroxyindoleaceacetic acid concentration in different brain regions of suicide victims: Comparison in chronic schizophrenic patients with suicide as cause of death.* Paper presented at the meeting of the International Society for Neurochemistry, Vancouver, British Columbia, Canada, July 14, 1983.

Langer, S. F., Briley, M. S., Raisman, R., et al. 3H-imipramine binding in human platelets: Influence of age and sex. *Naunyn Schmiedebergs Archivs für Pharmacologie*, 1980, *313*, 189–194.

Langer, S. F., & Raisman, R. Binding of [3H]imipramine and [3H]desipramine as biochemical tools for studies in depression. *Neuropharmacology*, 1983, *22*, 407–413.

Lloyd, K. G., Fraley, I. J., Deck, J. H. N., & Hornykiewicz, O. Serotonin and 5-hydroxyindoleacetic acid in discrete areas of the brainstem of suicide victims and control patients. In *Advances in biochemical psychopharmacology* (Vol. 2). New York: Raven Press, 1974.

Mann, J. J., Petito, C., Stanley, M., McBride, P. A., Chin, J., & Philogene, A. Amine receptor binding and monamine oxidase activity in postmortem human brain tissue: Effect of age, gender and postmortem delay. In G. D. Burrows, T. R. Norman, & L. Dennerstein (Eds.), *Clinical and pharmacological studies in psychiatric disorders*. London: John Libbey, 1985.

Mann, J. J., & Stanley, M. (Eds.). *Psychobiology of suicidal behavior*. New York: New York Academy of Sciences, 1986.

Mann, J. J., Stanley, M., McBride, P. A., & McEwen, B. Increased serotonin and beta-adrenergic receptor binding in the frontal cortices of suicide victims. *Archives of General Psychiatry*, 1986, *43*, 954–959.

McIntyre, I. M., & Stanley, M. Post mortem and regional changes of serotonin, 5-hydroxyindoleacetic acid and tryptophan in brain. *Journal of Neurochemistry*, 1984, *42*, 1588–1592.

Meltzer, H. Y., Nash, J. F., Ohmori, T., Kregel, L., & Arora, R. Neuroendocrine and biochemical studies of serotonin and dopamine in depression and suicide. In *International Conference on New Directions in Affective Disorders: Book of abstracts.* 1987.

Meyerson, L. R., Wennogle, L. P., Abel, M. S., Coupet, J., Lippa, S., Rauh, C. E., & Beer, B. Human brain receptor alterations in suicide victims. *Pharmacology, Biochemistry and Behavior*, 1982, *17*, 159–163.

Nemeroff, C. B., Widerlow, E., Bissett, G., Walleus, H., Karlsson, I., Eklund, K., Kilts, C. D., Loosen, P. T., & Vale, W. Elevated concentrations of CSF corticotropin-releasing factor-like immunoreactivity in depressed patients. *Science*, 1984, *226*, 1342–1344.

Owen, F., Cross, A. J., Crow, T. J., Deakin, J. F. W., Ferrier, I. N., Lofthouse, R., & Poulter, M. Brain 5-HT2 receptors and suicide. *Lancet*, 1983, *i*, 1256.

Owens, M. J., Stanley, M., Bissette, G., & Nemeroff, C. B. *CRF receptor number is decreased in the frontal cortex of suicide victims*. Paper presented at the meeting of the American College of Neuropsychopharmacology, Washington, D.C., 1986.

Pare, C. M. B., Yeung, D. P. H., Price, K., & Stacey, R. S. 5-Hydroxytryptamine, noradrenaline, and dopamine in brainstem, hypothalamus, and caudate nucleus of controls and patients committing suicide by coal-gas poisoning. *Lancet*, 1969, *ii*, 133–135.

Paul, S. M., Rehavi, M., Skolnick, P., & Goodwin, F. K. High affinity binding of antidepressants to a biogenic amine transport site in human brain and platelet; studies in depression. In R. M. Post & J. C. Bellinger (Eds.), *Neurobiology of mood disorders*. Baltimore: Williams & Wilkins, 1984.

Peroutka, S. J., & Snyder, S. H. Regulation of serotonin (5HT2) receptors labeled with [3H]spiroperidol by chronic treatment with antidepressant amitriptyline. *Pharmacology and Experimental Therapeutics*, 1980, *215*, 582–587.

Perry, E. K., Marshall, E. F., Blessed, G., Tomlinson, B. E., & Perry, R. H. Decreased imipramine binding in the brains of patients with depressive illness. *British Journal of Psychiatry*, 1983, *1412*, 188–192.

Rainbow, T. C., & Beigon, A. Distribution of imipramine binding sites in the rat brain studied by quantitative autoradiography. *Neuroscience Letters*, 1983, *37*, 209–214.

Rehavi, M., Ittah, Y., Price, K. L., et al. 2-Nitroimipramine: A selective irreversible inhibitor of [3H]serotonin uptake and [3H]imipramine binding in platelets. *Biochemistry and Biophysics Research Communications*, 1981, *99*, 954.

Robins, E., Murphy, G. E., Wilkinson, R. H., Jr., Gassner, S., & Kayes, J. Some Clinical considerations in the prevention of suicide based on a study of 134 successful suicides. *American Journal of Public Health*, 1959, *49*, 888–899.

Severson, J. A., Marwsson, J. O., & Osterburg, H. H. Elevated density of [3H]imipramine binding in aged human brain. *Journal of Neurochemistry*, 1985, *45*, 1382–1389.

Shaw, D. M., Camps, F. E., & Eccleston, E. G. 5-Hydroxytryptamine in the hind brain of depressive suicides. *British Journal of Psychiatry*, 1967, *113*, 1407–1411.

Stanley, M. Cholinergic binding in the frontal cortex of suicide victims. *American Journal of Psychiatry*, 1984, *141*, 11.

Stanley, M. *Presynaptic measures of serotonin in suicide*. Paper presented at the meeting of the American College of Neuropsychopharmacology, Washington, D. C., 1985.

Stanley, M., & Mann, J. J. Increased serotonin-2 binding sites in frontal cortex of suicide victims. *Lancet*, 1983, *i*, 214–216.

Stanley, M., McIntyre, I., & Gershon, S. *Post mortem serotonin metabolism in suicide victims*. Paper presented at the meeting of the American College of Neuropsychopharmacology, San Juan, Puerto Rico, 1983.

Stanley, M., Traskman-Bendz, L., & Dorovini-Zis, K. Correlations between aminergic metabolites simultaneously obtained from samples of CSF and brain. *Life Sciences*, 1985, *37*, 1279–1286.

Stanley, M., Virgilio, J., & Gerhson, S. Tritiated imipramine binding sites are decreased in the frontal cortex of suicides. *Science*, 1982, *216*, 1337–1339.

Thatcher-Britton, K., Lee, G., Vale, W. W., Rivier, J., & Koob, G. Corticotropin-releasing factor (CRF) receptor antagonist blocks activating and anxiogenic actions of CRF in the rat. *Brain Research*, 1986, *369*, 303–306.

Zanko, M. T., & Beigon, A. Increased adrenergic receptor binding in human frontal cortex of suicide victims. *Society for Neuroscience Abstracts*, 1983, Part 1, 210.

4

The Psychological Autopsy: Methodological Considerations for the Study of Adolescent Suicide

David A. Brent, MD
Western Psychiatric Institute and Clinic

The psychological autopsy is an intensive interview, or series of interviews, designed to reconstruct the social and psychological circumstances associated with the manner of death (Shneidman & Farberow, 1961). This technique was originally developed in Los Angeles as a method of augmenting the coroner's standard investigations of equivocal deaths (Curphey, 1968), but has been utilized by several groups of psychiatric investigators to characterize adults who complete suicide (Barraclough, Burch, Nelson, & Sainsbury, 1974; Dorpat & Ripley, 1960; Robins, Murphy, Wilkinson, Gassner, & Kayes, 1959). With the recent concern about suicide among youths, there has been renewed interest in this method as a means of shedding light on the nature of suicide in adolescents. In this chapter, previous efforts to employ this technique are reviewed, with particular attention to the methodological issues involved.

Why Psychological Autopsy Studies?

Epidemiological designs take two basic forms—prospective or case–control (Kleinbaum, Kupper, & Morgenstein, 1982). In a prospective design, a cohort is followed forward; those who develop a condition are compared to those who do not with respect to certain hypothesized risk

Preparation of this chapter was supported by National Institute of Mental Health (NIMH) Contract No. 278-85-0026 (OD). Support for this work was provided by grants from the following: the Health and Research Services Foundation (No. AA-81), the William T. Grant Foundation (No. 86-1063-86), and NIMH (no. KO8 MH00581-01). A revised version of this paper appeared in the *Journal of the American Academy of Child and Adolescent Psychiatry*, May 1988.

factors. Although prospective studies do not suffer from the sampling biases or retrospective assessment of risk of case–control studies, they are highly inefficient for the study of rare disorders and disorders in which the risk factors are not well delineated, such as suicide. Moreover, rates of adolescent suicide have shown pronounced secular trends (Shaffer & Fisher, 1981), that could confound the interpretation of a longitudinal study of any significant duration.

Given these constraints, an alternative strategy is to employ a case–control method, in which suicide victims ("cases") are compared to members of some other group ("controls"). The assumption underlying this design is that variables differentiating the two groups are likely to be risk factors for suicide. Alternatively, those members of the control group who most closely resemble completers are those likely to be at highest risk for the completion of suicide. One cross-sectional comparison study of adult suicide attempters and completers verified these assumptions through a longitudinal follow-up on the attempters (Pallis, Barraclough, Levey, et al., 1982; Pallis, Gibbons, & Pierce, 1984).

Since groups are identified by presence or absence of suicide, risk factors need to be assessed retrospectively, after the fact of the suicide. It is in this design that the psychological autopsy is absolutely necessary (Fisher & Shaffer, 1984). Furthermore, even in a prospective design, the psychological autopsy can add greatly to the information gleaned, since it is likely that some time would have elapsed between the last longitudinal assessment and suicide in a given subject.

The use of the psychological autopsy technique requires attention to several key methodological details. These include (1) the choice of informants; (2) the manner of approach to informants; (3) the effect of the time period between the suicide and the interview on the quality of information obtained; (4) integration of various data sources; (5) the choice of a control group; and (6) the choice of domains and assessment instruments.

Choice of the Informants

Psychological autopsy studies of adults have generally relied most heavily on spouses or first-degree relatives (Barraclough et al., 1974; Dorpat & Ripley, 1960; Robins et al., 1959) (see Table 4.1). In addition, many different types of secondary informants have been employed, including physicians, close friends, and bartenders (Barraclough et al., 1974; Robins et al., 1959). Psychological autopsy studies involving adolescents have generally augmented information obtained from parents and sib-

TABLE 4.1.   Interviews with Informants for Psychological Autopsy Studies

Study	First-degree relative or spouse	Friends	Other	Professional contact
Robins, Murphy, Wilkinson, Gassner, & Kayes (1959)	×	×	×	Record
Dorpat & Ripley (1960)	×	×		Record
Barraclough, Burch, Nelson, & Sainsbury (1974)	×	×	×	×
Shafii, Carrigan, Whittinghill, & Derrick (1985)	×	×	×	×
Rich, Young, & Fowler (1986)	×	×		Record
Shaffer & Gould (1984)[a]	×	×		Record
Fawcett & Clark (1987)[a]	×	×	×	×
Brent, Perper, Kolko, & Goldstein (1988)[a]	×	×		×

[a] Report from ongoing study.

lings with information from close friends (Brent, Perper, Kolko, & Goldstein, 1988; Fawcett & Clark, 1987; Shaffer & Gould, 1984; Shafii, Carrigan, Whittinghill, & Derrick, 1985). Interviews with physicians can shed light on the potentially preventive role that the primary physician can play with respect to suicide, in light of the large proportion of adults who visit a physician within a month of their suicide (Barraclough et al., 1974; Robins et al., 1959). This strategy is now being pursued in one psychological autopsy study of adolescents as well (Fawcett & Clark, 1987). Analogously, interviews with teachers of adolescent suicide victims may shed light on how these youths appear in school, and whether, in retrospect, these victims displayed certain warning signs that could have led to the prevention of their tragic behavior (Kerr & Schaeffer, 1986).

Similar-age informants have been found to be useful in our experience, particularly for descriptions of suicidal threats, drug and alcohol abuse, and affective symptomatology (Shaffer & Gould, 1984). For example, Brent et al. (1988) found that 50% of suicidal threats in the completer group were confided *only* to another peer. Similarly, information from peers raised our rates of drug and alcohol abuse by 9%.

TABLE 4.2.   Method of Approach for Psychological Autopsy

Method	Study	Compliance
Home visit, unannounced	Barraclough et al. (1974)	100%
Contact at funeral home, numerous follow-up visits	Shafii et al. (1985)	85%
Letter, home visit, or phone contact	Robins et al. (1959)	85%
	Dorpat & Ripley (1960)	94%
	Rich et al. (1986)	87%
	Shaffer & Gould (1984)	>80%
	Fawcett & Clark (1987)	>80%
	Brent et al. (1988)	77%

Approach to the Informants

Despite variable methods in the approach to the informants, most psychological autopsy studies have reported good compliance, generally over 80% (see Table 4.2). Informants have been approached at the funeral home (Shafii et al., 1984), at the home "unannounced" (Barraclough et al., 1974), by letter (Brent et al., 1988; Dorpat & Ripley, 1960; Fawcett & Clark, 1987; Robins et al., 1959; Shaffer & Gould, 1984), and by telephone (Rich, Young, & Fowler, 1986), all with apparently good success (e.g., compliance ≥ 77%). In several studies, the interval from the suicide and the interview is not specified, but Shafii and colleagues (Shafii et al., 1985; Shafii, Whittinghill, Dolen, Pearson, Derrick, & Carrigan, 1984) began the interviewing process within a week of the death and gathered information in subsequent follow-up interviews over the next year. In other studies of adolescent suicide victims, the family is contacted by a letter of condolence approximately 6–12 weeks after the suicide (Brent et al., 1988; Shaffer & Gould, 1984). The letter contains some information about the study, and the family is contacted via phone by an interviewer within a week of the letter. Other studies to interview have noted that compliance is greater in families where the suicide has occurred more recently (Cantor, 1975; Herzog & Resnick, 1968). Some research efforts are also linked to support groups or supportive therapy for the bereaved family members and friends, which probably tends to encourage compliance (Brent et al., 1988; Fawcett & Clark, 1987).

Shafii et al. (1984) have outlined some guidelines for the proper conduct of the psychological autopsy: (1) Remember that the informants are *not* patients; (2) even though semistructured instruments are employed, follow the family's lead; (3) avoid any guilt-inducing approach and be nonjudgmental; (4) give no false reassurances or platitudes; and (5) be flexible as to the length of the interview.

Interview Effects: Timing

There have been no previous systematic studies of the effect of the time interval between the death and the interview on the quality and quantity of data elicited in psychological autopsies. During the acute phase of grief, the request to complete a long interview protocol may appear insensitive and is perhaps unproductive. However, if too much time has elapsed between the death and the interview, recall of events may be indistinct, and the family's motivation in completing such an interview may no longer be optimal. Therefore, my colleagues and I have tried to interview families no earlier than 2 months after the death and no later than 6 months. In our pilot study of 27 completed adolescent suicides, the families were interviewed a median of 4 months after the suicide (Brent et al., 1988). We looked at the correlations of the interval between death and the interview with reported suicidal intent score and with number and type of diagnoses reported and found none to be significant (see Table 4.3). These data suggest that within the range of 2–6 months, there is no simple or consistent relationship between timing of the interview and the quality and quantity of data obtained. We also replicated this finding in comparable interviews with suicide attempters and their families (median interval between suicidal episode and interview = 21 days; range = 0–56 days).

Another issue related to the timing of the interview is the impact of the emotional state of the informant on the quality and quantity of data obtained during the interview. Within our sample, we looked at

TABLE 4.3.   Effects of Time Lapsed between Suicidal Event and Interview

	Completers[a]	Attempters[b]
Intent	−.09	−.13
Number of diagnoses	−.20	.14
Diagnosis of:		
Affective disorder	−.03	.03
Anxiety disorder	.17	−.01
Substance abuse	−.09	.11
Conduct disorder	−.01	.23

[a] $n = 27$; median time elapsed was 4 months.
[b] $n = 32$–38; median time elapsed was 21 days.

the relationship of the presence of a current affective disorder in the informant to number and type of diagnoses and to suicidal intent, and found no significant association, either for completers or for suicide attempters (see Table 4.4).

The knowledge of the suicide could influence the informant in one of two ways. First, the informant, to expiate his or her sense of guilt, might exaggerate the presence of psychopathology in the victim. However, the similarity in frequencies of various depressive symptoms between depressed completers and depressed patients belies this mechanism and suggests that the reporting of informants in psychological autopsy studies is in fact reliable and valid (Barraclough et al., 1974). One might also expect the reverse effect: That is, in an effort to idealize the victim, all the victim's psychological problems might be denied. However, all reported psychological autopsy studies describe psychiatric disorder in over 90% of completed suicide victims, so that this proposed "halo effect" does not seem to be significant (Barraclough et al., 1974; Brent et al., 1988; Dorpat & Ripley, 1960; Rich et al., 1986; Robins et al., 1959; Shafii et al., 1988; Shafii et al., 1985). Interview bias may play a role in the high rate of psychopathology elicited from informants. Nevertheless, this can be guarded against by the use of structured interview schedules, reliability checks, and diagnostic conferences (Barraclough et al., 1974). The rate of diagnoses is fairly comparable across a wide range of geographic samples (see Table 4.5; Barraclough et al., 1974; Dorpat & Ripley, 1960; Rich et al., 1986; Robins et al., 1959). Discrepancies may be accounted for in part by different diagnostic practices (e.g., the high rate of schizophrenia in Dorpat & Ripley's [1960] study) or secular trends in substance abuse (e.g., the high rate of alcohol use in Rich et al.'s [1986] study). Moreover, the prominence

TABLE 4.4. Effect of *Current* Parental Affective Disorder on Reporting in a Psychological Autopsy Study

	Completers[a]	Attempters[b]
Intent	.06	.03
Number of diagnoses	−.14	−.06
Diagnosis of:		
Affective disorder	−.24	.02
Anxiety disorder	−.10	.11
Substance abuse	.16	.03
Conduct disorder	—	−.13

[a] $n = 27$.
[b] n's ranged from 32 to 38.

TABLE 4.5. Validity of Diagnoses: Agreement among Studies

Study	Affective disorder	Alcohol abuse	Schizophrenia	Any disorder
Robins et al. (1959)	47%	25%	2%	94%
Dorpat & Ripley (1960)	30.5%	27%	12%	100%
Barraclough et al. (1974)	64%	15%	3%	93%
Rich et al. (1986)				
Age > 30	52%	55%	5%	91%
Age < 30	36%	54%	2%	92%

of alcoholism and affective disorders in completed suicide is confirmed by prospective studies, which do *not* suffer from the apparent biases of the psychological autopsy study (reviewed in Miles, 1977).

Another potential source of bias is that the presence of psychiatric illness in the victim may bias coroners to declare a death to be a suicide. If this were the case, it would artificially inflate the proportion of suicide victims who had a psychiatric disorder (Barraclough et al., 1974). This is not likely to be a major factor, because a coroner's investigations are usually far from detailed in regard to the assessment of psychiatric illness. In fact, the legal definition of suicide does not include a mention of psychiatric illness, but is simply based on the circumstances of intent (Barraclough et al., 1974). If a marginal case was declared a suicide because of the victim's psychiatric state, the family could always contest the verdict. Moreover, coroners are just as likely to classify a psychiatrically disturbed person's death as "undetermined" as they are to declare it a suicide (Holding & Barraclough, 1975).

Integration of Various Data Sources

Although the integration of various data sources is a common problem in psychiatry, it is a particularly salient issue in the administration and interpretation of the psychological autopsy. The absence of self-reported data from suicide victims means that symptoms referent to anxiety and affective disorder will probably be underreported (Herjanic & Reich, 1982). Siblings and peers will be able to add somewhat to the sensitivity of this procedure, but there is no doubt that this will still result in an underestimate of the extent and range of symptomatology. For example, by parent report alone, we estimated that 67.9% of attempters had an affective disorder and that 26.8% had affective disorder *with* comorbidity (Brent et al., 1988). When siblings' and peers' reports were combined with those of the parents, these rates became 82.1% and 41.1%, respectively. The relationship between direct and indirect interviews has been most carefully studied in comparisons of the family history (indirect) and family study (direct) methods (Andreasen, Rice, Endicott, Reich, & Coryell, 1986). The family history method, when compared with direct interviews, shows modest sensitivity (31–79%) but high specificity (66–100%). The sensitivity for the indirect method increases with the number of informants interviewed, and both sensitivity and specificity were higher when data was obtained from female informants. Extrapolation to the psychological autopsy technique suggests that diagnoses will be accurate but subject to some underascertainment, and that increasing the number of informants can boost the sensitivity of this procedure.

Choice of Comparison Groups

Barraclough et al. (1974) compared suicide victims to geographic controls selected from general practitioners' case registers. In addition, in this study, victims were compared with diagnostically similar psychiatric patients. Shafii and colleagues (Shafii, 1986b; Shafii et al., 1985) have compared victims to their close friends. It is of interest that the friends appear to be highly deviant, although not so much as the completers. Shafii et al. (1988) later reported that one of the friends committed suicide, which yielded a rate over 100 times that expected. Therefore, close friends of adolescent suicide victims may represent one "at-risk" population. The choice of close friends of the victims as a comparison group affords other advantages, insofar as these friends are frequently closely matched with the victims in race, sex, age, socioeconomic status, and neighborhood.

The classic comparison in suicidology is that of suicide attempters and completers. Suicide attempters are a group at high risk for suicide, although only a maximum of 10% of youthful attempters actually complete suicide (Otto, 1972). Characteristics that differentiate attempters and completers are likely to be risk factors for completed suicide (Pallis et al., 1982). Conversely, attempters who most closely resemble completers in these risk factors are likely to complete suicide (Pallis et al., 1984). A similar interview protocol can be administered to both groups, and some useful comparisons can be obtained, but the presence of the actual attempters makes direct contrast with the absent completers problematic unless the asymmetry of informants is controlled for in the data analyses. Furthermore, most samples of attempters or other psychiatric controls come from self-referred samples and so may not be directly comparable to completers who have never sought treatment.

Finally, one can compare completers to victims of accident, homicide, or sudden natural death, so that the psychological autopsy technique is applied in *all* groups. However, these results, while more methodologically sound, are not as clinically useful, insofar as the assessment of suicidal risk is a clinical problem in *clinical* populations. If a comparison group of accident victims is sampled, such potentially ambiguous accidents such as single-passenger vehicular deaths should be excluded, as some of these may be disguised suicides.

Asymmetry of Informants

Except for this last set of contrasts, most case–control studies involving psychological autopsy studies require a comparison of the suicide victims to members of some *live* control group. This highlights the most obvious asymmetry of the psychological autopsy procedure: A suicide victim cannot be interviewed, whereas a live suicide attempter can be a rich source of information. As noted above, best-estimate diagnoses, which integrate *all* data sources, are likely to provide *more* of an underestimate of some diagnoses in the completer group than in the live comparison group. This generalization is based upon our experience with the relative contribution of the attempters' self-report to the best-estimate diagnosis (Brent et al., 1988), as well as the data from comparison of indirect and direct interviews reported by Andreasen et al. (1986). Weissman, Kidd, and Prusoff (1982) addressed this methodological problem by controlling for interview status in any data analyses of family studies (e.g., direct vs. indirect, number of informants, etc.). A comparable procedure can be utilized in psychological autopsy studies. The comparison of the parent reports of both groups is the most conservative approach and should underestimate psychopathology in both groups to approximately the same degree. Comparison of best-estimate reports will underestimate psychopathology in the victims to a greater degree than in a live comparison group. Therefore, the *most* robust differences are those seen across *both* sets of contrasts; differences seen *just* across parent reports are also felt to be robust. Differences seen *just* across best-estimate diagnoses should be viewed with suspicion, as they are likely to be due to the asymmetry of reporting.

Choice of Domains and Assessment Instruments

Most psychological autopsy studies have tried to delineate circumstances of death, events leading up to the suicide, psychopathology, social adaptation and physical health, medical/psychiatric treatment, and family background. All reported psychological autopsy studies have employed semistructured interviews. In fact, only Barraclough et al. (1974) and Rich et al. (1986) have actually reported on interrater reliability.

Circumstances

Information required to delineate the circumstances of death are method, toxicology, precipitants, and suicidal intent. The definition of precipitants is difficult because it involves the attribution of a causal relationship between the stressor and the suicide. Therefore, it is important to define the time interval that can elapse between a so-called precipitant and a suicide. Paykel, Prusoff, and Myers (1975) noted that suicide *attempters* showed more stressors in the week and month prior to the attempt than psychiatric controls; Murphy, Armstrong, Hermele, Fisher, and Clendenin (1979) showed similar results with alcoholic suicide victims. Therefore, 1 month might seem a reasonable, albeit arbitrary, cutoff. On the other hand, Cohen-Sandler, Berman, and King (1982) showed that for child inpatients hospitalized for suicidal behavior, there was a greater number of stressors for the *year* prior to admission. Because of the potential bias involved in the attribution of a given stressor, it may be best to record stressors and precipitants separately and to note their occurrence as to the last year, month, week, or day, as well as the attribution of the informants.

The Suicidal Intent Scale of Beck, Schuyler, and Herman (1974) and the subsequent modification of this scale by Pierce (1981) are quite useful for recording the parameters of suicidal behavior. The first nine items in the Beck scale relate to observable behavior, and so parents or other informants can supply this information. Among the areas this measure taps are prior communication of suicidal intent, evidence of planning, note leaving, and behavior anticipating death (e.g., a will). This scale has been shown to predict reattempts in adults and adolescents (Beck et al., 1974; Hawton, Osborn, O'Grady, et al., 1982), as well as to predict completions in adults (Beck et al., 1974; Pierce, 1981).

Exposure to Suicidal Behavior

With the recent interest in and awareness of imitative suicides (Gould & Shaffer, 1986; Phillips & Carstensen, 1986), the study of the role of exposure to suicidal behavior represents a potentially fruitful area of inquiry. One of the weaknesses of the above-cited work is that the exposure and vulnerability characteristics of the suicide victims whose suicides *appear* to be imitative are unknown. However, quantification of exposure is difficult, particularly in retrospect. For example, if a 17-year-old boy has recently discovered that his mother died of suicide rather than of natural causes, as he has been led to believe since he was 8 years old, does this constitute exposure? If so, how does this compare to witnessing the suicide of a friend or going to the funeral of an acquaintance who died by suicide? Shafii et al. (1985) report greater exposure to suicidality among completers than controls, but they do not differentiate between familial and extrafamilial exposure, nor do they distinguish among suicide, suicide attempts, and threats. Any measure of exposure should allow for quantification of the intensity and timing of the exposure, the relationship of the victim to the suicidal person, *and* the type of suicidality displayed to which the victim was exposed.

Availability of Lethal Agents

The relationship between the availability of firearms and suicide (Boyd, 1983; Boyd & Mościcki, 1986) has attracted interest in recent years. Most studies have been ecological in nature, so that it is difficult to know whether individuals who commit suicide actually have a greater availability of guns than a comparison group. However, in case–control studies involving the psychological autopsy, the availability and accessibility of firearms can easily be ascertained. Accessibility can be categorized as follows: (1) guns loaded; (2) guns stored with ammunition, unlocked; (3) guns stored with ammunition, locked; (4) guns stored separate from ammunition, neither locked; (5) guns stored separate from ammunition, both locked; (6) guns broken down, need to be reassembled; (7) no guns. Also, the specific availability of handguns should be noted. In this way, the effects of availability and accessibility can be disentangled. Because of the likely correlation of firearms availability with rural locations, population density and distance from a metropolitan area should be reported (Brent et al., 1988).

Psychopathology

There are a variety of structured and semistructured interview schedules to elicit psychiatric symptomatology, such as the Diagnostic Interview for Children and Adolescents (DICA; Herjanic & Reich, 1982), the Schedule for Affective Disorders and Schizophrenia for School-Age Children, Forms E and P (K-SADS-E/P; Chambers, Puig-Antich, Hirsch, Paez, Ambrosini, Tabrizi, & Davies, 1985; Orvaschel, Puig-Antich, Chambers, Tabrizi, & Johnson, 1982), and the Interview Schedule for

Children (ISC; Kovacs, 1985). My colleagues and I have had good experience is using the K-SADS-E/P in our psychological autopsy protocol. The advantage of a semistructured as compared to a fully structured clinical interview is that the interviewer has greater flexibility to deal with the exigencies of interviewing bereaved informants.

One interesting question is whether suicidality should count as a symptom of depression in suicide victims. We only count suicidality as a symptom of depression if there is evidence of persistent and/or recurrent suicidal ideation over a 2-week period that coincides with other depressive symptoms. In this way, we do not automatically increase the likelihood that a suicide attempter or completer will meet criteria for major depression.

Two areas of psychopathology not covered under current interview schedules for children and adolescents are premenstrual syndrome and seasonal affective disorder. We have found preliminary evidence that two of six female adolescent suicide victims showed severe premenstrual mood disturbance, but found that it was difficult to quantify on the basis of the K-SADS-E/P. Similarly, given the seasonal fluctuation in suicide (Parker & Walter, 1982), it makes sense to augment current diagnostic interviews to assess seasonal affective disorder. Finally, personality characteristics are likely to contribute to risk for suicide (Frances, 1987), but assessment tools to tap this domain in adolescents have yet to be developed and field-tested.

Family History of Psychiatric Disorders and Suicide

Given that suicide and psychiatric disorders both show familial aggregation (Kety, 1986), family history is an important area of inquiry. However, it is unlikely that one could ever perform such an interview blind to the suicidal status of the index subject. The Family History Method using Research Diagnostic Criteria, and/or the Family Study Method (Andreasen, Endicott, Spitzer, & Winokur, 1977; Andreasen et al., 1986), enables the interviewers to gather data on the morbid risk for psychiatric disorders and suicidal behavior within the family and to estimate the relative effects of the transmission of psychiatric disorder and suicidality versus those of exposure and modeling.

Integration with Other Methods of Investigation

Postmortem studies of the brains of suicide victims provide evidence that suicide is associated with biochemical changes at the serotonergic receptor level (Stanley & Mann, 1983; Stanley, Virgilio, & Gershon, 1982). However, the relationship of psychological and psychiatric characteristics of these suicide victims to these biological findings remains completely unknown. It would be of great interest to learn whether impulsive, violent suicides are associated with the aforementioned changes or whether these biological changes are only found in the presence of an affective disorder. Similarly, it would be of interest to learn whether there is a relationship between imitative suicides and biochemical receptor changes postmortem.

Psychological autopsy studies can also be linked with statistical studies of time–space clustering of suicides (Davidson & Gould, 1986). The characteristics of suicides that appear as part of an "outbreak" can be compared to those of suicides that appear sporadically. This may give additional insight into the profile of adolescents at risk for engaging in imitative suicide.

Summary and Conclusions

The psychological autopsy has been employed to study risk factors for completed suicide for more than three decades. Despite a wide range in methods of approach to families and interview techniques, the studies show high compliance and remarkable consistency of results across a wide age range and diverse geographic samples. The convergent evidence is that the diagnostic information obtained is both reliable and valid, although it is likely that such an approach will be more specific than sensitive. Integration of data obtained through psychological autopsies with data obtained through biochemical, toxicological, and epidemiological approaches is likely to deepen our understanding of suicide. Successful completion of careful psychological autopsy studies should enable investigators to examine intensively patients who resemble suicide completers, thereby transcending the inherent limitations of this important first step in the investigation of suicide.

References

Andreasen, N. C., Endicott, J., Spitzer, R., & Winokur, G. The family history method using Research Diagnostic Criteria: Reliability and validity. *Archives of General Psychiatry*, 1977, *34*, 1229–1235.

Andreasen, N. C., Rice, J., Endicott, J., Reich, T., & Coryell, W. The family history method approach to diagnosis: How useful is it? *Archives of General Psychiatry*, 1986, *43*, 421–429.

Barraclough, B., Burch, J., Nelson, B., & Sainsbury, P. A hundred cases of suicide: Clinical aspects. *British Journal of Psychiatry*, 1974, *125*, 355–373.

Beck, A., Schuyler, D., & Herman, J. Development of suicidal intent scales. In K. Resnick & D. Letierri (Eds.), *The prediction of suicide*. Bowie, Md.: Charles Press, 1974.

Blumenthal, S. J., & Kupfer, D. J. Generalizable treatment strategies for suicidal behavior. In J. J. Mann & M. Stanley (Eds.), *Psychobiology of suicidal behavior*. New York: New York Academy of Sciences, 1987.

Boyd, J. H. The increasing rate of suicide by firearms. *New England Journal of Medicine*, 1983, *308*, 313–317.

Boyd, J. H., & Mościcki, E. K. Firearms and youth suicide. *American Journal of Public Health*, 1986, *76*, 1240–1242.

Brent, D. A., Perper, J. A., Kolko, D. J., & Goldstein, C. E. Risk factors for adolescent suicide: A comparison of adolescent suicide victims with suicidal inpatients. *Archives of General Psychiatry*, 1988, *45*, 581–588.

Cantor, P. The effects of youthful suicide on the family. *Psychiatric Opinion* 1975, *12*, 6–11.

Chambers, W., Puig-Antich, J., Hirsch, M., Paez, P., Ambrosini, P., Tabrizi, M., & Davies, M. The assessment of affective disorders in children and adolescents by semi-structured interview: Test–retest reliability of the K-SADS-P. *Archives of General Psychiatry*, 1985, *42*, 669–674.

Cohen-Sandler, R., Berman, A. L., & King, R. A.: Life stress and symptomatology: Determinants of suicidal behavior in children. *Journal of the American Academy of Child Psychiatry*, 1982, *21*, 178–186.

Curphey, T. J. The psychological autopsy: The role of the forensic pathologist in the multidisciplinary approach to death. *Bulletin of Suicidology*, July 1968, pp. 39–45.

Davidson, L., & Gould, M. S. *Contagion as a risk factor for youth suicide*. Paper presented for the Task Force on Youth Suicide, Work Group on Risk Factors, U.S. Department of Health and Human Services, Bethesda, Md., 1986.

Dorpat, T. L., & Ripley, H. S. A study of suicide in the Seattle area. *Comprehensive Psychiatry*, 1960, *1*, 349–359.

Fawcett, J., & Clark, D. *A psychological autopsy study of adolescent suicide* (Grant submitted to the National Institute on Drug Abuse, 1987.)

Fisher, P., & Shaffer D. Methods for investigating suicide in young children and adolescents: An overview. In H. S. Sudak, A. B. Ford, & N. B. Rushforth (Eds.), *Suicide in the young*. Littleton, Mass.: John Wright–PSG, 1984.

Frances, A. Personality and suicide. In J. J. Mann & M. Stanley (Eds.), *Psychobiology of suicidal behavior*. New York: New York Academy of Sciences, 1987.

Gould, M. S., & Shaffer, D. The impact of suicide in television movies: Evidence of imitation. *New England Journal of Medicine*, 1986, *315*, 690–694.

Hawton, K., Osborn, M., O'Grady, J., et al. Classification of adolescents who take overdoses. *British Journal of Psychiatry*, 1982, *140*, 124–131.

Herjanic, B., & Reich, W. Development of a structured psychiatric interview: Agreement between parent and child on individual symptoms. *Journal of Abnormal Child Psychology*, 1982, *10*, 307–324.

Herzog, A., & Resnick, H. C. P. A clinical study of parental response to adolescent death with recommendations for approaching survivors. In N. L. Farberow (Ed.), *Proceedings of the Fourth International Conference for Suicide Prevention*. Los Angeles: Suicide Prevention Center, 1968.

Holding, T. A., & Barraclough, B. M. Psychiatric morbidity in a sample of a London coroner's open verdicts. *British Journal of Psychiatry*, 1975, *127*, 133–143.

Kerr, M. M., & Schaeffer, A. *The Teacher Interview for Psychiatric Symptoms (TIPS)*. Unpublished manuscript, University of Pittsburgh, Western Psychiatric Institute and Clinic, 1986.

Kety, S. S. Genetic factors in suicide. In A. Roy (Ed.), *Suicide*. Baltimore: Williams & Wilkins, 1986.

Kleinbaum, D., Kupper, A., & Morgenstein, H. *Epidemiologic methods: Principles and quantitative methods*. London: Lifetime Learning, 1982.

Kovacs, M. The Interview Schedule for Children (ISC). *Psychopharmacological Bulletin*, 1985, *21*, 991–994.

Miles, C. Conditions predisposing to suicide. *Journal of Nervous and Mental Disease*, 1977, *164*, 231–246.

Murphy, G. E., Armstrong, J. W., Hermele, S. L., Fisher, J., & Clendenin, W. Suicide and alcoholism: Interpersonal loss confirmed as a predictor. *Archives of General Psychiatry*, 1979, *36*, 65–69.

Orvaschel, H., Puig-Antich, J., Chambers, W., Tabrizi, M., & Johnson, R. Retrospective assessment of prepubertal major depressive episode with the K-SADS-E. *Journal of the American Academy of Child Psychiatry*, 1982, *21*, 392–397.

Otto, V. Suicidal acts by children and adolescents: A follow-up study. *Acta Psychiatrica Scandinavica*, *48*, 1972 (Suppl. 233), 1–123.

Pallis, D. J., Barraclough, B. M., Levey, A. B., et al. Estimating suicide risk among attempted suicide: I. The development of new clinical scales. *British Journal of Psychiatry*, 1982, *141*, 37–44.

Pallis, D. J., Gibbons, J. S., & Pierce, D. W. Estimating suicide risk among attempted suicides: II. Efficiency of predictive scales after the attempt. *British Journal of Psychiatry*, 1984, *144*, 139–148.

Parker, G., & Walter, S. Seasonal variation in depressive disorders and suicidal deaths in New South Wales. *British Journal of Psychiatry*, 1982, *140*, 626–632.

Paykel, E. S., Prusoff, B. A., & Myers, J. K. Suicide attempts and recent life events: A controlled comparison. *Archives of General Psychiatry*, 1975, *32*, 327–337.

Phillips, D. P., & Carstensen, L. L. Clustering of teenage suicides after television news stories about suicide. *New England Journal of Medicine*, 1986, *315*, 685–689.

Pierce, D. W. Predictive validation of a suicide intent scale. *British Journal of Psychiatry*, 1981, *139*, 391–396.

Rich, C. L., Young, D., & Fowler, R. C. San Diego suicide study: I. Young vs. old subjects. *Archives of General Psychiatry*, 1986, *43*, 577–582.

Robins, E., Murphy, G. E., Wilkinson, R. H., Gassner, S., & Kayes, J. Some clinical considerations in the prevention of suicide based on a study of 134 successful suicides. *American Journal of Public Health*, 1959, *49*, 888–899.

Shneidman, E. S., & Farberow, N. L. Sample investigations of equivocal deaths. In N. L. Farberow & E. S. Shneidman (Eds.), *The cry for help*. New York: McGraw-Hill, 1961.

Shaffer, D., & Fisher, P. The epidemiology of suicide in children and young adolescents. *Journal of the American Academy of Child Psychiatry*, 1981, *20*, 545–565.

Shaffer, D., & Gould, M. *A study of completed and attempted suicide in adolescents* (NIMH Grant No. RO1 MH38198). New York: Columbia University.

Shafii, M. Dr. Shafii replies to "Handling threats in children and adolescents." *American Journal of Psychiatry*, 1986, *143*, 1193–1194.

Shafii, M., Steltz-Lenarsky, J., & Derrick, A. M. Comorbidity of mental disorders in the postmortem diagnosis of completed suicide in children and adolescents. *Journal of Affective Disorders*, 1988, *15*, 227–233.

Shafii, M., Carrigan, S., Whittinghill, J. R., & Derrick, A. Psychological autopsy of completed suicide in children and adolescents. *American Journal of Psychiatry*, 1985, *142*, 1061–1064.

Shafii, M., Whittinghill, J. R., Dolen, D. C., Pearson, V., Derrick, A., & Carrigan, S. Psychological reconstruction of completed suicide in childhood and adolescence. In H. S. Sudak, A. B. Ford, & N. B. Rushforth (Eds.), *Suicide in the young*. Littleton, Mass.: John Wright–PSG, 1984.

Stanley, M., & Mann, J. J. Increased serotonin-2 binding sites in frontal cortex of suicide victims. *Lancet*, 1983, *i*, 214–216.

Stanley, M., Virgilio, J., & Gershon, S. Tritiated imipramine binding sites are decreased in the frontal cortex of suicides. *Science*, 1982, *216*, 1337–1339.

Weissman, M. M., Kidd, K. K., & Prusoff, B. A. Variability in the rates of affective disorders in the relatives of affected probands. *Archives of General Psychiatry*, 1982, *39*, 1397–1403.

5

Studies of Suicidal Preadolescent and Adolescent Inpatients: A Critique of Research Methods

Cynthia R. Pfeffer, MD
Cornell University Medical College
New York Hospital–Westchester Division

Early clinical reports of suicidal children were descriptive observations of psychiatric inpatients (Bender & Schilder, 1937; Toolan, 1962). More recently, young suicidal psychiatric inpatients have been studied empirically. This chapter evaluates the research methodology of investigations of suicidal preadolescent and adolescent psychiatric inpatients. In addition, studies of suicidal preadolescents and adolescents who were admitted to medical inpatient facilities are discussed.

The research designs of these studies are considered in relation to whether they include components that will make it possible for the results to be replicated or compared with other studies. At least five components should be included in the research design of studies of suicidal youths:

1. Define and measure suicidal behavior.
2. Describe index sample to be studied.
3. Use appropriate comparison subjects.
4. Use standardized measures for data collection.
5. Document the limitations of the research design.

The severity of suicidal behavior should be defined and measured, whether by clinical interview or by standardized research instruments. There exist several reliable and easily administered measurement in-

---

Preparation of this chapter was supported in part by National Institute of Mental Health Contract No. 278-85-0026.

struments for suicidal behavior of children and adolescents, among which are the following:

1. Spectrum of Suicidal Behavior Scale (Pfeffer, 1986)
2. Schedule for Affective Disorders and Schizophrenia for School-Age Children (K-SADS; Chambers, Puig-Antich, Hirsch, Paez, Ambrosini, Tabrizi, & Davies, 1985)
3. Diagnostic Interview Schedule for Children (DISC; Costello et al., 1986)
4. Schedule for Affective Disorders and Schizophrenia (SADS; Endicott & Spitzer, 1978)
5. Children's Depression Inventory (CDI; Kovacs, 1982)
6. Scale for Suicide Ideation (Beck, Kovacs, & Weissman, 1979)
7. Suicide Intent Scale (Beck, Beck, & Kovacs, 1975; Beck, Weissman, Lester, & Trexler, 1976)

Some of these instruments are administered as part of an interview (Brent, Kalas, Edelbrock, Costello, Dulcan, & Conover, 1986; Chambers et al., 1985; Endicott & Spitzer, 1978; Pfeffer, 1986); others are administered as self-reports (Beck et al., 1975, 1976, 1979; Kazdin & Petti, 1982).

In addition to measuring the severity of suicidal behavior, the time between the expression of suicidal behavior and the time of the research assessment should be indicated. This clarifies whether the study involves recent, past, or lifetime suicidal behavior.

A representative sample of suicidal individuals is necessary. Ascertainment biases for inpatients may occur because of referral and admitting patterns. For example, some suicidal individuals who may be admitted to one hospital may not be admitted to another hospital, but instead may be treated in other clinical settings. Therefore, a detailed description of the demographic characteristics of the inpatient sample and of selection procedures is necessary. Furthermore, comparisons of suicidal inpatients with nonsuicidal inpatients are needed to control for features associated with inpatient status. Use of normal subjects also makes it possible to determine whether there are factors associated with suicidal behavior that are not found among normal subjects.

A variety of reliable research instruments with interview or self-report formats have been developed to evaluate preadolescent and adolescent psychiatric symptoms, behaviors, and disorders (Kazdin & Petti, 1982). These research instruments can be used to evaluate correlates of suicidal behavior. Furthermore, description of statistical techniques enables comparisons of effect sizes of findings between studies. Finally, the inherent limitations of the research design should be described, and approaches to overcome the limitations should be discussed.

Research with Psychiatric Inpatients

Several key questions that have been the focus for study among suicidal preadolescent and adolescent inpatients are as follows:

1. What are risk factors associated with suicidal ideas and or acts?
2. Is there a continuous spectrum of severity for suicidal behavior?
3. Are there continuities in factors associated with preadolescent and adolescent suicidal behavior?
4. What is the incidence of suicidal ideas and/or acts among previously suicidal preadolescents or adolescents?
5. What factors predict repeated suicidal acts?

The first three questions have been studied in cross-sectional investigations, and the last two questions have been evaluated with follow-up studies.

Cross-Sectional Studies of Suicidal Preadolescent Psychiatric Inpatients

Table 5.1 lists 12 studies of suicidal preadolescent psychiatric inpatients. The number of subjects ranged from 46 to 348. Most studies were of white males, and in 50% of the studies the subjects were of low socioeconomic status. All studies had a comparison group, which usually consisted of nonsuicidal inpatients.

Seventy percent of the studies provided a definition and/or a measurement of the severity of suicidal behavior. Most studies (Kazdin, French, Unis, Esveldt-Dawson, & Sherick, 1983; Myers, Burke, & McCauley, 1985; Orbach, Rosenheim, & Hary, 1987; Pfeffer, Conte, Plutchik, & Jerrett, 1979; Pfeffer, Plutchik, Mizruchi, & Lipkins, 1986; Pfeffer, Solomon, Plutchik, Mizruchi, & Weiner, 1982; Pfeffer, Zuckerman, Plutchik, & Mizruchi, 1984; Rosenthal, Rosenthal, Doherty, & Santora, 1986; Weiner & Pfeffer, 1986) included a broad range of suicidal tendencies from suicidal ideas, threats, or attempts. Others (Cohen-Sandler, Berman, & King, 1982b; Kosky, 1983) investigated suicide attempts, but neither of these designated the severity of the suicide attempt. One study (Carlson, Asarnow, & Orbach, 1987) did not describe the suicidal tendencies of the subjects.

Interviews of subjects were carried out in 90% of the studies and chart reviews were used in two investigations (Cohen-Sandler et al., 1982b; Myers et al., 1985). Standardized research instruments were used in 10 studies. These included the Child Suicide Potential Scales

TABLE 5.1. Studies of Suicidal Preadolescent Psychiatric Inpatients

Study	Total n	Demography	Comparison subjects	Measurement of suicidal behavior?	Type of assessment	Standard research instruments?	Statistics described?
Pfeffer et al. (1979)	58	88% male; 88% black or hispanic; low SES	Inpatients	Yes	Interview	Yes	Yes
Cohen-Sandler, Berman, & King (1982b)	76	65% male; 50% white; low SES	Inpatients	Yes	Chart review	Yes	Yes
Pfeffer et al. (1982)	65	73% male; 73% white; varied SES	Inpatients	Yes	Interview	Yes	Yes
Kazdin et al. (1982)	46	70% male; 70% white; middle–low SES	Inpatients	Yes	Interview	Yes	Yes
Kosky (1983)	70	75% male; middle–low SES	Inpatients	No	Interview	No	Yes
Pfeffer et al. (1984)	176	73% male; 73% white; varied SES	Inpatients and Nonpatients	Yes	Interview	Yes	Yes
Myers, Burke, McCauley (1985)	348	73% male; 86% white; low SES	Inpatients	Yes	Chart review	No	Yes
Pfeffer et al. (1986)	308	76% male; 74% white; varied SES	Inpatients Outpatients Nonpatients	Yes	Interview	Yes	Yes
Weiner & Pfeffer (1986)	106	70% male; 74% white; middle SES	Inpatients	Yes	Interview	Yes	Yes
Rosenthal et al. (1986)	51	90% male; 100% white; low SES	Outpatients	No	Interview	Yes	No
Orbach, Rosenheim, & Hary (1986)	75	27 preadol. inpts; 55% male; 60% black; 40% white	25 chronically ill medical outpts; 50% male; 60% white and 23 normal subjects; 74% female; 50% white	No	Interview	Yes	Yes
Carlson, Asarnow, & Orbach (1986)	85	32 older preadol. inpts; 72% male	26 normal preadols.; 28 young preadols. inpts; 25 adol. inpts	No	Interview	Yes	Yes

in the studies by my group (Pfeffer et al., 1979; 1982, 1984, 1986; Weiner & Pfeffer, 1986); the Life Stress Inventory, the Social Readjustment Scale for Children, and the Child Behavior Checklist in the study by Cohen-Sandler et al. (1982b); the Hopelessness Scale for Children, the Bellevue Index of Depression, the Depression Symptom Checklist, and the Coopersmith Self-Esteem Inventory in the study by Kazdin et al. (1983); the Rosenthal Preschool Depression Scale in the study by Rosenthal et al. (1986); the Suicidal Tendencies Test in the study by Orbach et al. (1987); and the Depression Self-Rating Scale, the Death/Suicide Interview, the K-SADS, the Child Behavior Checklist, and the Wechsler Intelligence Scale for Children in the study by Carlson et al. (1987). Statistical analyses were described in 11 studies; they predominantly included bivariate analyses using chi-square tests and analysis of variance. Relations between multiple variables were not evaluated statistically in most studies.

In summary, there are relatively few studies of suicidal behavior in preadolescent psychiatric inpatients. These 12 systematic studies represent research efforts of seven independent research groups. The strongest of these studies were those (Kazdin et al., 1983; Pfeffer et al., 1979, 1982; Pfeffer, 1984, 1986; Weiner & Pfeffer, 1986) that used comparison subjects, interviews of subjects with standardized research instruments, and a measure of severity of suicidal behavior.

Cross-Sectional Studies of Suicidal Adolescent Psychiatric Inpatients

Table 5.2 shows 11 studies of suicidal adolescent psychiatric inpatients. The number of subjects ranged from 34 to 867. The demographic features of the subjects were only minimally indicated in most of the studies. All the studies utilized nonsuicidal psychiatric inpatients as a comparison group. Suicidal behavior was defined or measured in most of the studies. In approximately 50% of the studies, the subjects were interviewed, and standardized research instruments were utilized. The research instruments included the SADS in the studies by Friedman, Clarkin, and associates (Clarkin, Friedman, Hurt, Corn, & Aronoff, 1984; Friedman, Aronoff, Clarkin, Corn, & Hurt, 1983; Friedman, Clarkin, Corn, Aronoff, Hurt, & Murphy, 1982; Friedman, Corn, Hurt, Fibel, Schulick, & Swirsky, 1984) and by Robbins and Alessi (1985a,b). In most of the studies, bivariate statistical analyses were used, although three reports described multivariate analyses (Pfeffer, Newcorn, Kaplan, Mizruchi, & Plutchik, 1988; in press; Robbins & Alessi, 1985a).

In summary, there are few studies of suicidal adolescent psychiatric inpatients. These studies have many methodological limitations, in-

TABLE 5.2. Studies of Suicidal Adolescent Psychiatric Inpatients

Study	Total n	Demography	Comparison subjects	Measurement of suicidal behavior?	Type of assessment	Standard research instruments?	Statistics described?
Stanley & Barter (1970)	76	70% female	Inpatients	Yes	Interview	No	Yes
Shneer, Perlstein, & Brozovsky (1975)	867	60% male; low SES	Inpatients	No	Chart review	No	No
Friedman, Clarkin, Corn, Aronoff, Hurt, & Murphy (1982)	76	Not given	Inpatients	Yes	Chart review	Yes	Yes
Inamdar, Lewis, Siomopoulous, Shanok, & Lamela (1983)	51	60% male low SES	Inpatients	No	Chart review	No	Yes
Friedman, Aronoff, Clarkin, Corn, & Hurt (1983)	53	81% female	Inpatients	Yes	Interview	Yes	Yes
Clarkin, Friedman, Hurt, Corn, & Aronoff (1984)	44	84% female	Inpatients	Yes	Interview	Yes	Yes
Friedman, Corn, Hurt, Fibel, Schulick, & Swirsky (1984)	34	Not given	Inpatients	Yes	Interview	Yes	Yes
Robbins & Alessi (1985a)	64	55% male	Inpatients	Yes	Interview	Yes	Yes
Robbins & Alessi (1985b)	45	50% female	Inpatients	Yes	Interview	Yes	Yes
Pfeffer, Newcorn, Kaplan, Mizruchi, & Plutchik (1988)	200	59% female; 85% white; middle SES	Inpatients	Yes	Chart review	No	Yes
Pfeffer, Newcorn, Kaplan, Mizruchi, & Plutchik (in press)	129	67% female; 90% white	Inpatients	Yes	Chart review	No	Yes

cluding insufficient characterization of the samples, minimal descriptions of suicidal behavior, use of retrospective chart reviews in many of the studies, and lack of standardized measurement of other factors in almost half of the studies. The variability in research methods makes it difficult to compare data between the studies.

Other Cross-Sectional Studies of Suicidal Psychiatric Inpatients

As shown in Table 5.3, three studies have combined psychiatric inpatients and outpatients. One study (Pfeffer, Plutchik, & Mizruchi, 1983) was of only preadolescent subjects, and the others (Brent et al., 1986; Carlson & Cantwell, 1982) included preadolescents and adolescents. Two studies (Brent et al., 1986; Pfeffer et al., 1983) described the demographic features of the subjects. All included comparison subjects, a measure of suicidal behavior, standardized research instruments, and details of data analysis. Suicidal behavior and other variables were measured with the CDI in the study by Carlson and Cantwell (1982); the Spectrum of Suicidal Behavior Scale and the Child Suicide Potential Scales in the study by Pfeffer et al. (1983); and the DISC in the study by Brent and colleagues (1986). Bivariate statistical analyses were used in two studies (Brent et al., 1986; Carlson & Cantwell, 1982) and multivariate statistics were used in the third study (Pfeffer et al., 1983).

Results of Cross-Sectional Studies of Suicidal Psychiatric Inpatients

Several studies of suicidal psychiatric inpatients in which suicidal behavior was measured and the patients were interviewed with standardized research instruments have provided reliable data for understanding youth suicidal behavior. We (Pfeffer et al., 1986) used the Child Suicide Potential Scales to compare suicidal and nonsuicidal preadolescent psychiatric inpatients and outpatients and nonpatients. The prevalence and severity of suicidal tendencies were greatest among the psychiatric inpatients. Of the 106 psychiatric inpatients, 34% attempted suicide; only 1% of the 101 psychiatric outpatients and 1% of the 101 nonpatients made mild suicide attempts. There was a relation between DSM-III disorders and suicidal behavior. Among the inpatients, suicidal behavior was associated with a diagnosis of Major Depressive Disorder, Adjustment Disorder, or Specific Development Disorder. Suicidal behavior among the outpatients was associated with Major Depressive, Dysthymic, and Borderline Personality Disorders. No diagnosis was associated with suicidal tendencies among the nonpatients—a

TABLE 5.3. Studies of Suicidal Preadolescent and Adolescent Psychiatric Inpatients and Outpatients

Study	Total n	Demography	Comparison subjects	Measurement of suicidal behavior?	Type of assessment	Standard research instruments?	Statistics described?
Carlson & Cantwell (1982)	102	62% male	Inpatients and outpatients	Yes	Self-report questionnaire	Yes	Yes
Pfeffer, Plutchik, & Mizruchi (1983)	102	83% male; 33% white; middle–low SES	Inpatients and outpatients	Yes	Interview	Yes	Yes
Brent, Kalas, Edelbrock, Costello, Dulcan, & Conover	231	66% male; 50% white; 50% low SES	Inpatients and outpatients	Yes	Interview	Yes	Yes

finding that may be related to the low number of diagnoses and the low prevalence of suicidal tendencies among the nonpatients.

Friedman, Clarkin, and associates (Clarkin et al., 1984; Friedman et al., 1984) studied suicidal depressed adolescent psychiatric inpatients with the SADS. Patients with Borderline Personality Disorder, compared to patients with other Axis II disorders, had more prevalent and lethal suicidal tendencies. Furthermore, Robbins and Alessi (1985a) used the SADS and found that symptoms of depression such as depressed mood, negative self-evaluation, anhedonia, insomnia, poor concentration, indecisiveness, lack of reactivity of mood, and psychomotor disturbance were associated with the seriousness of suicidal behavior. There was also an association between substance abuse and suicidal behavior among these inpatient adolescents.

Other correlates of suicidal behavior have been evaluated. Kazdin et al. (1983) reported that in preadolescent inpatients there was a relationship among suicidal behavior, depression, and hopelessness. Using the Hopelessness Scale for Children, these authors determined that suicidal preadolescent inpatients showed more hopelessness than nonsuicidal inpatients and that suicidal risk was correlated more with hopelessness than with depression.

Death concepts and preoccupations with death have been associated with suicidal preadolescents. We (Pfeffer et al., 1982, 1984, 1986) reported that suicidal preadolescents were consistently more preoccupied with fantasies about people dying than were nonsuicidal preadolescents. Orbach et al. (1987) compared 27 suicidal psychiatric inpatient preadolescents with 25 chronically ill preadolescents and 23 normal preadolescents. The suicidal preadolescents were more attracted to death as an alternative for decreasing problems than were either of the other groups of preadolescents. In addition, the suicidal preadolescents were more inflexible in their thinking about life and death. They gave fewer alternative problem-solving solutions to death as a solution than did the other two groups of youngsters.

Assessments of family psychopathology have yielded variable results, probably because relatives were not evaluated directly. Parental depression, suicidal behavior, and violence have been associated with suicidal behavior (Carlson & Cantwell, 1982; Cohen-Sandler et al., 1982b; Kosky, 1983; Myers et al., 1985; Pfeffer et al., 1979, 1982, 1983, 1984, 1986, in press-a, in press-b; Rosenthal et al., 1986).

There are some data regarding the question of whether suicidal tendencies can be considered along a continuum. We (Pfeffer et al., 1982) reported that the severity of general psychopathology, death preoccupations, and depression was greatest among preadolescents who attempted suicide, was intermediate among adolescents who thought

about suicide, and was least severe among nonsuicidal preadolescents. These findings suggest that suicidal behavior is on a continuum. In contrast, Carlson and Cantwell (1982) suggested that suicidal ideation is not on a continuum with suicide attempts, on the basis of their findings in a population of 102 preadolescent and adolescent psychiatric inpatients and outpatients. More specifically, using the CDI, these investigators observed that severity of depression was associated with severity of suicidal attempters. More recently, Brent et al. (1986) used the DISC and derived a hierarchy of suicidal ideation and suicidal behavior. Symptoms of depression and the syndrome of depression were correlated with the severity of suicidality. This study supported the concept that suicidal ideation and acts are on a continuum. The hypothesis that suicidal behavior is on a continuum requires additional investigation with cross-sectional studies that include youngsters who commit suicide, as well as with longitudinal assessments of previously suicidal youngsters.

Developmental characteristics of suicidal behavior have received little research attention. Myers et al. (1985), in a record review of 348 preadolescent psychiatric inpatients, found that suicidal behavior significantly increased with age. Carlson et al. (1987) evaluated 85 preadolescent and adolescent inpatients and 26 nonpatients. Using the Death/ Suicide Interview, these authors compared 8- to 10-year-old and 11- to 13-year-old patients who were either at or below grade level. These two groups were compared also with adolescents who were developmentally impaired and functioning below grade level. The results suggested that the least mature children were least convinced about the finality of death and least certain about the consequences of a suicidal method and motivation for suicide. Adolescents were consistent in their beliefs of what suicidal methods would be fatal, what they thought about doing, and what they actually enacted. Suicidal ideation and attempts increased with age, as did the understanding that death was final.

Follow-Up Studies of Suicidal Psychiatric Inpatients

A few follow-up studies of suicidal preadolescent and adolescent psychiatric inpatients have been reported. These are listed in Table 5.4. The total number of subjects in the initial samples ranged from 47 to 1,547, and at the time of follow-up information was obtained on 51% to 100% of the subjects. The follow-up times ranged from a mean of 1.5 years in one study (Cohen-Sandler et al., 1982a) to longer follow-

TABLE 5.4. Follow-Up (FU) Studies of Suicidal Psychiatric Inpatients

Study	n of initial subjects	Percentage of subjects at FU	Initial comparison subjects	Measurement of suicidal behavior?	FU time (years)	Type of assessment at FU	Standardized research instr. at FU?	Statistics described?
Barter, Swaback, & Todd (1968)	63 adolescents	71	Adolescents inpatients	Yes	0.3–3.7 (mean 1.8)	Telephone interview	No	Yes
Otto (1972)	1,547 adolescent medical and psychiatric patients	85	Adolescent medical and psychiatric patients	No	15	Chart review	No	Yes
Welner, Welner, & Fishman (1979)[a]	110 adolescents	70	Adolescent inpatients	No	8–10	Telephone interview	No	No
Cohen-Sandler, Berman, & King (1982a)	76 preadolescents	96	Preadolescent inpatients	Yes	0.5–3 (mean 1.5)	Telephone interview	Yes	Yes
Angle, O'Brien, & McIntire (1983)	47 adolescents	51	None	Yes	9	Telephone interview	Yes	Yes
Motto (1984)	122 adolescents	100	Adolescent inpatients	Yes	4–10	Coroner report	No	Yes

[a]This study was of adolescent psychiatric inpatients without a particular focus on their initial suicidal states.

up times of up to 15 years (Otto, 1972). A telephone interview was used to gather information in four studies (Angle, O'Brien, & McIntire, 1983; Barter, Swaback, & Todd, 1968; Cohen-Sandler *et al.*, 1982a; Welner, Welner, & Fishman, 1979), but standardized research instruments were used to gather data in only two studies (Angle et al., 1983; Cohen-Sandler et al., 1982). In two studies (Motto, 1984; Otto, 1972), follow-up data were taken from a record review. No studies used standardized research instruments to assess the subjects both initially and at follow-up.

Information in the rate of suicide at follow-up was obtained in all studies. It was 0% in three studies (Angle et al., 1983; Barter et al., 1968; Cohen-Sandler et al., 1982a). The low rate of suicide may have been due to the short follow-up time in two studies (Barter et al., 1968; Cohen-Sandler et al., 1982) and the low number of subjects in the follow-up phase in the third study (Angle et al., 1983). In two long-term studies, the suicide rates were 4.3% (Otto, 1972) and 9% (Motto, 1984). In another study (Welner et al., 1979), 77 adolescent psychiatric inpatients (out of an initial sample of 110) who were not studied for initial suicidal status were followed 8–10 years after discharge. Fifty-two percent were female. At the time of follow-up, six, or 8%, had committed suicide. Of the six who committed suicide, five were males. Two were schizophrenic, three had a bipolar disorder, and the one female had a primary depressive disorder. Diagnoses were based on Feighner criteria (Feighner, Robins, & Guze, 1972). A limitation of this study, as noted above, is that it did not provide information about the initial suicidal status of the patients.

Other outcome factors for suicidal psychiatric inpatients have been studied. In the only study to include preadolescents, Cohen-Sandler et al. (1982a) followed 73 patients who were initially 6–16 years old. The sample included 70% males, with an equal distribution of whites and nonwhites. A telephone interview occurred on an average of 18 months after discharge. The parents or legal guardians completed the Child Behavior Checklist and the Social Readjustment Scale for Children in the telephone interview. Suicidal behavior included a self-destructive act and the intent to injure self. At follow-up, a significantly greater proportion of nonsuicidal youngsters (70%) who were living with a biological parent at hospitalization remained in the parental home. By contrast, only 44% of the suicidal youngsters who were living with a parent at admission remained in the parental home. At follow-up, the suicidal and nonsuicidal youngsters had similar features of social adjustment on the Child Behavior Checklist. Twenty percent of the original 20 suicidal youngsters, compared to none of the 55 nonsuicidal youngsters, were suicidal after discharge. Suicidal repeaters were older (mean age 13.5 years) than the nonrepeaters (mean age 11 years). The initial suicidal behavior was greater for the repeaters than for the nonrepeaters. The repeaters were living less frequently in the parental home and had more psychosocial stress than the nonrepeaters.

Barter et al. (1968) reviewed hospital charts of 63 adolescents who attempted suicide and conducted a telephone follow-up interview with 45 adolescents who could be located. The demographic features of the sample were not described, and no standardized research instruments were used to gather follow-up information. Of the 45 adolescents, 42% made suicide attempts after discharge. Significantly more of the suicidal repeaters (58%) than the nonrepeaters (16%) were not living in the parental home after discharge. There was more parental loss due to death, divorce, or separation among the repeaters (63%) than the non-repeaters (37%). Sixty-eight percent of the repeaters, compared to 88% of the nonrepeaters, had an active social life. The suicidal repeaters (78%) had significantly more social agency contact after discharge than the nonrepeaters (35%). In addition to the limitations of record review methods, another limitation of this study was that there were no non-suicidal adolescent inpatients for comparison.

The most systematic assessment of early predictors of suicide among suicidal adolescent psychiatric inpatients was conducted by Motto (1984). He evaluated 122 male adolescent psychiatric inpatients who made initial suicide attempts when they were 10–19 years old. Data during hospitalization were obtained systematically with research instruments constructed for the study. Information about suicide was obtained from coroner records. Eleven adolescents committed suicide, with a suicide rate of 1.3% per year. A mean of 38 months elapsed between discharge and suicide. Psychosocial data collected during hospitalization were compared for the adolescents who did and those who did not commit suicide. A limitation of this study is that data on nonsuicidal psychiatric inpatients were not reported. Factors associated with suicide were that the adolescents at the time of their initial suicide attempt clearly com-municated intent to attempt suicide, had a fear of losing their minds, sought help before the suicide attempt, exhibited hypersomnia, had a negative attitude toward a mental health interviewer, had limited financial resources, had an ability to communicate, and had severe feelings of hopelessness and psychomotor retardation. Valuable infor-mation would have been obtained if the adolescents who committed suicide and those who did not had been assessed for psychosocial variables at the time of follow-up. Such information would elucidate proximal risk factors for suicide.

Studies of Suicidal Medical Inpatients

Only a few reports, listed in Table 5.5, describe suicidal preadolescents
and/or adolescents admitted to medical inpatient services. Hawton and
associates (Hawton, Cole, O'Grady, & Osborn, 1982; Hawton, O'Grady,
Osborn, & Cole, 1982; Hawton, Osborn, O'Grady, & Cole, 1982), working
in London, studied 50 adolescents aged 13–18 who were admitted to
the hospital after taking overdoses. The severity of the overdoses was
not described, and there were no nonsuicidal comparison subjects. For
comparison, the suicidal adolescents were divided into groups of 13- to
15-year-olds and 16- to 18-year-olds. A comprehensive interview of each
adolescent during hospitalization and at a 1-month follow-up was done.
Information 1 year after discharge was obtained from the hospital
register. Normative data from other sources were used to compare
information about these hospitalized adolescents. Compared to the normative data, the younger suicidal adolescents had a high rate of family
disturbance, frequent social agency care, and hospital admissions for
medical and surgical treatment. Problems with parents, school, and
peers were also associated with the younger adolescents who took overdoses. Twenty percent of the total of suicidal adolescents were mildly
depressed and had personality problems. Alcohol abuse was apparent
in 14% of the suicidal adolescents. The prevalence of these factors
among normal adolescents was not discussed. There was 66% improvement in social adjustment 1 month after discharge. One year after
discharge, 14% had repeated an overdose; most of the repeat overdoses
were among the older adolescents and occurred within 3 months of
discharge. The adolescents were classified into three levels of psychological disturbance. One group was normal with transient problems;
another group was chronically alienated and had problems with family
and friends; the third group had general problems with society and
chronic psychological problems.

Taylor and Stansfeld (1984a, 1984b) studied 50 youngsters aged 8–
17 years who were hospitalized for overdoses and compared them to
50 nonsuicidal adolescents referred for psychiatric outpatient treatment.
There were no controls who were nonsuicidal hospitalized adolescents.
The suicidal youngsters had more disturbed family relations, had more
depressive disorders, and ran away from home more often than the
psychiatric outpatients. Those suicidal youngsters who were compliant
with at least one follow-up outpatient treatment visit, compared to
those who were noncompliant, had higher levels of depression and more
positive parental attitudes toward treatment. The study was also limited
by the lack of description of the severity of the overdose.

TABLE 5.5. Studies of Suicidal Medical Inpatients

Study	Total n	Demography	Comparison subjects	Measurement of suicidal behavior	Type of assessment	Standard research instruments?	Statistics described?
Hawton, Cole, O'Grady, & Osborn (1982); Hawton, O'Grady, Osborn, & Cole (1982); Hawton, Osborn, O'Grady, & Cole (1982)	50	90% female; SES represented community distribution	Normative data for adolescents aged 13–15 and 16–18	None	Interview	No	Yes
Taylor & Stansfeld (1984a, 1984b)	100	70% female	Nonsuicidal preadolescent and adolescent psychiatric outpatients	None	Interview	No	Yes
Goldacre & Hawton (1985)	2,493	75% female	1- to 5-year follow-up of adolescents who repeated suicide attempts	None	Chart review	No	Yes
Brent (1986)	127	66% white; 66% female; 50% middle SES	Nonepileptic preadolescents and adolescents admitted for suicide attempts	Yes	Chart review	Yes	Yes

Goldacre and Hawton (1985) studied records of 2,493 adolescents aged 12–20 years who were hospitalized for overdoses, together with follow-up records of rehospitalizations that occurred 1–5 years later. Approximately 6.3% of the adolescents made a repeat suicide attempt that required hospitalization within 1 year of the initial admission. The highest repetition rates were among the younger teenage females and among the older males. Suicide rates were 0.7% for males and 0.1% for females. These rates were significantly higher than in the general population for this age group. A limitation of the study was that there were no data on repeat suicide attempters who were not hospitalized.

Brent (1986) reviewed the charts of 126 youngsters aged 7–14 years who were admitted to a pediatric service for a suicide attempt. Nine patients were epileptic; the proportion of epileptics in this sample was thus 15 times greater than in the general population. All eight epileptics who were being treated with phenobarbital used this medicine for the suicidal overdose. This study was limited by the use of a chart review, the small number of epileptic subjects, and the fact that the researcher knew the medical status of the subjects at the time other factors were being evaluated.

In summary, these studies have numerous limitations, including lack of appropriate comparison subjects, no measurement of suicidal behavior, and no standardized research instruments to measure other variables. Nevertheless, the results suggest that these suicidal youngsters had family disruption, depressive symptoms, prior medical illness, and past medical treatment.

Discussion

There have been few studies of preadolescents and adolescents admitted to psychiatric or medical inpatient services for suicidal behavior—a mental health problem that has increased dramatically within the last two decades. The greatest limitations of existing studies are that they do not define and measure the severity of suicidal behavior, do not evaluate subjects with standardized research instruments, and do not use appropriate controls (both nonsuicidal inpatients and normal subjects).

There are many advantages to studying psychiatric and/or medical inpatients. These patients are readily available, and comprehensive observations can be done while they are in the hospital. It is probable that inpatients exhibit the most serious suicidal tendencies and have the most extensive risk factors. It would be expected that the suicidal behaviors of many inpatients represent suicide attempts that failed to become suicides. Therefore, it may be that these subjects have characteristics similar to those of youngsters who commit suicide. However, because of the paucity of studies of youth suicide, it is not currently known how suicidal inpatients compare with youngsters who commit suicide. In addition, it is not clear how suicidal inpatients compare to suicidal youngsters in other settings and to nonsuicidal youngsters in other settings. Future investigations should incorporate comparison subjects that can help address these issues.

The number of follow-up studies of suicidal inpatients is minimal. There is a need to develop prospective follow-up of suicidal youngsters that evaluates outcome associated with suicidal behavior and other risk variables. A prospective research design can enhance the possibility that the subjects will remain in the study. Finally, the existing reports of suicidal inpatients suggest that multiple variables are associated with suicidal behavior. Some of these are as follows:

1. High prevalence and severity of suicidal behavior
2. Depressive, personality, and substance abuse disorders
3. Hopelessness
4. Preoccupations with death and inflexibility in thoughts about death
5. Problems with health, family, and friends
6. Family depression, suicidal behavior, and violence
7. Developmental correlates of age and cognitive maturity
8. Approximate suicide rate 4–9% in long-term follow-up
9. Repetition of suicidal behavior associated with:
   a. Not being in parental home
   b. Severity of initial suicidal behavior
   c. Age and gender
   d. Stress and loss

Numerous other issues that may affect risk have not been studied sufficiently among suicidal inpatients. These include family risk factors, biological variables, and treatment approaches.

References

Angle, C. R., O'Brien, T. P., & McIntire, M. S. Adolescent self-poisoning: A nine year follow-up. *Developmental and Behavioral Pediatrics*, 1983, *4*, 83–87.
Barter, J. T., Swaback, D. O., & Todd, D. Adolescent suicide attempts: A follow-up of hospitalized patients. *Archives of General Psychiatry*, 1968, *19*, 523–527.
Beck, A. T., Beck, R. & Kovacs, M. Classification of suicidal behaviors: I. Quantifying intent and medical lethality. *American Journal of Psychiatry*, 1975, *132*, 285–287.

Beck, A. T., Kovacs, M. & Weissman, A. Assessment of suicidal intention: The Scale for Suicide Ideation. *Journal of Consulting and Clinical Psychology*, 1979, *47*, 343–352.

Beck, A. T., Weissman, A., Lester, D., & Trexler, L. Classification of suicidal behaviors: II. Dimensions of suicidal intent. *Archives of General Psychiatry*, 1976, *33*, 835–837.

Bender, L., & Schilder, P. Suicidal preoccupations and attempts in children. *American Journal of Orthopsychiatry*, 1937, *7*, 225–234.

Brent, D. A. Overrepresentation of epileptics in a consecutive series of suicide attempts seen at a children's hospital, 1978–1983. *Journal of the American Academy of Child Psychiatry*, 1986, *25*, 242–246.

Brent, D. A., Kalas, R., Edelbrock, C., Costello, A. J., Dulcan, M. K., & Conover, N. Psychopathology and its relationship to suicidal isolation in childhood and adolescence. *Journal of the American Academy of Child Psychiatry*, 1986, *25*, 666–673.

Carlson, G. A., Asarnow, J. R., & Orbach, I. Developmental aspects of suicidal behavior in children: I. *Journal of the American Academy of Child and Adolescent Psychiatry*, 1987, *26*, 186–192.

Carlson, G. A., & Cantwell, D. P. Suicidal behavior and depression in children and adolescents. *Journal of the American Academy of Child Psychiatry*, 1982, *21*, 361–368.

Chambers, W. J., Puig-Antich, J., Hirsch, M., Paez, P., Ambrosini, P. J., Tabrizi, M. A., & Davies, M. The assessment of affective disorders in children and adolescents by semistructured interview. *Archives of General Psychiatry*, 1985, *42*, 696–702.

Clarkin, J. F., Friedman, R. C., Hurt, S. W., Corn, R., & Aronoff, M. Affective and character pathology of suicidal adolescent and young adult inpatients. *Journal of Clinical Psychiatry*, 1984, *45*, 19–22.

Cohen-Sandler, R., Berman, A. L., & King, R. A. A follow-up study of hospitalized suicidal children. *Journal of the American Academy of Child Psychiatry*, 1982, *21*, 398–403. (a)

Cohen-Sandler, R., Berman, A. L., & King, R. A. Life stress and symptomatology: Determinants of suicidal behavior in children. *Journal of the American Academy of Child Psychiatry*, 1982, *21*, 179–186. (b)

Costello, J., Edelbrock, C., & Costello, A. J. The validity of the NIMH Diagnostic Interview Schedule for Children: A comparison between pediatric and psychiatric referrals. *Journal of Abnormal Child Psychology*, 1985, *13*, 579–595.

Endicott, J., & Spitzer, R. L. A diagnostic interview: The Schedule for Affective Disorders and Schizophrenia. *Archives of General Psychiatry*, 1978, *35*, 837–844.

Feighner, J. P., Robins, E., & Guze, S. B. Diagnostic criteria for use in psychiatric research. *Archives of General Psychiatry*, 1972, *26*, 57–63.

Friedman, R. C., Aronoff, M. S., Clarkin, J. F., Corn, R., & Hurt, S. W. History of suicidal behavior in depressed borderline inpatients *American Journal of Psychiatry*, 1983, *140*, 1023–1026.

Friedman, R. C., Clarkin, J. F., Corn, R., Aronoff, M. S., Hurt, S. W., & Murphy, M. C. DSM III and affective pathology in hospitalized adolescents. *Journal of Nervous and Mental Disease*, 1982, *170*, 511–521.

Friedman, R., Corn, R., Hurt, S. W., Fibel, B., Schulick, J., & Swirsky, S. Family history of illness in the seriously suicidal adolescent: A life-cycle approach. *American Journal of Orthopsychiatry*, 1984, *54*, 390–397.

Goldacre, M., & Hawton, K. Repetition of self-poisoning and subsequent death in adolescents who take overdoses. *British Journal of Psychiatry*, 1985, *146*, 395–398.

Hawton, K., Cole, D., O'Grady, J., & Osborn, M. Motivational aspects of deliberate self-poisoning in adolescents. *British Journal of Psychiatry*, 1982, *141*, 286–291.

Hawton, K., O'Grady, J., Osborn, M., & Cole, D. Adolescents who take overdoses: Their characteristics, problems and contacts with helping agencies. *British Journal of Psychiatry*, 1982, *140*, 118–123.

Hawton, K., Osborn, M., O'Grady, J., & Cole, D. Classification of adolescents who take overdoses. *British Journal of Psychiatry*, 1982, *140*, 124–131.

Inamder, S. C., Lewis, D. O., Siomopoulos, G., Shanok, S. S., & Lamela, M. Violent and suicidal behavior in psychotic adolescents. *American Journal of Psychiatry*, 1982, *139*, 932–935.

Kazdin, A. E., French, N. H., Unis, A. S., Esveldt-Dawson, K., & Sherick, R. B. Hopelessness, depression, and suicidal intent among psychiatrically disturbed inpatient children. *Journal of Consulting and Clinical Psychology*, 1983, *51*, 504–510.

Kazdin, A. E., & Petti, T. A. Self-report and interview measures of childhood and adolescent depression. *Journal of Child Psychology and Psychiatry*, 1982, *23*, 437–457.

Kosky, R. Childhood suicidal behavior. *Journal of Child Psychology and Psychiatry*, 1983, *24*, 457–468.

Kovacs, M. Rating scales to assess depression in school-aged children. *Acta Paedopsychiatrica*, 1980, *46*, 305–315.

Motto, J. A. Suicide in male adolescents. In H. S. Sudak, A. B. Ford, & N. B. Rushforth (Eds.), *Suicide in the young*. Boston: John Wright–PSG, 1984.

Myers, K. M., Burke, P., & McCauley, E. Suicidal behavior by hospitalized preadolescent children on a psychiatric unit. *Journal of the American Academy of Child Psychiatry*, 1985, *24*, 474–480.

Orbach, I., Rosenheim, E., & Hary, E. Some aspects of cognitive functioning in suicidal children. *Journal of the American Academy of Child and Adolescent Psychiatry*, 1987, *26*, 181–185.

Otto, V. Suicidal acts by children and adolescents: A follow-up study. *Acta Psychiatrica Scandinavica*, 1972 (Suppl. *233*), 7–123.

Pfeffer, C. R. *The suicidal child*. New York: Guilford Press, 1986.

Pfeffer, C. R., Conte, H. R., Plutchik, R., & Jerrett, I. Suicidal behavior in latency age psychiatric inpatients: An empirical study. *Journal of the American Academy of Child Psychiatry*, 1979, *18*, 679–692.

Pfeffer, C. R., Newcorn, J., Kaplan, G., Mizruchi, M. S., & Plutchik, R. Suicidal and assaultive adolescent inpatients. *Journal of Child Psychiatry and Psychology*, in press.

Pfeffer, C. R., Newcorn, J., Kaplan, G., Mizruchi, M. S., & Plutchik, R. Suicidal behavior in adolescent psychiatric inpatients. *Journal of the American Academy of Child and Adolescent Psychiatry*, 1988, *27*, 357–361.

Pfeffer, C. R., Plutchik, R., & Mizruchi, M. S. Suicidal and assaultive behavior in children: Classification, measurement and interrelations. *American Journal of Psychiatry*, 1983, *140*, 154–157.

Pfeffer, C. R., Plutchik, R., Mizruchi, M. S., & Lipkins, R. Suicidal behavior in child psychiatric inpatients and outpatients and in nonpatients. *American Journal of Psychiatry*, 1986, *143*, 733–738.

Pfeffer, C. R., Solomon, G., Plutchik, R., Mizruchi, M. S., & Weiner, A. Suicidal behavior in latency-age psychiatric inpatients: A replication and cross validation. *Journal of the American Academy of Child Psychiatry*, 1982, *21*, 564–569.

Pfeffer, C. R., Zuckerman, S., Plutchik, R., & Mizruchi, M. S. Suicidal behavior in normal school children: A comparison with child psychiatric inpatients. *Journal of the American Academy of Child Psychiatry*, 1984, *23*, 416–423.

Robbins, D. R., & Alessi, N. E. Depressive symptoms and suicidal behavior in adolescents. *American Journal of Psychiatry*, 1985, *142*, 588–592. (a)

Robbins, D. R., & Alessi, N. E. Suicide and the dexamethasone suppression test in adolescence. *Biological Psychiatry*, 1985, *20*, 107–110. (b)

Rosenthal, P. A., Rosenthal, S., Doherty, M. B., & Santora, D. Suicidal thoughts and behaviors in depressed hospitalized preschoolers. *American Journal of Psychotherapy*, 1986, *15*, 201–212.

Schneer, H. I., Perlstein, A., & Brozovsky, M. Hospitalized suicidal adolescents: Two generations. *Journal of the American Academy of Child Psychiatry*, 1975, *14*, 268–280.

Stanley, E. J., & Barter, J. T. Adolescent suicidal behavior. *American Journal of Orthopsychiatry*, 1970, *40*, 87–96.

Taylor, E. A., & Stansfeld, S. A. Children who poison themselves: I. A clinical comparison with psychiatric controls. *British Journal of Psychiatry*, 1984, *145*, 127–135. (a)

Taylor, E. A., & Stansfeld, S. A. Children who poison themselves: II. Prediction of attendance for treatment. *British Journal of Psychiatry*, 1984, *145*, 132–135. (b)

Toolan, J. M. Suicide and suicidal attempts in children and adolescents. *American Journal of Psychiatry*, 1962, *118*, 719–724.

Weiner, A. S., & Pfeffer, C. R. Suicidal status, depression, and intellectual functioning in preadolescent psychiatric inpatients. *Comprehensive Psychiatry*, 1986, *27*, 372–380.

Welner, A., Welner, Z., & Fishman, R. Psychiatric adolescent inpatients: Eight to ten-year follow-up. *Archives of General Psychiatry*, 1979, *36*, 698–700.

6

The Iowa Record-Linkage Experience

Donald W. Black, MD
University of Iowa College of Medicine

The study of suicide has bedeviled clinicians and researchers alike. Because suicide is important from both personal and economic perspectives, particularly for psychiatric patients, multiple strategies have been developed over the past decades for its investigation. The ultimate goal of this research is to enable clinicians to predict—and, one hopes, to prevent—suicide. Some investigators have focused on retrospective "psychological autopsies" of suicide victims, including the now classic reports by Robins, Murphy, Wilkinson, Gassner, and Kayes (1959) and Barraclough, Bunch, Nelson, and Sainsbury (1974). Other strategies have included case–control designs (Roy, 1982; Winokur & Black, 1987) and prospective study designs (Helgason, 1964; Martin, Cloninger, Guze, & Clayton, 1985a,b; Rorsman, Hagnell, & Lanke, 1982). The latter are relatively uncommon because of the large numbers of patients who must be followed in order to witness the relatively rare suicide outcome, and the huge expense required to conduct such studies. On the other hand, another strategy has evolved to evaluate high-risk populations, such as psychiatric patients, using a historical prospective design (Black, Warrack, & Winokur, 1985a,b,c,d; Eastwood, Stiasny, Meier, & Woogh, 1982; Tsuang, 1978). This involves determining the outcome of persons at risk in an earlier decade. The determination of outcome can be performed in a variety of ways, such as making personal or telephone contact, or using the follow-up material found in available case notes. If the objective of follow-up is to study a predetermined outcome such as death, then the only concern may be whether the patient is deceased, and, if deceased, when the death occurred and what caused it. This type of study can be accomplished through a relatively simple record-

Preparation of this chapter was supported in part by National Institute of Mental Health Contract No. 278-85-0026. Requests for reprints should be sent to Dr. Donald W. Black, Psychiatric Hospital, 500 Newton Road, Iowa City, IA 52242.

linkage process, wherein the roster of patients is compared electronically with death certificates for a given period. This is merely one example of record-linkage study; other uses of record linkage are unlimited.

Historical Overview

Studies over the past 50 years have documented that psychiatric patients are at risk for excess mortality, particularly from suicide. These findings have been noted in many countries, in different decades, and in different groups, including both inpatients and outpatients (Babigian & Odoroff, 1969; Black et al., 1985a; Eastwood et al., 1982; Helgason, 1964; Innes & Millar, 1970; Martin et al., 1985a; Morrison, 1982; Roy, 1982). There has been a decline in mortality among psychiatric patients, due primarily to the decline in premature deaths from natural causes (Black, Winokur, & Nasrallah, 1987a; Martin et al., 1985b). In fact, premature death from natural causes may no longer be as significant a problem among psychiatric patients as it once was many years ago, particularly among the institutionalized. This may be due to improvements in the efficacy and availability of psychiatric treatments, better care of intercurrent medical problems, and the rarity of long-term hospitalization nowadays. Suicides and accidents continue to contribute to excess mortality, and there is recent evidence that suicide rates may be climbing, particularly in young white males (Weed, 1985).

The Iowa Record-Linkage Study

Few historical prospective studies of mortality in psychiatric patients have made age- and sex-adjusted comparisons with death rates in the general population. My coinvestigator, George Winokur, MD, had participated in the Iowa "500" study many years earlier, in which careful mortality studies were carried out with schizophrenic, manic, and depressed patients (Tsuang & Woolson, 1977). Because of the study design, patients in other diagnostic groups were not followed. We wanted to enlarge upon this experience and see how patients in all categories fared. Furthermore, because of secular trends noted by other investigators, we became interested in studying mortality in a relatively recent sample.

We began by obtaining a list of all patients admitted to our hospital over a 10-year period from 1972 through 1981. After duplicate names resulting from rehospitalizations were removed, our list consisted of 5,412 patients, including 2,933 (54.2%) women and 2,479 (45.8%) males.

The record included multiple identifiers, including name, sex, date of birth, and hospital number. This information was then linked by computer with all Iowa death certificates for the same period. A total of 331 deaths were identified; all matches were confirmed by manually checking the list of deceased individuals against hospital admission records. The cause of death listed on the death certificate was recorded. Each patient was then assigned a single psychiatric diagnosis from a hierarchical and shortened list of 10 psychiatric categories based on the *International Classification of Diseases*, ninth edition (U.S. Department of Health and Human Services, 1980):

1. Organic mental disorders (including alcoholic psychoses)
2. Schizophrenia (including paranoid disorders)
3. Acute schizophrenia (including schizoaffective disorder)
4. Affective disorder
5. Depressive neurosis
6. Neuroses
7. Alcohol and drug abuse
8. Adjustment disorders
9. Psychophysiological disorders and special symptoms (including eating disorders)
10. Personality disorders (including sexual disorders)

The diagnostic hierarchy was determined by Winokur, based on his clinical and research experience. We developed a computer program that reviewed each patient's clinical diagnosis (or diagnoses) made by the ward psychiatrist and picked the one with the highest priority in the hierarchy. For example, a patient with both schizophrenia and alcoholism would be assigned a research diagnosis of schizophrenia. In a case of multiple admissions, we used only information from the patient's last psychiatric hospitalization.

Our statistician (Giles Warrack, PhD) then constructed mortality tables adjusted for age, sex, and follow-up time among the patients, allowing us to compute expected numbers of deaths. We did not adjust for race, because so few Iowans (<3%) are nonwhite. The computations were based on Poisson's distribution, and the method has been fully described (Black et al., 1985a). Standardized mortality ratios (SMRs), representing the ratio of observed to expected mortality, were calculated and tested for significance using the chi-square statistic modified by Freeman–Tukey deviates. The Freeman–Tukey transformation was used because it is more conservative than the regular chi-square test, and many of our observed and expected numbers were quite small.

Findings from the Iowa Record-Linkage Study

Our findings are presented in Tables 6.1, 6.2, and 6.3. Relative risk for premature death was greatest among women and the young, particularly patients younger than 40 years. Risk was associated with all psychiatric diagnoses and was significantly higher among patients of either sex with an organic mental disorder or schizophrenia; women with acute schizophrenia, depressive neuroses, alcoholism, drug abuse, and psychophysiological disorders and special symptoms; and men with neuroses. Death from natural causes, especially from heart disease, was significantly excessive among women, while death from accidents and suicides was excessive for both men and women. The overall SMR was 1.65 ($p < .001$). Furthermore, and most importantly, we found that the greatest excess of mortality occurred within the first 2 years after hospital discharge. In fact, 188 (56.8%) of all deaths occurred during the early follow-up period, when only 59.8 (29.7%) had been expected. The data on excess deaths (observed death minus expected) showed that 98.7% occurred within the 2-year period; after that, the observed number of deaths approximated those expected.

TABLE 6.1. General Mortality Findings in the Iowa Record-Linkage Study

Variable	Observed deaths	Expected deaths	SMR
Sex			
Male	168	114.95	1.46**
Female	163	86.21	1.89**
Age			
<30 years	47	14.09	3.34**
30–69 years	207	84.54	2.45**
>69 years	77	102.53	0.75
Follow-up interval			
<2 years	188	59.83	3.14**
>2 years	143	141.33	1.01
Cause of death			
Natural	225	182.34	1.23*
Unnatural	106	18.82	5.63**
Total	331	201.16	1.65**

* $p < .01$.
** $p < .001$.

TABLE 6.2.   Data on Suicide in the Iowa Record-Linkage Study

Variable	Observed deaths	Expected deaths	SMR
Sex			
Male	37	2.47	14.98*
Female	31	0.75	41.33*
Age			
<30 years	24	0.82	29.27*
30–69 years	42	1.86	22.58*
>69 years	2	0.54	3.70
Follow-up interval			
<2 years	54	1.05	51.43*
>2 years	14	2.17	6.45*
Total	68	3.22	21.12*

* $p < .001$.

Among findings specific to suicide, both men and women in all age categories except the senium (over 69 years) were at significant risk for suicide. Patients were at great risk for suicide throughout the entire follow-up period, although 54 (79.4%) suicides occurred during the first 2 years of follow-up. Patients in all categories were at significant risk for suicide, except for patients with organic mental disorders, adjustment disorders, psychophysiological disorders, and special symptoms; men with depressive neuroses; and women with neuroses or personality disorders. The overall SMR (men and women combined) was 21.20 ($p < .001$). Thus, we were able to demonstrate that risk of mortality in general,

TABLE 6.3.   Suicide by Psychiatric Diagnosis in the Iowa Record-Linkage Study

Diagnosis	Observed deaths	Expected deaths	SMR
Organic mental disorders	1	0.42	2.38
Schizophrenia	14	0.37	37.84*
Acute schizophrenia	5	0.15	33.33*
Affective disorders	22	0.78	28.21*
Neuroses	5	0.17	29.41*
Depressive neuroses	5	0.16	31.25*
Personality disorders	7	0.54	12.96*
Alcohol and other drug abuse	6	0.32	18.75*
Adjustment disorders	3	0.21	14.29*
Other	0	0.09	—
Total	68	3.22	21.12*

* $p < .001$.

and risk of suicide specifically, differed according to age, sex, diagnosis, and portion of the follow-up.

Advantages and Disadvantages of the Iowa Record-Linkage Approach

Few research designs are infallible. The Iowa Record-Linkage Study is no exception, and its drawbacks involve patient sampling, death ascertainment, psychiatric assessment, and statistical inference. First, our sample included former adult inpatients hospitalized at a tertiary care facility. Although our sample was random in the sense that all patients in a given 10-year period were included (it was, in fact, a population), it was nonrandom in that we chose a highly select group of patients to study. Therefore, it is difficult to generalize our findings beyond the confines of our sample.

Next, death was ascertained using a record-linkage process that did not allow for personal follow-up. It is likely that our method underestimated the true number of deaths, as many patients would have emigrated from Iowa, changed their names, or died in other states, and follow-up data on them would thus not have been readily available. We determined that about 6% of our patients were from other states, but had no estimate on the number of persons who emigrated, changed their names, or died elsewhere, although it is generally recognized that Iowa's population is stable. Past studies (e.g., the Iowa "500") have demonstrated that even after 30 or 40 years, most Iowans remain in Iowa and are traceable. We relied on death certificates for death determination—a practice often fraught with difficulty, as there is no standardization in assignment of death cause, or even in who fills a death certificate out (e.g., physician, mortician). The difficulty of this assignment is illustrated by the case of a living cancer patient dying of pneumonia. Should the death be recorded as due to cancer or pneumonia? Information about death from unnatural causes (e.g., accidents, homicides, suicides) is probably less idiosyncratic, but still rests on the coroner's verdict. A coroner's expertise may vary from place to place, and verdicts often reflect administrative, economic, or other constraints, not merely medical fact.

Third, our psychiatric assessment was not based on an interview with each subject or on careful chart review, but rested on chart diagnosis. Each patient was assigned a single diagnosis; multiple diagnoses, however important they may have been, were not allowed. Also, diagnoses were assigned in a hierarchical fashion, so that certain disorders preempted others. For example, organic mental disorders were ranked first and were followed by schizophrenia, acute schizophrenia, affective disorders, and so on (see list above). Naturally, a hierarchy of this nature is arbitrary and minimizes the contribution to mortality that multiple diagnoses may make. For example, a patient with both affective disorder and alcoholism would have received a study diagnosis of affective disorder, yet alcoholism clearly contributes to excess mortality. Other rankings may have produced other findings.

Fourth, although our total sample was large, many subsamples were quite small after the total group was divided into different categories (e.g., sex, diagnosis), and both observed and expected numbers of deaths within the subsamples were even smaller. Naturally, drawing a statistical inference from such small numbers may not be warranted, even with the conservative Freeman–Tukey modified chi-square. For example, two females with acute schizophrenia committed suicide when 0.03 were expected. This is statistically significant, yet one wonders whether such small numbers merit any inference at all. Lastly, because there were no chart reviews or personal interviews, relevant risk factors (e.g., demographic, clinical treatment, etc.) could not be evaluated for their possible influence on mortality.

Several advantages can be cited in defense of our approach. Our study sample included all persons within a 10-year period who were hospitalized, and in this sense, it was unbiased. These adults comprised a group at high risk for early mortality—a group of great concern to all hospital-based clinicians. Therefore, the findings from this study are relevant to that select group of patients. Death ascertainment may have been incomplete, but because Iowa's population is relatively stable, it was probably not too far off the mark. We had to rely on death certificates for assignments of death causes, and, regardless of errors, not much could be done about them. One strategy we used was to look at death from either natural or unnatural causes. By creating two categories, we probably minimized the influence of any idiosyncratic practices on determining specific natural causes of death, or of the administrative, legal, and political concerns that plague ascertainment in cases of unnatural death. For example, a suicide may have been misclassified as accidental for political reasons. By classifying it as unnatural, we were able to ignore such concerns. (On the other hand, this method ignores the differences between suicides and accidents.) Other investigators have found this dichotomy useful as well (Martin et al., 1985a, 1985b). Although our use of a single, hierarchical diagnosis has been criticized (Martin, 1985), most patients did have a single psychiatric diagnosis.

Advantages of our approach are apparent. Record-linkage studies are simple and economical; a large staff is unnecessary. Using this approach allowed us to work with relatively large sample sizes not possible with prospective follow-up study designs. We used a statistically sound, actuarial approach for calculating expected numbers of deaths based on U.S. census and Iowa vital statistics data. Our computer programs could easily be updated for future studies. Furthermore, the programs were adjusted for age, sex, and duration of follow-up. The last of these is essential in studies such as ours, where some patients are followed for 1 year and others may be followed for 10 years. Naturally, a person followed for 10 years would have a greater cumulative risk for mortality than someone followed for 1 year.

Iowa Depression Study

As an offshoot of our original study, we became interested in learning about specific risk factors associated with mortality in affective disorders. In our original study, we had created a broadly defined affective disorders category. We were unable to look at subtypes, because we lacked specific diagnostic information. Furthermore, our original design did not allow us to look at risk factors associated with mortality other than age, sex, and duration of follow-up. Therefore, we initiated the still ongoing Iowa Depression Study. We reviewed the charts of all patients admitted to our hospital over a 12-year period (1970 through 1981) who had an affective disorder. Included were all patients with chart diagnoses of major depression, bipolar disorder, schizoaffective disorder, depressive neurosis, secondary depression, and so on. Our final sample consisted of 2,054 charts. Each chart was individually reviewed by a master's-level psychologist (Amelia Nasrallah). Each chart was systematically evaluated for demographic, diagnostic, clinical, treatment, and outcome data. In all, over 120 bits of information were obtained on each patient. Next, we conducted a record linkage, comparing the roster of affective disorder patients with Iowa death certificates through 1983, allowing at least a 2-year and at most a 14-year follow-up. Each patient was carefully diagnosed according to three sets of operationalized criteria: DSM-III, Research Diagnostic Criteria, and the St. Louis criteria. Multiple diagnoses were allowed, and medical illnesses were coded as well. Thus, we were able to correct some of the deficiencies of the Iowa Record-Linkage Study, such as lack of chart review, enabling us to evaluate multiple risk factors and look at specific diagnostic groups.

Findings of the Iowa Depression Study

As the study is still in progress, only preliminary data are available (Black, Winokur, & Nasrallah, 1987a,b,c). We have evaluated death

TABLE 6.4.　General Mortality in Major Affective Disorder

Subtype	Observed deaths	Expected deaths	SMR
Primary unipolar depression	77	58.60	1.31*
Secondary unipolar depression	38	16.34	2.33**
Bipolar affective disorder	42	22.51	1.87**
Bipolar, depressed type	17	8.15	2.09*
Bipolar, manic type	25	14.38	1.74*
Total	157	97.45	1.61**

* $p < .01$.
** $p < .001$.

rates in unipolar and bipolar affective disorders. A total of 157 deaths occurred in the sample, but only 97.5 were expected, yielding an SMR of 1.61 ($p < .001$). We found that overall mortality risk differed between subtypes (see Table 6.4), but much of the difference was attributable to physical illnesses. Patients with bipolar disorder and secondary depression were more likely to have a serious physical disorder than primary depressives (partly because of the definition we used). After deleting patients with these conditions from the analysis, we found death rates between the subtypes to be similar.

We found little evidence for a difference in risk for suicide among depressive subtypes (see Table 6.5). Among patients with primary unipolar depression, 31.2% of the deceased died from suicide; corresponding percentages among secondary unipolars and bipolars were 26.3% and 16.7%, respectively. Although it appears that bipolars were at less risk for suicide, it became clear after further study that this finding was simply a result of combining the manic and depressed bipolar patients into a single group. As manics have a very low risk for suicide, and depressed bipolars have a risk for suicide similar to that of primary

TABLE 6.5.　Suicide in Major Affective Disorder

Subtype	Observed deaths	Expected deaths	SMR
Primary unipolar depression	24	0.55	43.64*
Secondary unipolar depression	10	0.24	41.67*
Bipolar affective disorder	7	0.48	14.58*
Bipolar, depressed type	5	0.14	35.71*
Bipolar, manic type	2	0.34	5.88
Total	41	1.27	32.38*

* $p < .001$.

and secondary unipolar patients, the result is the appearance of lowered risk for bipolars. Our findings suggest that depression, regardless of specific subtype, leads to a high risk for suicide, although a diagnosis of mania does not. These findings appeal to common sense. Mania is not traditionally associated with risk for suicide, but depression is. Thus, a person with bipolar disorder who has both manic and depressive episodes may spend less time altogether at risk for suicide than a unipolar depressive who experiences only depressive episodes. At least in a short-term follow-up such as ours, bipolars appear to have a lower risk of suicide.

We also noted a trend for suicides to cluster near the beginning of the follow-up period. Nearly three-quarters of the suicides occurred during the first 2 years of follow-up. These findings are consistent with the Iowa Record-Linkage Study and suggest that the relative risk for suicide may be increased early in the course of illness, but continues throughout follow-up.

Future Directions

Studies of suicide risk continue to be important, because prevention of suicide is the ultimate goal of treatment. A knowledge of suicide and of factors influencing its risk is necessary before successful interventions can be systematically applied. Suicide remains a multidimensional problem and requires research designs and analytic methods suited for a multidimensional analysis. The method we have used in the Iowa Depression Study has allowed us to look at risk for suicide in patients with specific subtypes of affective disorder. With demographic, diagnostic, clinical, and treatment data gathered from the chart review, a multivariate study of correlations between these risk factors in suicide can be accomplished. We are now in the process of carrying this out.

The Iowa Record-Linkage Study has made clear the need for large-scale studies when investigating mortality, and has pointed to the need for careful diagnostic assessment. Our economical method has allowed us to gather a large number of data on many patients. We are now planning additional studies on other diagnostic groups, including patients with schizophrenia, sexual deviancy, and antisocial personality.

References

Babigian, H. M., & Odoroff, C. L.: The mortality experience of a population with psychiatric illness. *American Journal of Psychiatry*, 1969, *126*, 470–479.

Barraclough, B., Bunch, J., Nelson, B., & Sainsbury, P. A hundred cases of suicide: Clinical aspects. *British Journal of Psychiatry*, 1974, *125*, 355–373.

Black, D. W., Warrack, G., & Winokur, G. Excess mortality among psychiatric patients: The Iowa Record-Linkage Study. *Journal of the American Medical Association*, 1985, *253*, 58–61. (a)

Black, D. W., Warrack, G., & Winokur, G. The Iowa Record-Linkage Study: I. Suicides and accidental death among psychiatric patients. *Archives of General Psychiatry*, 1985, *42*, 71–75. (b)

Black, D. W., Warrack, G., & Winokur, G. The Iowa Record-Linkage Study: II. Excess mortality among patients with organic mental disorders. *Archives of General Psychiatry*, 1985, *42*, 78–81. (c)

Black, D. W., Warrack, G., & Winokur, G. The Iowa Record-Linkage Study: III. Excess mortality among patients with "functional" disorders. *Archives of General Psychiatry*, 1985, *42*, 82–88. (d)

Black, D. W., Winokur, G., & Nasrallah, A. Is natural death still excessive in psychiatric patients?: A study of 1593 patients with affective disorder. *Journal of Nervous and Mental Disease*, 1987, *175*, 674–680. (a)

Black, D. W., Winokur, G., & Nasrallah, A. Mortality in patients with primary unipolar depression. Secondary unipolar depression and bipolar affective disorder: A comparison with general population mortality. *International Journal of Psychiatry and Medicine* 1987, *17*, 351–360. (b)

Black, D. W., Winokur, G., & Nasrallah, A. Suicide in subtypes of major affective disorder: A comparison with general population suicide mortality. *Archives of General Psychiatry*, 1987, *44*, 878–880. (c)

Eastwood, M. R., Stiasny, S., Meier, H. M. R., & Woogh, C. M. Mental illness and mortality. *Comprehensive Psychiatry*, 1982, *23*, 377–385.

Helgason, T. The epidemiology of mental disorder in Iceland. *acta Psychiatrica Scandinavica*, 1984, *40*(Suppl. 173), 1–128.

Innes, G., & Millar, W. Mortality among psychiatric patients. *Scottish Medical Journal*, 1970, *15*, 143–148.

Martin, R. L. Methodologic and conceptual problems in the study of mortality in psychiatry. *Psychiatric Developments*, 1985, *4*, 317–333.

Martin, R. L., Cloninger, C. R., Guze, S. B., & Clayton, P. J. Mortality in a follow-up of 500 psychiatric outpatients: I. Total mortality. *Archives of General Psychiatry*, 1985, *42*, 47–54. (a)

Martin, R. L., Cloninger, C. R., Guze, S. B., & Clayton, P. J. Mortality in a follow-up of 500 psychiatric outpatients: II. Cause specific mortality. *Archives of General Psychiatry*, 1985, *42*, 58–66. (b)

Morrison, J. R. Suicide in a psychiatric practice population. *Journal of Clinical Psychiatry*, 1982, *43*, 348–352.

Robins, E., Murphy, G. E., Wilkinson, R. H., Gassner, S., & Kayes, J. Some clinical considerations in the prevention of suicide based on a study of 134 successful suicides. *American Journal of Public Health*, 1959, *49*, 888–899.

Rorsman, B., Hagnell, O., & Lanke, J. Violent death and mental disorders in the Lundby Study: Accidents and suicides in a total population during a 25 year period. *Neuropsychobiology*, 1982, *8*, 233–240.

Roy, A. Risk factors for suicide in psychiatric patients. *Archives of General Psychiatry*, 1982, *39*, 1089–1095.

Tsuang, M. T. Suicide in schizophrenia, manic depressives, and surgical controls: A comparison with general population suicide mortality. *Archives of General Psychiatry*, 1978, *35*, 153–155.

Tsuang, M. T., & Woolson, R. F.: Mortality in patients with schizophrenia, mania, depression, and surgical conditions. *British Journal of Psychiatry*, 1977, *130*, 162–166.

U.S. Department of Health and Human Services. *International classification of diseases* (9th ed., 2nd rev., Vol. 1). Washington, DC: U.S. Government Printing Office, 1980.

Weed, J. A. Suicide in the United States: 1958–1982. In C. A. Taube & S. A. Barrett (Eds.), *Mental health, United States, 1985.* Rockville, Md.: National Institute of Mental Health, 1985.

Winokur, G., & Black, D. W. Psychiatric and medical diagnoses as risk factors for mortality in psychiatric patients: A case control study. *American Journal of Psychiatry,* 1987, *144,* 208–211.

7

The Utility of Emergency Room Data for Record Linkage in the Study of Adolescent Suicidal Behavior

Eva Y. Deykin, DPH
Harvard School of Public Health

Investigations on the phenomenon of adolescent suicide have pointed to the paradoxical characteristics of suicide attempters and completers, with females outnumbering males about 6:1 among the attempters but males outnumbering females by 4:1 among the completers. The age distribution is also different, with age having an inverse relationship to attempts but a direct relationship to completed suicides (Cosand, Bourque, & Kraus, 1982; Hellon & Solomon, 1980; Holinger, 1978; Shaffer & Fisher, 1981). The different population characteristics of attempters and completers presents methodological difficulties in identifying the social, familial, and demographic variables that could be risk factors for completed suicide (Hawton, O'Grady, Osborn, & Cole, 1982; Taylor & Stansfield, 1984).

To a large extent, what is known of the epidemiology of suicide attempts comes from data collected from emergency rooms or admissions to hospitals (Deykin, Hsieh, Joshi, & McNamarra, 1986; Deykin, Perlow, & McNamarra, 1984; Goldacre & Hawton, 1985; Wexler, Weissman, & Kasl, 1978). Yet trying to understand the epidemiology of suicide attempts from such data is a little like estimating the height of a tree when one knows only the diameter of its trunk. Emergency room data currently provide the best available information on the epidemiology of suicide attempts, but, at best, they are incomplete and potentially biased. The data are incomplete because people admitted to the emergency room are those who by chance or design are still salvageable. Missing from such admissions are those whose suicide attempts succeeded

Preparation of this chapter was supported in part by National Institute of Mental Health Contract No. 278-85-0026. This study was supported in part by a grant from the Association of Schools of Public Health/Centers for Disease Control Cooperative Agreement and by the William T. Grant Faculty Scholars Award.

because of some miscalculation, those who recovered on their own without medical attention, and those treated by private physicians.

Emergency room data are also potentially biased because of the possibility of differential history taking when an admission is known to be precipitated by an intentional, self-inflicted injury. Emergency room data may not always be accurate with respect to diagnosis. This is particularly true in the case of adolescents, who are a population at high risk of accidents and who may be able to disguise a suicide attempt as an accident, thus avoiding inquiry by emergency room personnel. The fine line between accidents and suicidal injuries was noted in a study of emergency room admissions for nonfatal suicidal behavior among adolescents aged 13–17 (Deykin et al., 1984). The study reported a pattern of repeat emergency room visits in which the same individuals were treated at one time for suicidal injuries and at other times for more generic life-threatening events that could easily be classified as accidents. This admixture of the two classifications suggests the possibility that some forms of accidental self-inflicted injuries could be equivalent of suicidal attempts, despite the lack of stated suicidal intent.

A final drawback of emergency room data for epidemiological purposes is their scantiness. Part of the problem is the very nature of emergency medicine, which requires quick decisions and provides little time for a detailed history or analysis. The deficits in emergency room data were documented in a study by Adityanjee and Mohan (1987), which examined the recording of basic sociodemographic characteristics of psychiatric emergencies coming to the emergency room. Even when emergency room personnel were provided with a special recording form, data on education, occupation, and income went unrecorded 20–88% of the time. The authors conclude that in emergency settings, data that are not directly relevant for a diagnostic and treatment formulation remain unrecorded, even though such data would be elicited in less frenetic medical settings.

Despite the multiple drawbacks of emergency room data, they can still provide a valuable information base, especially in the area of record linkage. In this chapter, I describe a method of record linkage using emergency room logs in the study of adolescent suicidal behavior.

Record linkage is a process by which data collected for different purposes on the same individual are brought together to provide new information not available without the linkage. There are at least three advantages to record linkage. First, the data contained in each of the different record sets were collected for reasons unrelated to the question under current investigation, and thus are not likely to be biased. Second, the data contained in two or more records have usually been collected and recorded prior to the research at hand, allowing for assessment of a temporal relationship between risk factor and outcome. Third, record linkage has the advantage of reducing or eliminating the problem of interviewer or observation bias.

Linkage of records is a well-established epidemiological procedure frequently used in etiological research. For example, certain kinds of cancers have been associated to specific occupational exposures by linking medical records to prior employment histories. Important information on the predictors of infant mortality has also been gleaned by linking infant death records to the respective birth records.

In the psychiatric field, an outstanding example of record linkage has been the work of Kety, Rosenthal, Wender, and Schulsinger (1969), who assessed the type and prevalence of mental illness in the biological and adoptive families of adopted schizophrenics. This seminal work, conducted in Denmark, was made possible by linking the information held by three high-quality registries: an adoption registry, a change-of-address registry, and a psychiatric registry.

In the United States, however, such comprehensive registries do not exist, and record access is often difficult if not legally restricted. Generally, U.S. records fall into one of three major categories: public records (e.g., town lists, marriage or death records), which are easily accessible; semipublic records (e.g., birth records, criminal records, military records), which may be obtainable under certain circumstances; and closed records (e.g., medical/psychiatric records, adoption records, child abuse records), which are not accessible to persons outside the hospitals or agencies holding the records.

My interest in applying the record-linkage method in the study of adolescent suicidal behavior was sparked by an observation made from the emergency room records during the course of an intervention designed to reduce the occurrence of suicidal, self-destructive behavior among high-risk adolescents. The intervention program focused on youths aged 13–17 who received medical treatment in emergency rooms for a variety of self-inflicted injuries.

There were four categories of study eligibility: suicide attempts; suicide gestures; life-threatening, self-destructive behavior; and suicide ideation. Suicide attempts were defined as self-inflicted injuries accompanied by stated suicidal intent, even if the injuries were not severe enough to be fatal. Suicide gestures were intentional self-inflicted injuries without a statement of suicidal purpose. Life-threatening behavior was the term applied to a variety of injuries resulting from risk-taking behavior, drug or alcohol abuse, or noncompliance with medically prescribed medication. For a youth's behavior to be classified in this category, there had to be reasonable evidence that the youth knew the potential consequences of his or her act. Finally, suicide ideation was reserved for subjects who sought help for recurrent, overwhelming thoughts of suicide but who had not inflicted any physical harm on themselves.

As part of the research component of the intervention study, a comparison was made of the hospital records of the suicidal youths and those of age- and sex-matched adolescents who had been treated in the emergency ward for various medical illnesses or injuries unrelated to suicidal behavior. Although the medical records of the proband and comparison groups were very similar with respect to sociodemographic characteristics, prior utilization of health care, and method of payment, the records of the suicidal probands frequently contained notations of family violence, child abuse, and removal of the subjects from their family homes. Such notations were rarely present in the medical records of the comparison subjects.

This observation raised the possibility that exposure to violence or child abuse might be an important risk factor in adolescence. On a number of theoretical points, this hypothesis had a good measure of validity. First of all, violence as a means of coping with frustration or anger is a learned response. Thus, exposure to violence at any early age could be associated to self-aggressive, destructive behavior at a later age. Second, low self-esteem has been identified as a characteristic of both abused children and suicidal individuals. If low self-esteem is a necessary component of suicidal ideation, then persons with low self-esteem, for whatever reason, could be at increased risk of self-destructive behavior. Finally, an indirect association of child abuse and suicidal behavior could exist through the action of foster home placement. Depending on the age of the child and the duration of foster home placement, disruptions of bonding, leading to a sense of separateness and a diminished ability to establish meaningful relationships, could result. Emotional and social disconnectedness have also been noted among suicidal individuals and are believed to be important predictors of suicidal behavior.

Despite the attractiveness of these theories, it was also possible that the observed high frequency of child abuse or family violence notations in the medical records of the suicidal group could be entirely due to differential history taking in the suicidal and comparison group. An illness or injury that requires emergency treatment may also dictate the kind of history taken and the discipline of the history taker. Adolescents who require medical treatment for suicidal injuries are likely to be seen by a psychiatrist, social worker, or psychologist who will elicit information on family history and dynamics. Conversely, an adolescent who has suffered a sports injury will not be seen by a psychiatrist, nor will any notation be recorded on the social dynamics of his or her family. Because of this systematic bias, the medical records could not be used as a data base to assess whether exposure to family violence and child abuse were risk factors for adolescent suicidal behavior.

Methods

An unbiased test of the hypothesis required a data source that not only was independent of the emergency room, but also contained information gathered prior to the self-destructive act or medical event that identified the adolescent as either a proband or comparison subject. In Massachusetts, such a data source existed in the Massachusetts Department of Social Services (DSS), the only agency in the state empowered to collect, investigate, and act on reports of child abuse and neglect. In hopes of linking the names of study subjects (both probands and comparison) to the registry held by the DSS, a letter was sent to the commissioner of the DSS, explaining the purpose of the study and the need for the linkage. Despite interest in the study, the commissioner replied that state law prohibited access to DSS records to anyone outside the agency, and that even redacted or abstracted records were prohibited to outsiders, since it might be possible to guess the identity of a child from the details of the case. The commissioner stated that if a method could be devised to link the names of the study adolescents to the DSS registry within the legal restraints, the linkage might be possible.

Accordingly, the following method was devised. Each study subject was given a six-digit identification number. The first three digits provided information on the sex of the subject, the type of suicidal behavior exhibited by the proband, and whether the individual was a proband or a comparison subject. The last three digits linked the triplet set, which consisted of a suicidal proband and two comparison subjects. Next, we obtained from the emergency room records basic identifying data on all subjects, including date of birth, parents' names, current address, and any known prior addresses for all of the probands and comparison subjects. Lastly, on three separate sheets of paper we typed out the name and identifying information for each study subject, with the first sheet containing the name of the proband and the second and third sheets containing the names of the two matched comparison subjects. There were five names per sheet, arranged in such a manner that when the first, second, and third sheets were placed next to one another, the triplet sets would be horizontally in line.

A staff member at the DSS, who was unaware of the status of subjects, searched the central registry to determine whether the subjects had had contact with the DSS prior to the emergency room admissions that led to study enrollment. The presence or absence of prior contact with the department was indicated by a "1" or a "0" next to a subject's name. When all the subjects' names had been searched, the staff assistant was instructed, without changing page order, to align the first three sheets of paper in such a manner that subjects with the same last three digits were next to one another. For each triplet set, one of eight possible combinations was recorded: 100, 110, 101, 111, 010, 011, 001, and 000. The same process was repeated for all subsequent pages. Since the name of the proband appeared on the first page, and the names of the comparison subjects appeared on the second and third pages, a "1" in the hundreds column indicated that the proband was known to the DSS, and a "1" in either of the other two columns indicated that a comparison subject had had contact with the DSS (see Table 7.1).

Each of the eight possible combinations was summed over the entire sample, and the data were subjected to a matched analysis (Mantel & Haenszel, 1959). The odds ratio was calculated as the measure of association between prior contact with the DSS and subsequent suicidal behavior.

Results

The probands in each type of suicidal behavior were compared to their own age- and sex-matched comparison subjects with respect to prior contact with the DSS. Table 7.2 shows the association of adolescent suicidal behavior with prior contact with the DSS, according to the four categories of study eligibility.

For every category of suicidal behavior, the probands were more than twice as likely to have been known to the DSS prior to their emergency room admission as were the comparison subjects. In three of the four categories of suicidal behavior, the difference was statistically significant. In the fourth category—that of suicidal ideation—the risk was elevated, but because of very small numbers in this category, the difference was not significant.

Discussion

This study utilizing record linkage has documented the importance of emergency room data in providing the basis for new information. This particular study employed a methodology designed to obtain data without infringing on the legal restrictions imposed on child abuse records. It is possible that this methodology could be employed to obtain other

TABLE 7.1. Example of Data Layout

	Subjects			Triplet combinations						
				100	110	101	111	010	011	001
I.D.	101001	111001	121001							
Name	John Doe	Ted Doe	Bob Doe							
DSS contact	0	1	0					×		
I.D.	101002	111002	121002							
Name	Al Doe	Dave Doe	Frank Doe							
DSS contact	1	0	0	×						
I.D.	101003	111003	121003							
Name	Bill Doe	Stan Doe	Fred Doe							
DSS contact	1	0	1			×				
I.D.	101004	111004	121004							
Name	Chet Doe	Ken Doe	Will Doe							
DSS contact	1	1	1				×			

TABLE 7.2.   Association of Suicidal Behavior and Prior Contact
with the Department of Social Services (DSS), According to the Four Categories
of Study Eligibility

	DSS contact			Odds ratio	95% confidence interval	χ^2 (1 dF)
	Yes	No	Total			
Suicide attempts						
Probands	34	125	159			
Comparison subjects	27	291	318	2.93	1.7–5.0	15.8*
Total	61	461	477			
Suicide gestures						
Probands	23	97	120			
Comparison subjects	12	228	240	4.50	2.3–9.0	18.3*
Total	35	325	360			
Self-destructive behavior						
Probands	20	82	102			
Comparison subjects	10	194	204	4.73	2.2–10.0	16.6*
Total	30	276	306			
Suicide ideation						
Probands	2	13	15			
Comparison subjects	1	29	30	4.50	0.4–47.6	1.6
Total	3	42	45			

*$p < .001$.

kinds of information, such as educational achievement, psychiatric treatment, medical history, or other data that are legally protected.

The present study indicated only a higher risk of DSS contact for the probands, but did not prove that the contacts were due to child abuse or neglect, since a name could have appeared on the central registry for reasons other than abuse or neglect. Nevertheless, the DSS devotes over 90% of its resources to child protective services. Because of these initial findings, the DSS has allowed an extension of the study to include abstracting of information from the actual case records of the subjects whose names appear on the central registry. Of the 129 subjects whose names appeared on the registry, the case records of 110 were found and abstracted. These new data will be analyzed to determine whether the probands and comparison subjects' contacts with the DSS were for different reasons, or whether there were differences between probands and comparison subjects with regard to the number and duration of out-of-home placements, services offered to the families, or basic sociodemographic characteristics. It is possible that such analyses may yield information on risk factors experienced in early childhood that will lead to a better understanding of adolescent suicidal behavior.

References

Adityanjee, N. N. W., & Mohan, D. Non-recording of sociodemographic variables in the emergency room setting. *International Journal of Social Psychiatry*, 1987, *33*, 30–32.

Cosand, B. J., Bourque, L. B., & Kraus, J. F. Suicide among adolescents in Sacramento County, California, 1950–1979. *Adolescence*, 1982, *17*, 917–929.

Deykin, E. Y., Hsieh, C. C., Joshi, M., & McNamarra, J. J. Adolescent suicidal and self destructive behavior: Results of an intervention study. *Journal of Adolescent Health Care*, 1986, *7*, 88–95.

Deykin, E. Y., Perlow, R., & McNamarra, J. Non-fatal suicidal and life threatening behavior among 13 to 17 year old adolescents seeking emergency suicidal care. *American Journal of Public Health*, 1984, *75*, 90–92.

Goldacre, M., & Hawton, K. Repetition of self poisoning and subsequent death in adolescents who take overdoses. *British Journal of Psychiatry*, 1985, *146*, 395–398.

Hawton, K., O'Grady, J., Osborn, M., & Cole, D. Adolescents who take overdoses: Their characteristics, problems and contacts with helping agencies. *British Journal of Psychiatry*, 1982, *140*, 118–123.

Hellon, C. P., & Solomon, M. I. Suicide and age in Alberta, Canada, 1951–1977. *Archives of General Psychiatry*, 1980, *37*, 505–510.

Holinger, P. C. Adolescent suicide: An epidemiologic study of recent trends. *American Journal of Psychiatry*, 1978, *135*, 754–756.

Kety, S. S., Rosenthal, D., Wender, P. H., & Schulsinger, F. The types and prevalence of mental illness in the biological and adoptive families of adopted schizophrenics. In D. Rosenthal & S. S. Kety (Eds.), *Transmission of schizophrenia*. Oxford: Pergamon Press, 1969.

Mantel, N., & Haenszel, W. Statistical aspects of the analysis of data from retrospective studies of disease. *Journal of the National Cancer Institute*, 1959, *22*, 719–748.

Shaffer, D., & Fisher, P. Suicide in children and young adolescents. In C. F. Wells & I. R. Stuart (Eds.), *Self-destructive behavior in children and adolescents*. New York: Van Nostrand Reinhold, 1981.

Taylor, E. A., & Stansfield, S. A. Children who poison themselves. *British Journal of Psychiatry*, 1984, *145*, 127–135.

Wexler, L., Weissman, M. M., & Kasl, S. V. Suicide attempts 1970–1975: Updating a U.S. study and comparison with international trends. *British Journal of Psychiatry*, 1978, *132*, 180–185.

8

Studying Adolescent Suicidal Ideation and Behavior in Primary Care Settings

Felton Earls, MD
Washington University School of Medicine

Because suicide is the second most frequent cause of death among adolescents and young adults, it is essential for health personnel to make active efforts to detect suicidal ideation and behavior in youths. As yet, however, there is little knowledge on how to assess the risk of completed suicide among youths who have thoughts about death or who have attempted suicide. Enough is known to enable us to suspect strongly that risk assessment should not be based on the results of studies of adults. What makes the demographic picture of adolescent suicide particularly confusing is the discrepancy between suicide attempters and completers. Attempters are predominantly female, and the frequency of this behavior decreases with age. Completers, on the other hand, are mostly male, and their death rates increase during the period of late adolescence and young adulthood.

The clinician is faced with a difficult problem in attempting to select youths at the highest risk for completed suicide from the much larger group of youths who manifest some evidence of suicidal thoughts and behavior. Such decisions are probably based on individual experience and training more than on empirically based, logical appraisal. Given the absence of a scientific foundation on which to base decisions, many clinicians may choose an overinclusive strategy, in which most suicidal behavior is regarded as serious and life-threatening, or an underinclusive strategy, in which the assessment of seriousness is based on characteristics of the event (e.g., the degree of medical lethality associated with the event) or characteristics of the patient (e.g., the presence of previous attempts or the presence of a psychiatric disorder).

Preparation of this chapter was supported by National Institute of Mental Health (NIMH) Contract No. 278-85-0026. Support for this research was provided by the Robert Wood Johnson Foundation and NIMH Grant No. MH31302.

The purpose of this chapter is to discuss strategies involved in conducting research on the detection and treatment of suicidal ideation and behavior in primary health care settings. In such settings, the detection of youths who are suicidal typically occurs in the process of evaluating or treating unrelated problems for which they are seeking help. In fact, only about 5% of youths attending primary care facilities have a mental health problem as their presenting complaint (Robins, in press). Thus, the disclosure of suicidal ideation must occur rapidly and in a manner that is nonthreatening. Some of the problems and results from an ongoing study of adolescent health care (Stiffman, Earls, Robins, & Jung, 1988) are used to focus this discussion.

The study was initiated in 1984 to evaluate the impact that consolidated and comprehensive services for young people had on improving health outcomes. Three years earlier, in 1981, the Robert Wood Johnson Foundation had funded several medical schools to link hospital-based and community-based clinics into a consolidated system that would provide comprehensive services to adolescents. The rationale for targeting adolescents was provided in prevailing health statistics, which indicated this age group to be at high risk for a constellation of health conditions that seemed beyond the capacity of traditional health programs to deal with effectively (Blum, 1987). In response to this need, the foundation sought out medical schools that either already had adolescent medicine training programs or had the resources to begin one. It also required the schools to provide evidence that a consolidated service would serve a population of young people who were at higher than the national average risk for several targeted health conditions: suicide, depression, homicide, accidents, alcohol and substance abuse, pregnancy, and sexually transmitted diseases (Lear, Foster, & Wylie, 1985). This requirement was easily met by most applicants, since medical schools are typically located in central parts of large cities.

During the years of funding, the programs developed as a set of demonstration projects. There were no specific prescriptions for what constituted a consolidated program, so the different arrangements that evolved were reflections of local resources, ingenuity, and organizational efforts. All the programs were associated with training programs in adolescent medicine. Some clinics were primarily based in hospitals, others were community-based, and still others were situated in schools.

Research Design, Methods, and Sampling

By 1984, when the evaluation study began, all of the funded programs had matured into comprehensive health care networks. In designing the evaluation study, a number of decisions were made. First, it was decided that the consolidated clinics would be compared to traditional clinics providing categorical services. These traditional clinics were distinct in not being especially designed for adolescents and not being associated with an adolescent medical training program. Second, the emphasis of the evaluation would be on directly measuring change in the health status of youths using the consolidated and traditional services. Third, the age range of those served would be restricted to 13–18. Although many of the programs treated young people over this age, it was believed that the greatest impact of the consolidated approach would occur during the teenage years.

Seven consolidated clinics and three comparison (or traditional) clinics were selected for inclusion in the study. Each was located in a different city, to insure that youths using one clinic would not use another clinic included in the study. Between 150 and 300 youths were randomly sampled from each of the clinics. They were interviewed by trained interviewers using a structured protocol designed to detect physical and mental disorders, patterns of health care utilization, past and present living arrangements, recent stressful life events, social adjustment, and family background.

The study was conducted independently of the youths' use of the various health services. An initial interview, designed to provide a descriptive baseline on the sample, was followed by a second interview 12 months later. Following the second interview, the medical records of each youth were systematically reviewed. This method allowed us to compare the youths' own reports about their health problems and the amount and type of care they were receiving to what was documented in their records by their care providers.

The initial sample of 2,787 consisted largely of black youths (71%) and females (77%). Eighty-seven percent, or 2,425, of the initial sample were reinterviewed 12 months following the first interview. The over-representation of females influenced the types of presenting health problems most commonly seen in these settings. Other sources of variation that influenced the frequency and types of presenting problems were geographic location, setting (hospital, neighborhood, or school-based), age, and race.

The topic of this chapter was addressed by a series of related questions:

1. How frequent is suicidal ideation and behavior in this population?
2. How does it rank with other health problems and risk factors?
3. How efficiently can suicidal behavior be predicted from one year to the next in adolescents?

4. To what extent is suicidal ideation and behavior recognized and treated by health personnel?
5. Is the rate of recognition and treatment higher in centers that are specialized to deal with adolescent patients than in traditional clinics?

Results

In addressing the first question, regarding the frequency of suicidal ideation and behavior, we examined responses to the interview questions designed to elicit these symptoms. The questions were included in a section of the interview aimed at characterizing symptoms associated with major depressive disorder and dysthymia as outlined in DSM-III. This section of the interview was the same as that contained in the Diagnostic Interview Schedule (DIS; Robins, Helzer, Croughan, & Ratcliff, 1981). Four questions were used to elicit suicidal ideation and attempts:

1. Has there ever been a period of 2 weeks or more when you thought [Did you think] a lot about death—either your own, someone else's, or death in general?
2. Has there ever been a period of 2 weeks or more when you felt [Did you feel] like you wanted to die?
3. Have you ever felt [Did you feel] so low you thought of committing suicide?
4. Have you ever attempted [Did you attempt] suicide?

Table 8.1 shows the frequency of these four symptoms by age, sex, and race groups. These data reflect the 12-month prevalence of these symptoms in patients who continued to use these health clinics into the second year of our study. The sample was restricted to this group of persons making multiple visits to a clinic, in order to maximize the chance that their suicidal ideation and behavior would be detected and treated. Even for this sample of nearly 2,000 patients, the number of suicidal males was too small to permit us to make comparisons confidently with females (who outnumbered males 3:1 in clinic attendance). Overall, twice as many youths admitted to having "thought a lot about death" as reported "thoughts of committing suicide." The more specific questions about suicidal ideation and suicidal attempts should select a higher-risk group than the first two questions in the sequence.

Table 8.2 shows the results when a longer time interval was used to examine change and persistence of suicidal ideation (i.e., "thought of committing suicide") and actual suicide attempts. About 19% of the

TABLE 8.1. Frequency (in Percentages) of Suicidal Ideation and Behavior in Adolescent Medical Patients by Sex, Race, and Age

| | Females | | | | Males | | | | Total |
| | Black | | White | | Black | | White | | |
Symptom	13–16 (n = 577)	17–18 (n = 487)	13–16 (n = 220)	17–18 (n = 177)	13–16 (n = 152)	17–18 (n = 113)	13–16 (n = 40)	17–18 (n = 17)	1,783
Thought a lot about death	18	16	26	24	15	19	(13)	(12)	19
Wanted to die	11	7	14	12	(3)	(7)	(10)	—	9
Thought of committing suicide	8	4	14	8	(3)	(7)	(5)	(18)	7
Attempted suicide	2	(2)	(4)	(4)	—	(1)	(2)	—	2

Note. The sample was restricted to 1,783 patients who visited clinics in the 12-month period between Wave I and Wave II. Parentheses indicate cell size < 10.

TABLE 8.2. Combining Suicidal Ideation and Behavior over
a 24-Month Period in Adolescent Medical Patients ($n = 2,425$)

Ideation/behavior	%	Combined %
No thoughts or attempts	81.1	
Thoughts at Wave I	6.1 ⎱	
Attempts at Wave I	5.4 ⎰	11.5
Thoughts at Wave II	2.1 ⎱	
Attempts at Wave II	0.6 ⎰	2.7
Thoughts at both waves	1.6	
Attempts at both waves	1.1	
Thoughts at Wave I; attempts at Wave II	0.7	4.8
Thoughts at Wave II; attempts at Wave I	1.4	

youths admitted to suicidal ideation and behavior over a 2-year period.
More than half of this group were youths who experienced ideation or
an attempt only in the first 12-month period. About 5% of the youths
remained at risk for suicide over the entire 24-month period.

A previous paper (Robins, in press) demonstrated how 90% of suicide
attempters could be identified from responses to 11 questions included
in our research interviews. These items were the ones most highly
correlated with suicidal behavior. The questions were arranged in a
sequence that would permit a clinician working in a busy medical clinic
to efficiently gather the information from adolescent patients seeking
help for a variety of reasons. Because of the two-wave prospective
design of our project, we were able to evaluate the predictive efficiency
of this list of questions. As shown in Table 8.3, each of these risk factors
existed in a small minority of patients, and only 4 out of the 11 items
("ever run away," "feelings of worthlessness," "feelings of hopelessness,"
and "been beaten or threatened") predicted more than one-third of the
57 youths who made a suicide attempt in the 12-month period between
the Wave I and Wave II interviews. When the items were combined,
however, 82% of the suicidal youths were selected. This level of prediction
came at a cost of misidentifying a large number of nonsuicidal youths.
To permit us to identify the 2% of youths who attempted suicide in the
12-month follow-up interval, 42% of the sample became false positives.
However, considering the importance of suicidal behavior in the adolescent age group and the efficient and nonthreatening way in which
these questions can be used, they may still have a place in helping
clinicians identify suicidal youths. More research on this issue is needed.

The final question to address has to do with the actual detection and
treatment of suicidal youths in medical settings. Results from the study
are presented in Table 8.4. These data illustrate that only a minority

TABLE 8.3. Prevalence of Items Predicting Suicide Attempt in the 12-Month Interval between Wave I and Wave II

Predictors	Prevalence in sample (n = 57) %	All attempters with this problem %
Ever run away	17	40
Feelings of hopelessness	15	49
Been beaten/threatened	13	37
Feelings of worthlessness	12	37
Does not live with relative or spouse	10	18
Drunk 3+ times in past year	7	16
Used illicit drugs most weeks in past year	6	11
Family member committed suicide	5	16
Been arrested	5	18
Used hallucinogens, T's, blues, barbiturates, or glue	5	19

of youths who admitted to having thoughts of committing suicide or who made a suicidal attempt told anyone at the clinics they attended. Only about a quarter did so at the two types of consolidated clinics (neighborhood-based and school-based clinics). An even smaller number of youths who reported suicidal ideation or behavior in the interview had documentation of this problem in their medical records. Thus, the number of youths for whom treatment could have been offered was

TABLE 8.4. Prevalence and Recognition of Suicidal Thoughts and Attempts in Youths Attending Consolidated and Comparison Clinics in a 12-Month Period

Type of clinic[a]	Prevalence of problem reported in interview		If reported, told clinic %	If reported, found in chart %
	n	%		
Consolidated, NH[b] (n = 751)	164	22	27	15
Consolidated, S[c] (n = 412)	70	17	23	16
Comparison, NH[b] (n = 620)	104	17	<1	<1

[a] Numbers are restricted to those who visited the clinics at least once in the 12-month period between Wave I and Wave II.
[b] Neighborhood- or hospital-based.
[c] School-based.

much smaller than the number who reported the problem in the research interview.

Because of the low proportion of suicidal youths who were recognized, an effort was made to see whether some index of severity might improve our ability to detect them. This was done in two ways. First, only those youths with persisting suicidal symptoms were examined. These were the ones who reported thoughts of committing suicide or a suicide attempt at both interviews. The results shown in Table 8.4 were not significantly changed. Second, we examined the comorbidity of suicidal symptoms with other psychiatric symptoms, such as alcohol and drug abuse, antisocial behavior, and depressive symptoms (unrelated to suicidal ideation). In this instance, the number who told someone at the clinic was increased to nearly 50%, and somewhat more evidence of documentation in the medical records was found. Nevertheless, half or more of suicidal youths were still not being detected.

Conclusions

The frequency of suicidal ideation and behavior varies considerably in adolescents. Depending on the types of questions asked and the individuals' sex, the number of youths considered to be at risk for suicide could range from 25% to less than 1%. It is well established that females have higher rates of attempted suicide than males, but variation in suicidal ideation by sex is less clear. Unfortunately, our sample of adolescent medical patients provided too low a proportion of males to permit confident comparisons with females. In fact, the low proportion of males using neighborhood and hospital-based health clinics requires that efforts to prevent or treat suicidal behavior in this group develop a different approach to sampling. School-based clinics are an alternative, but males using such facilities are probably not those at highest risk.

Our sample of patients using urban public health facilities also selected different strata of the general population by race. Black youths were more closely representative of the communities in which these clinics operated than were white youths. The selection of a higher-risk sample of white youths is at least partially explained by the fact that many had left their families because of unbearable conflict and tension. There may also be reasons other than sampling bias that account for differences in the rate of suicidal ideation and behavior, since representative samples of persons completing suicide show higher rates in whites than in blacks.

With a small set of questions regarding psychiatric symptoms, drug use, and social circumstances, over 80% of teenagers who will make a suicide attempt over a 12-month period can be identified. Despite the fact that suicidal youths are not difficult to detect, clinicians in primary care settings appeared to be inefficient in recognizing youths who reported suicidal ideation or behavior in our interviews. Even when these youths experienced persistent suicidal thoughts or multiple attempts, less than a quarter of them were identified in their medical records.

It is not apparent from our study what accounts for the low identification of suicidal youths. Perhaps suicidal thoughts and behavior are most readily recognized when they occur in the context of other psychiatric or social problems. The next step in clinical research strategies should be a more direct effort to assess what information clinicians use in evaluating the need for intervention in suicidal youths. So far in this project, we have not been able to probe this question in much depth, because only a small number of youths reporting suicidal ideation or behavior in our interview have had these problems acknowledged and documented by their care providers.

References

Blum, R. Contemporary threats to adolescent health in the United States. *Journal of the American Medical Association*, 1987, *257*, 3390–3395.

Lear, J. G., Foster, H. W., & Wylie, W. G. Development of community-based health services for adolescents at risk for sociomedical problems. *Journal of Medical Education*, 1985, *60*, 777–785.

Robins, L. N. Suicide attempts in adolescent medical patients. In *Proceedings of NIMH/ CDC Conference on Youth Suicide*. Rockville, Md.: National Institute of Mental Health, in press.

Robins, L. N., Helzer, J. E., Croughan, J., & Ratcliff, K. S. The NIMH Diagnostic Interview Schedule: Its history, characteristics and validity. *Archives of General Psychiatry*, 1981, *38*, 381–389.

Stiffman, A. R., Earls, F., Robins, L., & Jung, K. Problems and help-seeking in high-risk adolescent patients of health clinics. *Journal of Adolescent Health Care*, 1988, *9*, 305–309.

9

Evaluation of Suicide Risk among Youths in Community Settings

Mary J. Rotheram-Borus
Columbia University College of Physicians and Surgeons

Suicide among youths has increased threefold over the last 10 years (Frazier, 1985). The psychiatric community and other professionals who are likely to be in contact with suicidal youths (teachers, recreation leaders, staff members in runaway shelters, and ministers) want to be able to identify and to intervene with suicidal youths. The goals of this chapter are to review the screening procedures that have been developed to evaluate youths at high risk for suicide; to suggest strategies for increasing the utility of such procedures; and to outline challenges that still face researchers attempting to validate risk evaluation procedures in community settings.

Existing Strategies for Evaluating Risk

Researchers have generally focused on the evaluation of suicidal risk among adults, typically already identified suicide attempters. The unique developmental characteristics of adolescents suggest that the findings with adults cannot be transferred directly to adolescents (Trautman & Rotheram-Borus, 1987). Moreover, as Pallis, Barraclough, Levy, Jenkins, and Sainsbury (1982) have shown, risk factors are even specific to subgroups of adult attempters. Despite a lack of substantial empirical support and concern about developmental differences, the adult literature has served as the model for the few studies currently being conducted with children (Pfeffer, 1984; Shaffer & Gould, 1985). Four basic strategies have been applied to the evaluation of suicidal risk: matching the social demographics of suicidal persons; conducting psychometric assessments;

This chapter was prepared with the support of the Office of Human Development Services Grant No. 90CY0412/01 and National Institute of Mental Health Contract No. 278-85-0026.

identifying psychological profiles of high risk; and identifying specific
high-risk groups.

Matching the Social Demographics of Suicidal Persons

Researchers have used three strategies to generate profiles of suicidal
adults: (1) psychological autopsies of completed suicides, and longitudinal
follow-up of suicide attempters (Ettlinger, 1975); (2) the construction
of risk indices based on circumstances surrounding a suicide attempt
(e.g., isolation and precautions against discovery) and the intent of the
attempter (Pierce, 1977); and (3) demographic factors (Pallis et al.,
1982). Although studies of completed adolescent suicides are only currently being conducted (Brent, 1986; Gould & Shaffer, 1986), the preliminary results of these studies suggest the utility of psychological
autopsies with youths (see Brent, chapter 4, this volume). Researchers
report considerable overlap with the adult literature; yet there appear
to be subpatterns that are related specifically to the adolescent developmental process. For example, the Pierce (1977) suicide risk index
was not related to hopelessness and depression among adolescents
(Rotheram-Borus & Trautman, 1986), as is typically found in adults
(Dyer & Kreitman, 1984).

Conducting Psychometric Assessments

The Minnesota Multiphasic Personality Inventory (MMPI) and semantic differential scales (Beck, Schuyler, & Herman, 1974; Blau, Farberow, & Grayson, 1967) have been used to indirectly assess risk for
suicide. The findings using these instruments have often been inconsistent. For example, some investigators report that the MMPI is quite
helpful (Foster, 1975), and others report that it is not (Tarter, Templer,
& Perley, 1975). In general, analysis of response patterns, rather than
scores, has been the most useful approach (Clopton, Pallis, & Birtchnell,
1979; Clopton, Post, & Larde, 1984; Leonard, 1977). There have been
no studies, however, cross-validating the prediction of suicides on the
basis of psychometric assessments.

Identifying Psychological Profiles

Identifying psychological profiles of high risk is the only strategy
that has been employed with children (Pfeffer, Conte, Plutchik, & Jerrett,

1979). Depression (Cohen-Sandler, Berman, & King, 1982; Matson, Seese, & Hawkins, 1969; Pfeffer, 1981; Trautman, Rotheram, Chatlos, & Sdrugias, 1984) and anger are the most frequently reported patterns among suicidal children. The strength of the association between suicide and depression in children is unclear: Reports have varied from 25% to 65% across investigators. The base rate of depressed feelings among adolescents is high (Teri, 1982); however, a method of diagnosing depression in children and adolescents has only recently been established (Kazdin, 1981; Puig-Antich, 1980), perhaps accounting for earlier disparities in rates. Furthermore, clinicians have disputed whether hyperactive or delinquent behaviors mask depression in adolescents (Cytryn & McKnew, 1972; Poznanski & Zrull, 1970; Toolan, 1962). In fact, the psychiatric community has begun to examine whether suicide is associated more closely with anger than with depression (Kovacs & Beck, 1977; Shaffer & Gould, 1985).

Other psychological factors have also been proposed to evaluate suicidal risk. These include intense emotional reactions, low frustration tolerance, and suggestibility (Shaw & Schelkun, 1965); borderline psychotic states (Ackerly, 1967); family stressors (Sabbath, 1969, 1971); parental suicidal behavior (Shaffer, 1974); family disorganization (Morrison & Collier, 1969); and marital discord (Lukranowicz, 1968).

Psychological profiles as a means of identifying suicide risk lead to overprediction. For example, when extensive psychological batteries were administered to psychiatrically disturbed, hospitalized latency-age children to identify risk factors (Pfeffer et al., 1979), 72% appeared at high risk of suicide. Such high estimates of risk lead one to question how to distinguish which psychiatrically disturbed children will and will not attempt or complete suicide.

Identifying Specific High-Risk Groups

Rather than focusing on risk in the general population, another strategy focuses on subgroups of adolescents who appear to be at high risk (Shaffer & Gould, 1986): suicide attempters, runaways, pregnant teens, and teens with HIV-positive antibody. For example, approximately 46% of the completed child and adolescent suicides in one study had been preceded by threats or attempts of suicide (Shaffer, 1974). We can estimate that half of the adolescent suicide attempters will repeat the attempt (Stanley & Barter, 1970), although the estimates vary from 31% to 50% (Chowdburry, Hicks, & Kreitman, 1973; Greer & Bagley, 1971; Kreitman, 1977; McIntire & Angle, 1972). Although there are few follow-up studies on adolescent attempters, the existing research identifies adolescent attempters as a group at risk for a variety of psychiatric problems, suggesting that interventions might be particularly cost-effective. Barter, Swaback, and Todd (1968) found 42% of hospitalized attempters to have inadequate peer relations and 28% to be performing inadequately in school 22 months later. This is consistent with the findings of Cohen-Sandler et al. (1982), who judged 40% to have below-average social and behavioral adjustment 1.5 years after the attempt.

Similar patterns are reported for other identified subgroups. Thirty percent of adolescent runaways in one study had attempted suicide, and an additional 28% had active suicidal ideations (Shaffer & Caton, 1983). By concentrating on youths who have previously attempted suicide, on runaways, and/or on other high-risk groups, one can tailor intervention efforts to the needs of specific populations being targeted. For example, evaluation procedures that involve families are not particularly useful for runaways, 40% of whom do not have families. Therefore, assessments of runaways require a focus on other treatment-related factors.

However, targeting populations does not reduce the problem of falsely identifying as suicidal adolescents who are not. As there are estimated to be 65,000 runaways a year in the United States, how can one determine who among this population is at high risk for suicide, or when it might occur? This calls for a redefinition of what is to be evaluated.

Redefining Suicide Risk and Imminent Danger

Problems with Evaluating Risk

There are a number of problems involved in each of the existing statistically based strategies for evaluating suicidal risk:

1. Developmental differences between adults and adolescents are likely to yield different predictors in suicide risk profiles for each group. There are no data available on which to match adolescent attempters to completers, and few data available based on psychometric assessments of youths. Even when such data become available, it is likely that their predictive ability in developing screens for suicidal risk will be low, as has been the case with adults (Motto & Heilbron, 1976).

2. Suicide risk is inevitably overpredicted, given the base rates for suicide in the population and the differential consequences for clinicians who make false-negative (evaluating a suicidal adolescent as nonsuicidal) and false-positive predictions (Pallis et al., 1982; Rosen, 1954; Rotheram-Borus, 1987).

3. Suicide risk is based on the environmental stressors and social supports available to youths. Each of the current evaluation strategies has been based on a model of individual psychopathology. Epidemiologists (Braucht, 1979; Carstairs & Brown, 1958; Phillips & McCulloch, 1966) have demonstrated that person and environmental variables must be considered in evaluating suicidal risk. For example, suicide attempters have been found to be different from others in the catchment area in which they live. Although the importance of situational contexts in clinical prediction has long been asserted (Meehl, 1954; Mischel, 1968), none of the methods of risk evaluation consider or specify environmental contexts in which an adolescent is likely to be suicidal. Similarly, researchers have not considered that the adolescent may present quite differently in the evaluation setting than in the situations likely to elicit the suicidal act. At best, there should be a correlation of about .40 in behavior across settings (Bem & Allen, 1974).

4. Suicide risk is a time-limited concept. Suicide risk is linked to highly unstable emotional states of depression and anger (Shaffer & Fisher, 1984). Therefore, clinicians are only capable of making short-term predictions regarding suicide risk; this is similar to the limits of their ability to predict other high-risk behaviors, such as violence (Monahan, 1981).

5. Evaluators in community settings are not likely to have sophisticated clinical skills. The majority of the screening methods that have been evaluated base a clinical judgment on the results of psychological testing. In many community settings, such as schools, runaway shelters, police departments, or community mental health centers, staff members are likely to be overburdened and without the skills and resources to conduct psychometric evaluations. It is therefore critical to streamline as much as possible the accurate identification of suicidal risk. To aid in this process, it is necessary to re-establish the difference between "imminent danger to self" and "suicidal risk."

Suicidal Risk versus a Model of Imminent Danger

Elsewhere (Rotheram-Borus, 1987), I suggest that attempts to predict risk of suicide be limited to those children and adolescents in "imminent danger." Imminent danger of suicide is an evaluation that can only be made in temporal proximity to the act, with an evaluation of the youth's emotional state, and with reference to specific situational contexts. "Suicide risk" is a global term that can be used to select populations of youths who may potentially become an imminent danger to themselves at some future point, but for whom overprediction is inevitable, and

for whom cost-effectiveness of prevention efforts is low. Whereas statisticians might facilitate the selection of individuals or groups of youths who are suicide risks, clinical judgments are the basis for evaluating imminent danger (Meehl, 1954).

Assessing imminent danger for suicide leads one to develop evaluation procedures that focus on "current" ability to cope in a nonsuicidal manner, with a recognition that this ability will fluctuate with time. Procedures must consider environmental stressors and supports, as well as identify situational contexts that are likely to elicit suicidal behavior. Evaluations must also be brief, must yield low rates of false positives and of false negatives, and must be easily administered by staff members in community settings (school counselors, runaway shelter staff).

One Potential Evaluation of Imminent Danger

Elsewhere, I (Rotheram-Borus, 1987) have proposed a two-tier evaluation procedure for suicide risk and imminent danger, based on a cognitive–behavioral model of assessment and intervention. A flow chart describing the process is presented in Figure 9.1. First, an evaluator assesses suicide risk on the basis of a youth's background: (1) history of depression; (2) history of antisocial behavior; (3) past suicide attempt; (4) a past attempt using a method other than ingestion, which places the youth at higher risk; (5) suicides by close peers and other family members; (6) frequent use of drugs and/or alcohol; and (7) current suicidal ideation and/or plans. A youth with current ideation and/or plans, or one with more than five risk factors, is considered potentially to be in imminent danger, and his or her ability to cope in a nonsuicidal manner is then assessed.

The evaluator determines whether the youth can (1) deliver compliments to self and others, demonstrating hopefulness about the future; (2) identify a range of situations and feelings using Wolpe's (1958) Subjective Units of Discomfort Scale (some situations will be potentially suicide-eliciting, and others will be quite neutral); (3) identify suicide-eliciting situations and make concrete plans regarding alternative actions in such stressful situations; (4) identify three alternative sources of social support and community resources that the youth would feel comfortable about contacting when under stress; and (5) write a commitment for no suicidal behavior in a specified period of time.

This evaluation procedure was utilized by intake workers to assess risk in 518 runaway youths at four runaway shelters in New York City (Rotheram-Borus & Bradley, 1987). The intake workers, primarily

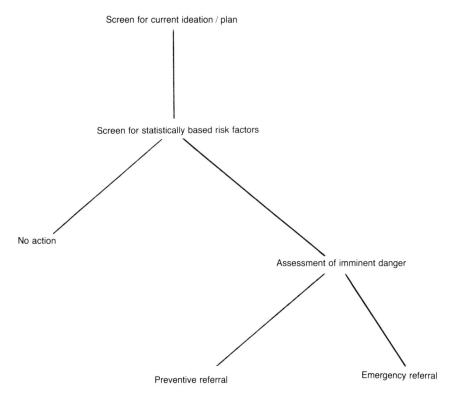

Figure 9.1.   Flowchart of triage process.

bachelor's-level paraprofessionals, gave the youths risk ratings similar
to those used by psychiatric personnel and research staff. The runaways
were 16 years old on average, half male, and predominantly from minority
groups; half were enrolled in school. Runaways reported a number of
stressful problems: 85% had serious family conflict; 10% had been thrown
out of their homes; 44% had no permanent housing; 23% reported
parental abuse; 13% were working as prostitutes; and 19% had medical
problems.

On the basis of background variables, 59% of these runaway youths
would be considered at high risk for suicide: 30% had previously attempted suicide; 2% had made more than one attempt; 16% had tried
a method other than ingestion; 28% reported active suicide ideation
and/or planning in the last week; 33% had a history of antisocial behavior;
44% had a history of depression; 12% reported suicide or suicide attempts
by family members; and 11% reported suicide attempts or completed
suicide by peers. These reports were highly consistent with an epide-

miological study with runaways (Shaffer & Caton, 1983), except in runaways' reports of drug and alcohol use. However, acknowledging drug and alcohol use at intake is likely to result in nonadmittance to a runaway shelter.

When the second-stage criterion of imminent danger was assessed, fewer than 2% were referred to psychiatrists for evaluation. Almost all youths were able to act in a nonsuicidal manner, completing the five tasks outlined above. Those youths who failed the tasks (i.e., those who appeared from the screening procedure to be in imminent danger of suicide) were evaluated by psychiatrists and hospitalized for suicidality in all but one case. The number of suicide attempts in the shelters over a period of 1 year dropped dramatically from 16 in a 3-month baseline to 2 in the year following staff training.

This procedure appears to be one approach for defining suicide risk that gives consideration to levels of risk, current emotional states, situational contexts, timing, and level of staff skills in community settings. As is the case for other risk evaluation procedures, however, there is no analysis of the predictive validity of such a procedure.

Research Issues

The suicide screening procedure outlined above addresses many of the problems that confront clinicians attempting to identify potentially suicidal youths. It does not require sophisticated clinical skills; environmental stressors and support are considered; time is included as a dimension; and the percentage of youths identified as potentially in imminent danger is low.

Simultaneously, when the definitions of imminent danger and suicide risk are clarified, a number of problems in the validation of suicide screens are highlighted. This cognitive–behavioral conceptualization of risk assumes that imminent danger for suicide fluctuates over time within a subgroup of adolescents at high risk (see Figure 9.2). Assessment of risk depends on situational contexts, family and social support resources, and access to lethal weapons, as well as on the personality and background variables that are typically assessed.

Predictive validity of any screening instrument for youths necessitates repeated measures of functioning in a longitudinal design of an extremely large sample—a design that includes nonintervention with those who may be at high risk for suicide. It is likely that such a study would be both fiscally and ethically unfeasible. To improve the cost–benefit ratio, studies of depression and other psychiatric disorders are most likely to have indirect benefits for the prediction of suicide risk. Such studies

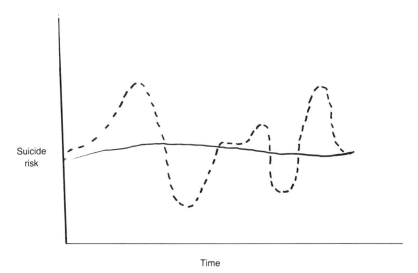

Time

Figure 9.2. The hypothetical relationship between suicide risk and imminent danger of suicide. Solid line, suicide risk based on statistical and background factors; dashed line, imminent danger of suicide.

will potentially provide accurate predictors of the covariates of suicide risk and states of imminent danger of youth suicide.

Prevention researchers are faced with quite different problems than are interventionists. The low incidence of suicide in the general population makes screening of all youths an impractical goal. A researcher would need a sample size of 15,000 to potentially achieve a sample of 150, and the power would be too low with even that sample size to estimate the most important predictors of youth suicide.

The best strategy for identifying youths at high risk appears to be to limit individual evaluations to those in high-risk groups—runaways, pregnant teens, suicide attempters, and teens who are HIV-positive (Shaffer & Gould, 1986). It appears that it is most important to use procedures for evaluating imminent danger for suicide with these groups. A cognitive–behavioral model would suggest that screening among high-risk groups focus on identifying suicide-eliciting situations for these youths and on increasing coping skills in stressful situations. In a strategy of evaluating imminent danger, researchers must validate clinical evaluations that are time-limited—a difficult task (Monahan, 1984). Such a model has been adopted by researchers attempting to validate predictions of violence (Monahan, 1981, 1984). Like suicide, violence is a rare behavior, and the consequences to the evaluator for false-negative and false-positive assessments are very different. It may be useful for researchers interested in suicide to borrow from those conducting research on violence.

Summary

Identifying youths in imminent danger of suicide and in need of emergency psychiatric services is a difficult task. Although clinicians have often described the psychiatric profile of youths at risk for suicide, there is little empirical evidence of successful strategies for identifying suicidal risk. Researchers are faced with a number of problems when attempting to validate risk evaluation procedures: Suicide risk profiles vary with age and developmental stage; there appear to be several patterns or subtypes of suicidal patterns; suicidality depends on one's current emotional state; evaluators are likely to be biased in the direction of overestimating risk and are not likely to have extensive clinical training; imminent danger for suicide is time-limited; and a youth's risk will depend on surrounding environmental stressors and supports.

These considerations force researchers to assume a strategic approach in defining levels of suicide risk and imminent danger of suicide. An example of a potential strategy for identifying risk among youths is outlined in this chapter. Although this strategic approach appears useful, researchers continue to be faced with major problems in validating such procedures. Determining the predictive validity of potential suicide screening procedures requires researchers to evaluate and to follow longitudinally a large sample of youths, while deliberately refraining from intervening to help those youths who appear to be in crisis.

References

Acklerly, W. C. Latency age children who threaten or attempt to kill themselves. *Journal of the American Academy of Child Psychiatry*, 1967, *6*, 242–261.

Barter, J., Swaback, D., & Todd, D. Adolescent suicide attempters: A follow up study of hospitalized patients. *Archives of General Psychiatry*, 1968, *19*, 523–527.

Beck, A. T., Schuyler, D., & Herman, I. Development of suicide intent scales. In A. T. Beck, H. L. P. Resnik, & A. J. Lettier (Eds.), *The prediction of suicide*. Bowie, Md: Charles Press, 1974.

Bem, D., & Allen, A. On predicting some of the people some of the time: The search for cross-situational consistence in behavior. *Psychological Review*, 1974, *81*, 506–520.

Blau, K. P., Farberow, N. L., & Grayson, H. M. The semantic differential as an indicator of suicidal behavior and tendencies. *Psychological Reports*, 1967, *21*, 609–612.

Braucht, G. Interactional analysis of suicidal behavior. *Journal of Consulting and Clinical Psychology*, 1979, *47*, 653–669.

Brent, D. *A study of psycho-autopsies among adolescent suicide attempters*. New York: William T. Grant Foundation, 1986.

Carstairs, G. M., & Brown, G. W. A census of psychiatric cases in two contrasting communities. *Journal of Mental Science*, 1958, *104*, 72–81.

Chowdburry, N., Hicks, R. C., & Kreitman, N. Evaluation of an aftercare service for parasuicide attempted suicide patients. *Social Psychiatry*, 1973, *8*, 67–81.

Clopton, J. R., Pallis, D. J., & Birtchnell, J. MMPI profile patterns of suicide attempters. *Journal of Consulting and Clinical Psychology*, 1979, *47*, 135–139.

Clopton, J. R., Post, R. D., & Larde, J. Identification of suicide attempters by means of MMPI profiles. *Journal of Clinical Psychology*, 1984, *31*, 868–871.

Cohen-Sandler, R., Berman, R., & King, R. A. A follow-up study of hospitalized suicidal children. *Journal of the American Academy of Child Psychiatry*, 1982, *214*, 398–403.

Cytryn, L., & McKnew, D. H., Jr. Proposed classification of childhood depression. *American Journal of Psychiatry*, 1972, *129*, 149–155.

Dyer, J. A. T., & Kreitman, N. Hopelessness, depression, suicidal intent in parasuicide. *British Journal of Psychiatry*, 1984, *144*, 127–133.

Ettlinger, R. Evaluation of suicide prevention after attempted suicide. *Acta Psychiatrica Scandinavica*, 1975 (Suppl. 260), 5–135.

Foster, L. L. MMPI correlates of suiciding patients. *Newsletter for Research in Mental Health and Behavioral Sciences*, 1975, pp. 9–10.

Frazier, S. *Preventing youth suicide: A collaborative effort*. Paper presented at the National Conference on Youth Suicide, Washington, D.C., June 1985.

Gould, M., & Shaffer, D. The impact of suicide in television movies: Evidence of imitation. *New England Journal of Medicine*, 1986, *315*, 690–694.

Greer, S., & Bagley, C. Effects of psychiatric intervention in attempted suicide. *British Medical Journal*, 1971, *i*, 310–312.

Kazdin, A. Assessment techniques for childhood depression. *Journal of the American Academy of Child Psychiatry*, 1981, *20*, 358–375.

Kovacs, M., & Beck, A. T. An empirical clinical approach towards a definition of childhood depression. In J. G. Schulterbrandt & A. Raskin (Eds.), *Depression in children*. New York: Raven Press, 1977.

Kreitman, N. *Parasuicide*. New York: Wiley, 1977.

Leonard, C. V. The MMPI as a suicide predictor. *Journal of Consulting and Clinical Psychology*, 1977, *45*, 367–377.

Lukranowicz, N. Attempted suicide in children. *Acta Psychiatrica Scandinavica*, 1968, *44*, 415–435.

Matson, A., Seese, L. R., & Hawkins, J. W. Suicidal behavior as a child psychiatric emergency. *Archives of General Psychiatry*, 1969, *20*, 100–109.

McIntire, M., & Angle, C. R. Psychological "biopsy" in self-poisoning of children and adolescents. *American Journal of Diseases of Children*, 1972, *126*, 42–46.

Meehl, P. *Clinical versus statistical prediction: A theoretical analysis and a review of the evidence*. Minneapolis: University of Minnesota Press, 1954.

Mischel, W. *Personality and assessment*. New York: Wiley, 1968.

Monahan, J. *Predicting violent behavior*. Beverly Hills, Calif.: Sage, 1981.

Monahan, J. The prediction of violent behavior. *American Journal of Psychiatry*, 1984, *141*, 10–15.

Morrison, G. C., & Collier, J. G. Family treatment approaches to suicidal children and adolescents. *American Journal of Psychiatry*, 1969, *8*, 140–153.

Motto, J. A., & Heilbron, D. C. Development and validation of scales for estimation of suicide risk. In E. S. Shneidman (Ed.), *Suicidology: Contemporary developments*. New York: Grune & Stratton, 1976.

Pallis, D. J., Barraclough, B. M., Levy, A. B., Jenkins, J. S., & Sainsbury, P. Estimating suicide risk among attempted suicides: The development of new clinical scales. *British Journal of Psychiatry*, 1982, *141*, 37–44.

Pfeffer, C. R. The family system of suicidal children. *American Journal of Psychotherapy*, 1981, *353*, 330–341.

Pfeffer, C. R. Clinical assessment of suicidal behavior in children. In H. Sudak, A. Ford, & N. Rushforth (Eds.), *Suicide in the young*. Littleton, MA: John Wright–PSG, 1984.

Pfeffer, C. R., Conte, H. R., Plutchik, R., & Jerrett, I. Suicidal behavior in latency-age children: An empirical study. *Journal of the American Academy of Child Psychiatry*, 1979, *19*, 679–692.

Phillips, A. E., & McCulloch, J. W. The use of social indices in psychiatric epidemiology. *British Journal of Preventive and Social Medicine*, 1966, *20*, 122–126.

Pierce, D. W. suicidal intent in self injury. *British Journal of Psychiatry*, 1977, *130*, 377–385.

Poznanski, E., & Zrull, J. P. Child depression. *Archives of General Psychiatry*, 1970, *23*, 8–15.

Puig-Antich, J. Affective disorders in childhood. *Psychiatry Clinics of North America*, 1980, *3*, 403–424.

Rosen, D. H. Detection of suicide patients: An example of some limitations in the prediction of infrequent events. *Journal of Consulting Psychology*, 1954, *18*, 397–403.

Rotheram-Borus, M. Evaluation of imminent danger for suicide among youth. *American Journal of Orthopsychiatry*, 1987, *57*, 102–110.

Rotheram-Borus, M., & Bradley, J. Evaluation of imminent danger and suicide risk. In M. Rotheram-Borus & J. Bradley (Eds.), *Planning to live: Evaluating and treating suicidal teens in community settings*. Tulsa: University of Oklahoma Press (in press).

Rotheram-Borus, M. J., & Trautman, P. *Cognitive behavior therapy with suicidal adolescents: A therapy training manual*. Unpublished manuscript, 1986.

Sabbath, J. C. The suicidal adolescent: The expendable child. *Journal of the American Academy of Child Psychiatry*, 1969, *8*, 272–289.

Sabbath, J. C. The role of the parents in adolescent suicidal behavior. *Acta Paedopsychiatrica*, 1971, *38*, 221–220.

Shaffer, D. Suicide in childhood and early adolescence. *Journal of Child Psychology and Psychiatry*, 1974, *15*, 275–291.

Shaffer, D., & Caton, C. L. *Runaway and homeless youth in New York City*. New York: Ittleson Foundation, 1983.

Shaffer, D., & Fisher, P. The epidemiology of suicide in children and young adolescents. *Journal of the American Academy of Child Psychiatry*, 1984, *20*, 545–565.

Shaffer, D., & Gould, M. *A study of completed suicide in the greater New York area*. Study in progress, funded by the National Institute of Mental Health, 1985.

Shaffer, D., & Gould, M. *A study of completed and attempted suicide in adolescents*. Paper presented at the National Conference on Youth Suicide, Oakland, Calif., 1986.

Shaw, C. R., & Schelkun, R. F. suicidal behavior in children. *Psychiatry*, 1965, *28*, 157–168.

Stanley, E. J., & Barter, J. T. Adolescent suicidal behavior. *American Journal of Orthopsychiatry*, 1970, *40*, 87–96.

Tarter, R. E., Templer, D. I., & Perley, R. L. Social role orientation and pathological factors in suicide attempts of varying lethality. *Journal of Community Psychology*, 1975, *3*, 295–299.

Teri, L. The use of the beck depression inventory for adolescents. *Journal of Abnormal Child Psychology*, 1982, *10*, 277–284.

Toolan, J. M. Depression in children and adolescents. *American Journal of Orthopsychiatry*, 1962, *32*, 404–415.

Trautman, P., & Rotheram-Borus, M. Cognitive behavior therapy with children and adolescents. In F. Allen (Ed.), *American Psychiatric Press review of psychiatry* (Vol. 7). Washington, D.C.: American Psychiatric Press, 1987.

Trautman, P., Rotheram, M. J., Chatlos, C., & Sdrugias, V. *Differences among normal, psychiatrically disturbed, and suicide attempting adolescent females*. Paper presented at the meeting of the American Academy of Child Psychiatry, Toronto, 1984.

Wolpe, J. *Psychotherapy by reciprocal inhibition*. Stanford, Calif.: Stanford University Press, 1958.

___ ___dy of Suicidal Behavior in the Schools

Carol Z. Garrison, PhD
University of South Carolina

Little is known about suicidal behaviors in the youthful nonpsychiatric population. Most of the existing data have been derived from the study of (1) general mortality statistics; (2) youths who commit or attempt suicide while under psychiatric care; (3) psychological autopsies of consecutive suicides in a given geographical region; or (4) those attempted suicides reaching medical, police, or social service attention. These data do not provide information regarding what is occurring in the wider population, nor do they address the question of how many youths experience suicidal thoughts and behaviors but never seek professional help. Both are important issues, as studies suggest that only a fraction of young suicide attempters do in fact seek medical or other attention (Smith & Crawford, 1986). Information on the range of suicidal behavior in nonpatient populations can be important. Such data provide a perspective against which to evaluate suicidal behavior that occurs in both psychiatric and nonpsychiatric populations (Leonard & Flinn, 1972).

The study of suicidal behavior in school settings is one approach wherein an attempt is being made to gather data on so-called normative populations. The major goal of these studies has been to determine the frequency and determinants of suicidal ideas, threats, and attempts, as opposed to completions (though a group of studies has addressed the frequency with which college students commit suicide). The lack of focus on completed suicides has stemmed principally from the infeasibility of studying a low-frequency event in a cross-sectional or prospective fashion. The numbers of subjects required for such an approach is generally prohibitive. College students have predominated, though a few studies of adolescents and younger school-age children have been

Preparation of this chapter was supported in part by National Institute of Mental Health Contract No. 278-85-0026.

reported. Samples have usually included small groups of volunteers, and as such have not clearly represented any larger population. Only a few of the studies (those dealing with the precollege population) have provided information on the racial/ethnic characteristics of their participants, and most (the college studies) have grouped students of various levels and ages (both graduate and undergraduate) together. A cross-sectional approach, whereby subjects have been asked to report on current or past (anywhere from 1 week to lifetime) thoughts and behaviors, has been most common. The accuracy of self-report (usually anonymous) data and the possibility that subjects may forget important details or distort the nature of emotionally charged events are problems inherent to this approach. Although all the studies have focused on the same general area—that of suicidal thoughts and behaviors—the definition, categorization, and time frame of behaviors (as well as the year in which the investigations have occurred) have varied considerably, further raising the issue of the comparability of study results.

Studies of Suicidal Behavior in Precollege Students

Studies of suicidal behavior among elementary, middle, and high school students indicate increasing rates of such behavior with advancing school grade. Pfeffer, Zuckerman, Plutchik, and Mizruchi (1984) reported on a study of suicidal behavior in a randomly selected sample of 101 nonpatient school children (aged 6–12) from a large urban community. This study was unique in that it compared the sample of school children with a systematically studied group of child psychiatric inpatients (Pfeffer, Solomon, Plutchik, Mizruchi, & Weiner, 1982). The sample of school children, which had been matched by age, race, and sex distribution to the inpatient sample, included 71 males, 30 females, 76 whites, and 25 nonwhites. Data was collected by parental (usually mother) and child interviews. Suicidal behavior was assessed using the Spectrum of Suicidal Behavior Scale. Suicidal behavior was defined as thoughts or actions that might lead to death or serious injury of the child and was categorized into one of two groups: thoughts and threats or actions. The time frame for which these behaviors were reported is not clear.

Among the 101 school children, 8.9% evidenced suicidal ideas or threats, while 3% reported previous attempts. This 11.9% prevalence of suicidal tendencies among school children was significantly lower than the researchers' previous results for psychiatric inpatients (78.5%) and outpatients (33%) (Pfeffer, Conte, Plutchik, & Jerrett, 1979; Pfeffer et al., 1982). Although most of the suicidal tendencies among school children were ideas (thus, the major focus of this study was on children who showed suicidal ideas and who were not suicidal at all), among patients there was a near-equal distribution of ideas, threats, and attempts. No differences in suicide behavior scores were noted between girls and boys. Among the 12 children who had acknowledged suicidal tendencies, 7 had distinct ideas of a method.

Suicidal school children differed from nonsuicidal school children in having greater and more recent depressive symptomatology (though none had a diagnosed major depressive disorder), more suicidal impulses in their mothers, greater preoccupation with death, and greater tendency to use introjection as an ego defense. These factors were similar to those uncovered by a comparison of suicidal and nonsuicidal inpatients. The researchers concluded that suicidal behavior is not a usual phenomenon among school children, but that among those children in whom suicidal thoughts are detected, the variables identified above can be considered an index of suicidal risk.

Albert and Beck (1975) found the prevalence of suicidal ideation to be higher among a small sample of seventh- and eighth-graders than that reported by Pfeffer et al. (1982) for the younger children. These researchers administered the short form of the Beck Depression Inventory during class time to 63 students in a parochial school in suburban Philadelphia. All but one student were white; 27 were female and 36 were male. Eighty-two percent of the sample were living with both parents; the average number of siblings was five; and there was an even division between children of blue- and white-collar workers. Thirty-five percent of the sample acknowledged current suicidal ideation, with 30% endorsing the statement "I have thoughts of harming myself but would not carry them out," and 5% endorsing the statement "I feel I would be better off dead." In addition, over 30% of the sample scored above the cutoff point used to detect clinical depression in adults. The most serious problems noted by the students were social (42%), school (26%), home (18%), and independence (14%). The relationship between suicidal ideation and depression scores or the problems noted was not discussed.

Smith and Crawford (1986) studied suicidal behaviors among 313 high school students in the Midwest. Participants were enrolled in human relations classes at one of four public high schools and a private girls' school. The sample was 66% female and 88% white. Only two students declined to participate. Students completed a self-administered questionnaire comprised of the Beck Depression Inventory and a survey of behaviors thought to relate to suicide. The time frame assessed was not specified. In the analysis, the students were divided into four mutually exclusive groups: nonsuicidal (those who reported no suicidal ideation or behavior); ideators (those who considered suicide but never made a plan or an attempt); planners (those who felt suicidal enough to have developed a plan for killing themselves, but had never made an attempt); and attempters (Those who had made one or more past suicide attempts). The seriousness of reported attempts was appraised by the Lethality of Suicide Attempt Rating Scale (Smith, Conroy, & Ehler, 1984).

Sixty-three percent of students reported some ideation. Eleven percent ($n = 33$) reported making one or more attempts. Since females made 5.6 attempts for every 1 male attempt, adjusting estimates for the overrepresentation of females in this sample lowered the attempt figure to 8.4%. All but three of the attempts were rated as low in lethality. Given the findings, this study provided information about youngsters who make low-lethality attempts, but not about seriously suicidal persons. Only 12% of the attempters received medical treatment after their attempts, suggesting that most low-lethality adolescent suicide attempters will not be identified by medical contacts. Attempters reported more depressive symptomatology, more chaotic home environments, more problems with both parents, and the highest percentage of unpleasant changes in their lives. When these serious indicators were considered, planners and attempters resembled each other, as did ideators and nonsuicidal students.

Studies of Suicidal Behaviors in College Students

Most of the data regarding suicidal behaviors in school populations have come from studies of college students. Interest in this population has stemmed from the belief that suicidal behavior among college students is higher than among same-age noncollege peers—a contention most recently disputed by Schwartz and Reifler (1980) and discussed in a later section of this chapter.

In one of the earlier studies, Leonard and Flinn (1972) investigated the frequency of suicidal behavior among young persons in college ($n = 352$) and military populations ($n = 128$). Four different types of students (undergraduate psychology and music majors, graduate engineering students, and first- and second-year medical students) and Air Force basic trainees were included. Comparisons were made to a military psychiatric group ($n = 123$). The sample included 447 males and 156 females. Ninety percent of the subjects were under 25, with a median age of 19 for the military group and 21 for the students. No information was given regarding response rates. Data was collected via a group-administered questionnaire, the Suicidal Incidence Survey. No differentiation was made between past and present behavior, and no attempt was made to ascertain reasons underlying reported behavior.

Eighteen percent of students reported having moderate to serious suicidal impulses, including 10% who had made a suicide threat, gesture, or attempt, and 8% who had entertained serious suicidal intent but had committed no overt act. Fifty-nine percent of the student population reported experiencing suicidal behavior in others, 13% with suicidal behavior in relatives. Significant differences were found among the subgroups. Medical students reported the least suicidal behavior (5%), and psychology students reported the most (30%). The rate among engineering students (16%) closely resembled that of basic military trainees (18%). Forty-two percent of the military clinic group reported moderate or severe suicidal behavior sometime in their lives. Subgroup differences were more important than age and sex, suggesting that one's choice of occupation and the personality characteristics reflected therein may be more important in understanding suicidal behavior than general age and sex characteristics.

Mishara (1982; Mishara, Baker, & Mishara, 1976) has reported on two studies regarding suicidal behavior in college students. In both investigations, data were collected on the lifelong prevalence of suicidal behavior. In the first investigation (Mishara et al., 1976), 293 undergraduate students from three separate and geographically distant universities were surveyed. The sample included 193 females and 100 males recruited from psychology classes. Response rates and other demographic characteristics were not mentioned. Participants anonymously filled out a questionnaire that focused on lifetime suicidal behavior. Open-ended questions about attempts, thoughts, and methods were included. Fifteen percent of respondents reported a previous attempt (which in every case had occurred in the preceding 5 years), and 65% reported contemplating a suicide attempt on at least one occasion. A number (25%) of the contemplated suicides involved automobile accidents; this supports investigations suggesting that many automobile accidents are intentional or subintentional suicides. Also common were meticulously planned and carefully described procedures leading to certain death, with an explanatory remark at the end ("but I would never do it").

In a second study, Mishara (1982) recruited 140 students (56% response rate) enrolled in undergraduate psychology courses in the Boston area. Students completed and returned by mail an anonymous questionnaire distributed during class. Students were asked whether they had considered suicide themselves, or told anyone they were thinking of suicide. They were also asked to describe their own suicide attempts. The rate of suicide attempts (14%) approximated the rate of the earlier study (15%). Forty percent of the students indicated that they would try again. The researchers questioned the validity of their data, because of the low response rate (those who did not return the questionnaires may have had no suicidal or different suicidal experiences) and the equivocal accuracy of self-reports of retrospective emotionally charged situations.

Bernard and Bernard (1982) attempted to delineate the factors in college life responsible for suicidal behaviors. They surveyed via self-administered questionnaires 838 volunteers (including 81 graduate students) from the departments of home economics, psychology, sociology, and counseling in a large urban university. The questionnaire inquired into previous suicidal behavior, defining a threat as "having actually told someone you were considering taking your life" and an attempt as "actually having tried to take your life." Twenty percent ($n = 167$) reported threats or attempts or both. For analyses, these individuals were combined into a single group. Of the 167, 75 stated that the suicidal behavior had occurred while they were in college, but only 1 individual reported that the behavior had been noted by school officials. Social and family problems accounted for 75% of all attempts; academic pressures accounted for only 7%. The most commonly reported feeling associated with suicidal behavior was depression (46%). The investigators concluded that membership in the young adult group, where social and family problems are commonplace, is more important in understanding suicidal behavior than is anything peculiar about college students per se.

Schotte and Clum (1982) focused on the relationship among life stress, poor problem-solving skills, and suicidal behavior in 175 student volunteers (87 males and 88 females) enrolled in introductory psychology classes at a Southern university. The study was labeled and presented to students as a "suicide study." Suicide ideation was operationally defined by the subjects' affirmative response to several items concerning the presence of suicide ideation within the past month on a self-report adaptation of the Scale for Suicide Ideation (Beck, Kovacs, & Weissman, 1979). A total of 96 subjects (49 women and 47 men) met the criteria for ideation. Of these ideators, 65 (but no controls) then participated in an interview session. Among the ideators, the poor problem solvers under high stress were found to be significantly higher in suicide intent than any other group.

Addendum: Studies of Completed Suicides in College Students

The school studies discussed earlier in this chapter have utilized self-report data and have focused on suicidal ideas, threats, and attempts. Other investigations involving university populations have not relied on self-reported data of suicidal behavior, but have looked specifically at completed suicides. Reports on suicide rates for students in American, British, and Canadian colleges appeared as early as 1937 (Raphael, Power, & Berridge, 1937). Since 1951, published reports, most of which have primarily or exclusively relied on the records of college or university health services for data, have suggested that the incidence of suicide among college students is higher (perhaps 50% so) than that found among a comparison population of those not in college (Seiden, 1969). Subsequent researchers have attempted to delineate those factors in college life contributing to this disparity (Creswell, 1972; Knott, 1973; Seiden, 1966).

Schwartz and Reifler (1980) recently questioned the accuracy with which the suicide rates for college students have been determined and generalized. These researchers summarized the data on the incidence of suicide at American colleges from 1920 to 1961. Several features of their summary are relevant. First, the sample of colleges reporting has been small ($n = 6$) and hardly representative. Two-thirds of the suicides came from two all-male schools, so few data on women are available. Random years were not selected for study; rather, in most cases, an unusually high rate of suicide in a brief interval seemed to prompt investigation. As such, study intervals are thought not to be representative, but rather to overestimate the general rate for a given institution. Finally, the number of suicides reported for half the studies has been so small that confidence limits surrounding the estimates have been large. The definition of who should be designated *students* at risk (all those at risk or just full-time students?), the definition of the interval when suicide by a person designated at risk should be considered a student suicide (just during the academic year, or during vacations and summer too?), the thoroughness of the procedures used to identify student suicides (one estimate of the accuracy of health service records as a source of data about student suicide is 70%), and the appropriate comparison group (census data suggest that among the white population, 40–50% of 18- to 19-year-olds and 20% of 20- to 24-year-olds are presently enrolled in college) are additional concerns raised by these researchers.

In an attempt to address these issues systematically, Schwartz and Reifler (1980) reported data obtained for 1971–1976 through the Mental Health Annual Program Survey of the American College Health Association. Questionnaires were mailed to 400 health services located at 2- and 4-year universities. Only 53 of the target institutions responded and were included in analyses. The number of student suicides were derived from the answer given by respondents to the question, "How many known suicides occurred among students during the reporting year?" Demographic characteristics of the students at risk were carefully delineated. Results indicated that student suicides occurred less frequently than suicides among the comparison group. A total of 116 suicides and a total of 1,663,000 student-years at risk were reported. These figures yield a rate of 7 suicides per 100,000 college students (95% confidence interval = 5.8–8.5). A suicide rate of 17.3 (95% confidence interval = 16.7–17.9) was found for a sex-matched comparison group of white males and females in the 20–24 age range. The researchers suggest that it may be more appropriate, although not without problems, to generalize from this sample of 53 institutions than from the experience of 6 select schools. Alternately, these results provide some evidence supporting the conjecture that the frequency of student suicide may be notably different at different institutions.

Using an approach similar to that of Schwartz and Reifler (1980), Rockwell, Rockwell, and Core (1981) surveyed all (116) U.S. medical schools to ascertain the frequency with which medical students attempted suicide, completed suicide, and sought psychiatric treatment. Data were requested on the classes graduating or expecting to graduate in 1974 through 1981. Usable responses were received from 88 schools, who reported a total of 52 suicides. Of these 88 schools, 52 reported no suicides, 25 reported one suicide, and 11 schools reported multiple suicides. The annual suicide rate for male students was 16 per 100,000, a rate comparable to that of age-mates in the national population. The rate for female students (19 per 100,000) surpassed that of the male students and was three to four times that of their age-mates. Seventy-six percent of the suicides were committed by sophomore and junior students, and 50% were committed in November, December, or January. Fewer than 30% of the schools provided estimates of the number of students receiving psychiatric treatment; estimates ranged from 0% to 43%. A total of 54 suicide attempts were reported, giving an attempt-to-completion ratio of approximately 1:1. Usual minimum rates of attempts to completion are 7:1 or 8:1. In addition, one might speculate that the nonresponding schools were more likely than responding schools to have had suicides.

One last investigation of completed suicide is noteworthy. Paffenbarger and Asnes (1966) attempted to identify in-college characteristics predictive of subsequent suicide. These researchers compared the college academic and medical records of 225 male suicides, from a cohort of over 41,000 individuals having attended one of two Ivy League universities between 1926 and 1950, with 450 controls matched for year and school of attendance. The sample included both undergraduate and graduate students. Death notification was obtained from the alumni office and included deaths occurring through 1965. Identification of suicides was based on death certificate data. A number of physical, sociocultural, and psychological characteristics differentiated eventual suicides from their surviving classmates. The strongest indicators were psychological traits. Other characteristics seemed important chiefly through their psychological implications. Outstanding among the psychological precursors of eventual suicide were worry, self-consciousness, and a complex of anxiety–depression traits. In addition, the role of the father assumed special prominence, since paternal deprivation was a significant predictor and maternal loss was not.

Summary and Conclusion

The studies reviewed indicate that suicidal behavior is infrequent among school children (12%), but increases progressively among junior high (35%), high school (65%), and college students (50–65%). Though considerable, these values are lower than those of similar-age psychiatric populations. Estimates of the rate of actual attempts were 3% for elementary students, 11% for high school students, and 15–18% for college students. Most were low-lethality attempts for which medical or other attention was not sought. Accordingly, the vast majority of suicide attempts will not be uncovered by investigations dealing solely with clinical or medically identified populations. The most commonly identified correlates of suicidal behaviors included depressive symptoms, social problems, family disorganization and problems, life stress, and poor problem-solving skills. Academic problems were not as important.

These findings must be interpreted in light of methodological constraints. Response rates have been low, samples have been small, minorities have been underrepresented, nonstudents have been ignored, and volunteers of unreported characteristics have predominated. The representativeness of such groups is questionable. The definition and categorization of behaviors have varied considerably, making between-study comparisons difficult. The differences among thoughts, threats, and attempts (the most frequently used categories) have often not been taken into account. Rather, in analyses, these behaviors have been treated as if they were homogeneous entities and grouped together. Where attempters have been separated from ideators, they too have been treated as a single entity. Many deliberately survived attempts are manipulative and oriented toward the benefits the individual survivors expect. Such attempts probably differ substantially in nature from those attempts where survival is not intended. Understanding of this phenomenon could be enhanced by a comparison of the characteristics of those with high- and low-lethality attempts. Similarly, a third group of behaviors—that of chronic behavior patterns that potentially hasten death (alcoholism, drug abuse, self-mutilation, and risk taking)—has not been adequately addressed in terms of its relationship to more discrete suicidal events.

Data have generally been obtained via anonymous self-administered questionnaires. The accuracy of retrospective self-reports on emotionally laden events is suspect. Only in two instances have self-reported questionnaire data been validated via interviews with subjects alone or subjects and their families. The time frames on which the referent behaviors has been collected have included "last week," "last month," "last year," "lifetime," and not specified. The longer the interval between the occurrence of the behavior and the report, the greater the likelihood that some reporting inaccuracies may occur. A second time-related issue centers on the years in which these studies were conducted. The reports span a 15-year period, over which the rates of completed suicide have increased dramatically. Furthermore, Schwartz and Reifler (1980) suggest that the time interval included in most reports is not randomly selected. Rather, an unusually high rate of suicide catalyzes systematic study, thereby resulting in overestimation of true long-term rates.

The major focus of the investigations to date has been on identifying the frequency of suicide behavior, with less emphasis placed on identifying the correlates or predictors of these behaviors. Where correlates have been investigated, their definitions have been broad. Noticeably absent are data on drug and alcohol use. Also missing are data regarding past psychiatric diagnosis and family history of suicide behavior. In addition, the cross-sectional approach precludes definitive statements regarding the temporality of identified associations. Prospective studies are needed to provide this perspective.

In summary, knowledge in this area can be improved by employing larger populations of randomly selected individuals. The pooling of data from separate investigations with standardized research protocols could provide larger numbers of individuals with more discrete types of suicidal behaviors, allowing consideration of more homogeneous entities. Careful attention to the inclusion of minorities and precollege students, and to the reporting of the sample characteristics and the time frame in and on which data is collected, is needed. Clearer, more standardized definitions of the various categories of suicidal behavior would increase comparability across investigations. Validation of self-administered questionnaire responses through interviews and additional data sources could provide additional insights. A case–control approach, whereby all those reporting suicidal behaviors are compared with a sample of those reporting no such behavior on a screening questionnaire, could be used.

References

Albert, N., & Beck, A. T. Incidence of depression in early adolescence: A preliminary study. *Journal of Youth and Adolescence*, 1975, *4*, 302–307.

Beck, A. T., Kovacs, M., & Weissmann, A. Assessment of suicidal intention: The scale for suicide ideation. *Journal of Consulting and Clinical Psychology*, 1979, *47*, 343–352.

Bernard, J. L., & Bernard, M. Factors related to suicidal behavior among college students and the impact of institutional response. *Journal of College Student Personnel*, 1982, *23*, 409–413.

Creswell, F. A. Factors associated with radical behavior amongst students. *International Journal of Psychiatry*, 1972, *18*, 219–224.

Knott, J. E. Campus suicide in America. *Omega: Journal of Death and Dying*, 1973, *4*, 65–71.

Leonard, C. V., & Flinn, D. E. Suicidal ideation and behavior in youthful nonpsychiatric populations. *Journal of Consulting and Clinical Psychology*, 1972, *38*, 366–371.

Mishara, B. L. College students' experience with suicide and reactions to suicidal verbalizations: A model for prevention. *Journal of Community Psychology*, 1982, *10*, 142–150.

Mishara, B. L., Baker, A. H., & Mishara, T. T. The frequency of suicide attempts: A retrospective approach applied to college students. *American Journal of Psychiatry*, 1976, *133*, 841–844.

Paffenbarger, R. S., & Asnes, A. B. Chronic disease in former college students: III. Precursors of suicide in early and middle life. *American Journal of Public Health*, 1966, *56*, 1026–1036.

Pfeffer, C. R., Conte, H. R., Plutchik, R., & Jerrett, I. Suicidal behavior in latency-age children: An empirical study. *Journal of the American Academy of Child Psychiatry*, 1979, *18*, 679–692.

Pfeffer, C. R., Solomon, G., Plutchik, R., Mizruchi, M. S., & Weiner, A. Suicidal behavior in latency-age psychiatric inpatients: A replication and cross-validation. *Journal of the American Academy of Child Psychiatry*, 1982, *6*, 565–569.

Pfeffer, C. R., Zuckerman, S., Plutchik, R., & Mizruchi, M. S. Suicidal behavior in normal school children: A comparison with child psychiatric inpatients. *Journal of the American Academy of Child Psychiatry*, 1984, *23*, 416–423.

Raphael, T., Power, S. H., & Berridge, W. L. The question of suicide as a problem in college mental health. *American Journal of Orthopsychiatry*, 1937, *7*, 1–14.

Rockwell, F., Rockwell, D., & Core, N. Fifty-two medical student suicides. *American Journal of Psychiatry*, 1981, *138*, 198–201.

Schotte, D. E., & Clum, G. A. Suicidal ideation in a college population: A test of a model. *Journal of Consulting and Clinical Psychology*, 1982, *50*, 690–696.

Schwartz, A. J., & Reifler, C. B. Suicide among American college and university students from 1970–71 through 1975–76. *Journal of the American College Health Association*, 1980, *28*, 205–210.

Seiden, R. H. Campus tragedy: A study of student suicide. *Journal of Abnormal Psychology*, 1966, *71*, 389–399.

Seiden, R. H. Suicide among youth. *Bulletin of Suicidology*, December 1969 (Suppl.).

Smith, K., Conroy, R. W., & Ehler, B. D. Lethality of suicide attempt rating scale. *Suicide and Life-Threatening Behavior*, 1984, *14*, 215–242.

Smith, K., & Crawford, S. Suicidal behavior among normal high school students. *Suicide and Life-Threatening Behavior*, 1986, *16*, 313–325.

11

Epidemiologic Surveys as Tools for Studying Suicidal Behavior: A Review

Eve K. Mościcki, ScD, MPH
Division of Clinical Research, National Institute of Mental Health

The purpose of this chapter is to discuss the usefulness of epidemiologic surveys in studying suicidal behavior in the population. The chapter first presents a brief overview of the purpose and characteristics of the epidemiologic survey. It summarizes five relatively recent community surveys that estimated the prevalence and correlates of suicidal behaviors in various communities. Similarities and differences among studies are discussed, and explanations for some of the differences are proposed. Finally, I address the advantages, disadvantages, and perspective the epidemiologic survey provides in studying suicidal behavior.

One of the fundamental pursuits of epidemiology is the search for causes (Lilienfeld & Lilienfeld, 1980). To this end, epidemiologic surveys are conducted to estimate not only the rate of occurrence of a disease or disorder in a population, but also its correlates or risk factors. In general, a probability sample is drawn so as to be representative of the underlying population. The epidemiologist gathers data from the sample regarding the disorder of interest and other characteristics in a stan-

The Epidemiologic Catchment Area Program (ECA) is a series of five epidemiologic research studies performed by independent research teams in collaboration with staff at the Division of Biometry and Epidemiology of the National Institute of Mental Health (NIMH). The NIMH principal collaborators are Darrel A. Regier, MD, MPH; Ben Z. Locke, MSPH; and Jack D. Burke, Jr., MD, MPH. The NIMH project officer is William J. Huber. The principal investigators and coinvestigators from the five sites are as follows: Yale University, UO1 MH 34224—Jerome K. Myers, Myrna M. Weissman, Gary L. Tischler; Johns Hopkins University, UO1 MH 33870—Morton Kramer, Sam Shapiro, Ernest Gruenberg; Washington University, St. Louis, UO1 MH 33883—Lee N. Robins, John Helzer; Duke University, UO1 MH 35386—Dan Blazer, Linda K. George; University of California at Los Angeles, UO1 MH 35865—Marvin Karno, Javier Escobar, M. Audrey Burnma, Dianne M. Timbers.

Correspondence should be addressed to Dr. Eve K. Mościcki, Epidemiology and Psychopathology Research Branch, Division of Clinical Research, National Institute of Mental Health, Room 10C-05, 5600 Fishers Lane, Rockville, MD 20857.

dardized manner, most often by interviewing the respondents. The investigator either develops an instrument for this purpose or uses one that has already been developed, in order to standardize the collection of information and apply case definition criteria in a systematic manner. On the basis of the data from the survey, the epidemiologist interprets the findings and draws conclusions regarding the rate of occurrence and correlates of the disorder of interest. The findings are generalized from the sample to the population from which it came (Backstrom & Hursh-César, 1981).

How have epidemiologic surveys contributed to our knowledge of suicidal behavior? Few studies have surveyed suicidal behavior in the community. With one exception, these surveys were primarily concerned with outcomes other than suicidal behavior, and therefore differed widely in their case definitions. In spite of their differences, however, the range of prevalence estimates and the major correlates identified are remarkably similar. The prevalence estimates for suicidal ideation and suicide attempts are presented first, followed by the correlates of these behaviors.

Prevalence

The classic community study of suicidal behavior was conducted by Paykel and his colleagues (Paykel, Myers, Lindenthal, & Tanner, 1974) in New Haven, Connecticut, in 1969. This was part of the larger New Haven Study, a multiwave psychiatric epidemiologic survey of the New Haven population. Data gathered included psychiatric diagnoses based on the Schedule for Affective Disorders and Schizophrenia and the Research Diagnostic Criteria (Myers & Weissman, 1986) and sociodemographic characteristics. During the second wave of the study, 720 adults aged 18 and over were asked about "suicidal feelings" and behavior that included both suicidal ideation and suicide attempts. The questions were as follows:

1. Have you ever felt that life was not worth living?
2. Have you ever wished you were dead?—for instance, that you could go to sleep and not wake up?
3. Have you ever thought of taking your life, even if you would not really do it?
4. Have you ever reached the point where you seriously considered taking your life, or perhaps made plans how you would go about doing it?
5. Have you ever made an attempt to take your life?

The order of questions implied a hierarchy of seriousness of intent, from feelings that life was not worth living and passive desire for death through an active attempt to take one's life. Questions 3 and 4 made an important distinction between casual and more serious suicidal ideation. The lifetime and 1-year prevalence estimates of suicidal ideation and attempts from this survey appear in Table 11.1. The estimates of suicidal ideation represent positive responses to question 3, with the assumption that positive responses to question 4 are included. Not shown in Table 11.1 are lifetime and 1-year estimates of suicidal ideation based on question 4 alone, which asked about serious suicidal ideation (including a plan). These were 2.6% and 1.5%, respectively.

The second study was conducted in 1972 in northern Florida by Schwab, Warheit, and Holzer (1972). These investigators interviewed 1,645 adults (ages not given) as part of a study measuring social psychiatric impairment and evaluating the county's mental health needs and services. The questions were part of a structured interview and asked about current occurrence of suicidal ideation and lifetime history of suicide attempts:

1. How often do you think about suicide? Would you say—never, seldom, sometimes, often, or all the time?
2. Have you ever tried to commit suicide? If so, how many times? How long ago?

Note that the question on suicidal ideation required more than a yes–no response by asking about the frequency of ideation; this could be used as a simple measure of the severity of the ideation or the seriousness of intent. The questions asking about suicide attempt tried to establish not only whether the respondent had ever attempted suicide, but also the number of attempts and their relative recency. There were difficulties with both the ideation and attempt questions, however. The ideation questions asked about current behavior only, and did not ask about behavior that occurred in the past. On the other hand, the attempt questions asked about past behavior. The response format was open-ended, which introduced bias by relying on the accuracy of the respondent's recall of events.

Table 11.1 shows that Schwab et al. (1972) found a prevalence of 15.9% for suicidal ideation and 2.7% for attempts. They also reported a 1-year prevalence of 0.4% for suicide attempts.

A third study of suicidal behavior was published by Vandivort and Locke (1979). These investigators inquired about suicidal ideation as part of the Community Mental Health Epidemiology Program, a survey of 3,935 adults aged 18 and over in the early 1970s in Kansas City,

TABLE 11.1. Suicidal Ideation and Attempts in Community Studies

Study	n (response rate)	Instrument/method	Time reference	Prevalence per 100	
				Ideation	Attempts
Paykel, Myers, Lindenthal, & Tanner (1974) New Haven, CT	720 (NA[a])	Structured interview	Lifetime 1 year	4.8 2.3	1.1 0.6
Schwab, Warheit, & Holzer (1972) Northern Florida	1,645 (84%)	Structured interview	Lifetime 1 year	15.9	2.7 0.4
Vandivort & Locke (1979) Kansas City, MO Washington Co., MD	3,935 (75%) (80%)	Structured interview	1 month	5.4	
Goldberg (1981)[b] Kansas City, MO Washington Co., MD	489	Structured interview	1 month	9.6	
Ramsey & Bagley (1985) Calgary, Alberta, Canada	679 (61%)	Semistructured interview	Lifetime 1 year	13.4 3.9	4.2 0.8
Mościcki et al. (1988) 5 ECA sites[c]	18,571 (76%)	Diagnostic Interview Schedule	Lifetime 1 year[d] 1 month[d]	10.7 2.6 0.8	2.9 0.3 0.1
New Haven, CT	5,034		Lifetime	10.2	2.4
Baltimore, MD	3,481		Lifetime	7.6	3.4
St. Louis, MO	3,004		Lifetime	10.6	3.1
Piedmont area, NC	3,921		Lifetime	10.0	1.5
Los Angeles, CA	3,131		Lifetime	14.6	4.3

[a]Information not available.
[b]Analysis of data from 18 to 24-year-old respondents to survey described by Vandivort and Locke.
[c]Epidemiologic Catchment Area Study.
[d]Excludes New Haven and St. Louis.

Missouri and Washington County, Maryland. The purpose of the survey was to study the extent of current depressive symptomatology in the community, based on the Center for Epidemiologic Studies Depression Scale (CES-D; Radloff, 1977). The structured interview included questions on sociodemographic information and two questions on suicidal ideation:

1. About how often did you think about suicide in the last month? (Very often, fairly often, occasionally, rarely, or never?)
2. In your opinion, how often do most people think about suicide? (Never, less than once a year, several times a year, once a month, about once a week, or every day?)

The question on projection of frequency of ideation in others is not discussed here. Note that the time frame in the question about one's own suicidal ideation referred to the past month. As with Schwab et al.'s questions, the respondent was asked about the frequency of the behavior, thus making possible a rough estimate of severity. The authors considered any response other than "never" as indicating some level of suicidal ideation, and did not report the frequency distribution of all responses to the question. The 1-month prevalence of any ideation, from "rarely" to "very often," was 5.4% (Table 11.1).

Goldberg (1981) used the Kansas City and Washington County data to investigate suicidal ideation and projection of frequency of ideation in others among 489 young adults aged 18–24 years. She found the 1-month prevalence of any level of suicidal ideation to be 9.6% in this age group, substantially higher than the estimate for all ages. Like Vandivort and Locke (1981), Goldberg did not report the frequency distribution of the responses, so it is not known what proportion of the suicidal ideators reported that they "rarely" thought about suicide.

The only study to specifically survey suicidal behaviors was conducted in 1984 in Calgary, Alberta, Canada, and was reported by Ramsay and Bagley (1985). Respondents were asked in a semistructured interview about sociodemographic characteristics, childhood history, social ties, religiosity, stress, health, "suicidal behaviors," and "suicidal actions":

1. Have you ever felt that life was not worth living?
2. Have you wished that you were dead—for instance, that you could go to sleep and not wake up?
3. Have you ever thought of taking your life, even if you would not really do it?
4. Have you ever reached the point where you seriously considered taking your life or perhaps made plans how you would go about doing it?

5. Have you ever deliberately harmed yourself, but in a way that stopped short of a real intent to take your life?
6. Have you ever made an intentional attempt to take your life?

The first four questions were identical to those used in the New Haven Study by Paykel et al. (1974). The final question from Paykel et al. was modified to establish degree of lethality of attempt. This is the only known community survey that has addressed the important distinction between deliberate self-harm without intent to die, which the authors called "parasuicide," and a lethal suicide attempt. The lifetime and 1-year prevalence rates for less serious suicidal ideation were 37.8% and 6.0%, respectively. Lifetime and 1-year prevalence rates for parasuicide were 5.9% and 1.3%, respectively. These are not shown. The rates in Table 11.1 reflect the responses to questions 4 and 6, and indicate the estimated proportion of persons who seriously considered taking their lives or made a serious attempt to do so. This survey, unfortunately, had a very low response rate of 61%, and the estimates therefore need to be interpreted cautiously. The authors emphasized that suicidal behaviors must be studied with a context of social values and beliefs.

The largest community study in which suicidal behaviors have been measured is the NIMH Epidemiologic Catchment Area (ECA) Study, conducted from 1980 to 1985. This is a five-site, multiwave survey of selected psychiatric disorders in the population, and is the largest such study of its kind ever undertaken (Blazer, George, Landerman, Pennybacker, Melville, Woodbury, Manton, Jordan, & Locke, 1985; Boyd, Burke, Gruenberg, Holzer, Rae, George, Karno, Stoltzman, McEvoy, & Nestadt, 1984; Burnam, Hough, Escobar, Karno, Timbers, Telles, & Locke, 1987; Eaton, Holzer, von Korff, Anthony, Helzer, George, Burnam, Boyd, Kessler, & Locke, 1984; Eaton & Kessler, 1985; Hough, Landsverk, Karno, Burnam, Timbers, Escobar, & Regier, 1987; Karno, Hough, Burnam, Escobar, Timbers, Santana, & Boyd, 1987; Myers, Weissman, Tischler, Holzer, Leaf, Orvaschel, Anthony, Boyd, Burke, Kramer, & Stoltzman, 1984; Regier, Myers, Kramer, Robins, Blazer, Hough, Eaton, & Locke, 1984; Robins, Helzer, Weissman, Orvaschel, Gruenberg, Burke, & Regier, 1984; Shapiro, Skinner, Kessler, von Korff, German, Tischler, Leaf, Benham, Cottler, & Regier, 1984). A total of 18,571 adults aged 18 years and over were surveyed in New Haven, Connecticut; Baltimore, Maryland; St. Louis, Missouri; the Piedmont region of North Carolina; and Los Angeles, California. The Diagnostic Interview Schedule (DIS; Robins, Helzer, Croughan, & Ratcliff, 1981; Robins, Helzer, Croughan, Williams, & Spitzer, 1981) was administered by highly trained lay interviewers, who gathered information on psychiatric symptoms, sociodemographic characteristics, and mental health care utilization. Diagnoses for selected psychiatric disorders were generated by computer algorithm. Questions on thoughts of death, desire to die, suicidal ideation, and suicide attempt were asked of each respondent:

1. Has there ever been a period of 2 weeks or more when you thought a lot about death—either your own, someone else's, or death in general?
2. Has there ever been a period of 2 weeks or more when you felt like you wanted to die?
3. Have you ever felt so low you thought of committing suicide?
4. Have you ever attempted suicide?

The questions did not overtly distinguish between more or less lethal outcomes. Table 11.1 shows the weighted lifetime prevalence estimates of suicidal ideation, based on question 3, and suicide attempt, based on question 4, for all five sites combined (Mościcki, O'Carroll, Rae, Roy, Locke, & Regier, 1988). Combined 1-year and 1-month estimates are shown for Baltimore, the Piedmont region, and Los Angeles, the three sites where information on recency of occurrence was obtained. Lifetime prevalence estimates for both suicidal behaviors are also shown by site. Suicidal ideation ranged from 7.4% in Baltimore to 14.6% in Los Angeles. Suicide attempts ranged from 1.5% in the Piedmont area to 4.3% in Los Angeles.

Risk Factors for Suicidal Ideation

Various methods were used in the community studies reviewed here to examine risk factors, or correlates, for suicidal behaviors. Multivariate analyses, which permit simultaneous control for the effects of multiple variables, are not always feasible in studies where the outcome behavior results in small numbers. Table 11.2 summarizes the correlates of suicidal feelings and/or ideation from the studies in which they were reported. The "×'s" represent statistically significant positive associations; the "—'s" represent correlates that were tested but were not significant. A blank indicates that the variable was not examined. Three of the studies reviewed—the New Haven Study (Paykel et al., 1974), Goldberg's (1981) analysis of the data from the Community Mental Health Epidemiology Program, and the ECA Study (Mościcki et al., 1988)—reported the results of multivariate analyses. No risk factor analyses were reported for the Calgary Study (Ramsay & Bagley, 1985).

TABLE 11.2. Correlates of Suicidal Feelings and/or Ideation in Community Studies

Study	Female gender	White race	Younger age	Disr. marr.	Single	Unemployment	Student	Low SES	Social adjmt.	Life stress	Psych. sx/dx	Separ. mother	Site
Paykel et al. (1974)[a] New Haven, CT	×	—	—	—	—				×	×	×		
Schwab et al. (1972) Northern Florida	—	×	×	×	×			—					
Vandivort & Locke (1979) Kansas City, MO Washington Co., MD	—	—	×	×	×	—	×				×		
Goldberg (1981)[b] Kansas City, MO Washington Co., MD	—	—		—	—		×	—			×	×	—
Mościcki et al. (1988) [5 ECA sites[c]]	×	×	×	×	×	—		—			×		×

Note. Disr. marr., disrupted marriage (widowed, separated, or divorced); Social adjmt., social adjustment; Psych. sx/dx, psychiatric symptoms or psychiatric diagnosis; Separ. mother, separated from mother before age 16.
[a] Includes attempters.
[b] Analysis of data from 18- to 24-year-old respondents to survey described by Vandivort & Locke.
[c] Epidemiologic Catchment Area Study: Baltimore, MD; Los Angeles, CA; New Haven, CT; Piedmont area, NC; St. Louis, MO.

It is not possible to distinguish between risk factors for ideation and attempts in the New Haven Study (Paykel et al., 1974), since the authors grouped outcomes into one category of "suicidal feelings" because of the very small number of respondents ($n = 64$) who reported any degree of suicidal feelings in the past year. The investigators used cross-tabulations to examine the effects of sociodemographic characteristics, and multivariate analyses to examine the effects of psychosocial variables. Correlates significantly associated with suicidal feelings in the New Haven Study included female gender, social adjustment (which included social isolation and absence of religiosity), life stress, and psychiatric symptoms. Correlates not associated with suicidal feelings were white race, younger age, and a disrupted or single marital status.

Schwab et al. (1972) used gamma, a statistic that measures the degree of association between ordered pairs, to show that white race, age under 30, and disrupted and single marital status were significantly associated with suicidal ideation. Not associated were female gender and lower socioeconomic status.

Vandivort and Locke (1979), using chi-square analyses, identified ages 18–24, disrupted and single marital status, student status, high educational achievement (beyond high school) for males only, and high levels of depressive symptoms as measured by the CES-D as being significantly associated with some degree of suicidal ideation during the past month. Female gender, white race, and unemployment were not significantly associated with the outcome. Because the investigators did not employ multivariate analyses, it is not possible to determine whether each of these variables independently contributed to the outcome. For example, student status is known to be associated with younger age, and one of these variables could have been a confounder.

Goldberg (1981) used a binary variable multiple-regression procedure to examine the effects of sociodemographic and selected psychosocial variables on suicidal ideation in the 18–24 age group who participated in the Community Mental Health Epidemiology Program. She found that student status, high levels of depressive symptoms as measured by the CES-D, childhood bereavement (defined as separation from mother before age 16), and overt aggression during the past week were significantly associated with reported suicidal ideation. Race, gender, age, education, marital status, and geographic site (Kansas City vs. Washington County) were not significantly associated with ideation.

Ramsay and Bagley (1985) did not report any specific correlates for either ideation or attempts. Instead, they suggested that a fairly stable and affluent population with high suicide rates is unusual. They reported that a substantial proportion of their sample experienced high rates of childhood and adult separations for long periods of time, marked stress in the past 6 months, lack of close social contacts, and family histories of suicidal behaviors. These observations were ecological, however, and were not tested in a multivariate model. The authors implied that higher socioeconomic status could be a significant risk factor for suicidal behavior. They further suggested that the prevalence rates reported by others in less affluent geographic areas could be underestimates. This notion remains to be empirically tested.

We (Mościcki et al., 1988) used weighted logistic regression analyses to examine the independent effects of selected risk factors on lifetime prevalence of suicidal behavior in the ECA Study. In order to increase the power of the analyses, data from the five sites were combined, and site was included as an independent variable. We found that female gender, white race, younger age, disrupted and single marital status, the Los Angeles site, and lifetime diagnosis of psychiatric disorder were independent risk factors for suicidal ideation. Unemployment and socioeconomic status were not significantly associated with suicidal ideation.

On the whole, the five studies shown in Table 11.2 report mixed findings. It is difficult to draw conclusions regarding the relative contributions of the risk factors considered here, because of the small number of community studies that have investigated suicidal behaviors. Nonetheless, some cautious generalizations can be made. Younger age, a disrupted or single marital status, and high levels of psychiatric symptoms or a psychiatric diagnosis appear to be important risk factors for suicidal ideation.

Risk Factors for Suicide Attempts

Only two studies examined risk factors for suicide attempts: the survey in northern Florida (Schwab et al., 1972) and the ECA (Mościcki et al., 1988) (see Table 11.3). Since even the lifetime prevalence of suicide attempts in the community is apparently less than 5%, the small numbers of suicide attempters make detailed analyses very difficult. This was the problem experienced in the New Haven Study (Paykel et al., 1974), which precluded separate analyses for ideators and attempters. Schwab et al. (1972) found a higher proportion of suicide attempts among females, whites, persons under 30, those with a disrupted marital status, and those with lower incomes. They did not test for significance, however. The investigators did find a statistically significant relationship between the number of respondents who reported suicidal ideation and those who had attempted suicide.

TABLE 11.3. Correlates of Suicide Attempts in Community Studies

Study	Prevalence per 100	Female gender	White race	Younger age	Disr. marr.	Unemployment	Low SES	Psych. sx/dx	Site
Schwab et al. (1972) Northern Florida	2.7	×	×	×	×		×	×[a]	
Mościcki et al. (1988) [5 ECA sites[b]]	2.9	×	×	—	×	—	×	×	×

Note. Disr. marr., disrupted marriage (widowed, separated, or divorced); Psych. sx/dx, psychiatric symptoms or psychiatric diagnosis.
[a]Suicidal ideation.
[b]Epidemiologic Catchment Area Study: Baltimore, MD; Los Angeles, CA; New Haven, CT; Piedmont area, NC; St. Louis, MO.

The ECA Study included large enough numbers of respondents to permit multivariate analyses without compromising power. We (Mościcki et al., 1988) found that female gender, white race, disrupted marriage, lower socioeconomic status, the Los Angeles site, and lifetime diagnosis of psychiatric disorder were significant risk factors for suicide attempts. The strongest risk factor was lifetime diagnosis of psychiatric disorder. Unemployment and younger age were not associated with suicide attempts in this model.

Factors Accounting for Differences in Findings

There are several reasons for differences in findings among the studies, ranging from differences in the populations studied to differences in the method used.

Underlying Population

The underlying populations that were surveyed differ a great deal from one another on a number of parameters. One is geographic location or region. Consider, for example, the port of New Haven, Connecticut, on the East Coast (Paykel et al., 1974) vis-à-vis the landlocked oil boom town of Calgary, Alberta, at the foot of the Canadian Rockies (Ramsay & Bagley, 1985). Another parameter is that of the culture and beliefs of each community that distinguish it from all others. For example, among the studies reviewed, two very different ECA communities are the Piedmont site, which is Southern and predominantly rural (Blazer et al., 1985), and urban, cosmopolitan Los Angeles (Burnam et al., 1987; Hough et al., 1987; Karno et al., 1987). Finally, the sociodemographic composition of a community also contributes to the uniqueness of its population, and presumably to the prevalence of certain behaviors. Examples of two sociodemographically different communities in the same study are nearly all-white Washington County, Maryland, and racially mixed Kansas City, Missouri (Goldberg, 1981; Radloff, 1977; Vandivort & Locke, 1979).

Method

A great many differences in findings between studies can be attributed to differences in methodology. One important difference lies in the sample drawn and the sampling techniques used to get the sample. Factors that need to be considered in any discussion of samples include the type and size of the sample, and the representativeness of the sample with respect to the population from which it was drawn. Although each of the surveys reviewed here collected data from a probability sample of the population, the type of probability sample used differed with each study. The New Haven Study used a systematic household sample (Paykel et al., 1974); the Community Mental Health Epidemiology Program used a simple random sample (Vandivort & Locke, 1979); the ECA used complex, multistage samples, which also differed by site (Eaton et al., 1984). The size of the sample is also an important factor in comparing findings across studies. For example, consider the 720 respondents in the 1969 New Haven Study (Paykel et al., 1974), compared with 5,034 respondents in the 1981 New Haven ECA Study (Eaton et al., 1984).

The most crucial sampling issue in any survey is, of course, the representativeness of the sample. Did the demographic composition of the sample match the demographic composition of the underlying population? Was the response rate substantial enough to assure confidence in the findings? If the response rate is too low, the investigator's ability to generalize the findings back to the population is compromised. For example, the response rate of the northern Florida study was reported to be 84% (Schwab et al., 1972), which is considered very good. The response rate achieved in the Calgary study was 61% (Ramsay & Bagley, 1985). With nearly 40% of the sample missing, it is difficult to draw conclusions from the findings of this study, and sampling bias cannot be ruled out.

A second major category of differences in methodology can be attributed to differences in instrumentation, especially as they apply to case definition. This is clearly demonstrated by the variety of questions employed in the surveys to operationalize suicidal behavior. Although only six studies were reviewed, four types of suicidal behaviors were defined: suicidal feelings, suicidal ideation, parasuicide, and suicide attempt. The time reference for these four types of behaviors represented three different periods: 1 month, 1 year, and lifetime. The number of questions asked ranged from one to six.

Finally, secular trends and cohort effects can also play a role in different findings among studies. For example, the two New Haven surveys (Paykel et al., 1974; Mościcki et al., 1988) were conducted nearly 15 years apart. The differences between the 1969 and 1984 rates may be explained in part by changes over time in the amount of risk associated with the factors defining the groups at greatest risk for suicidal behavior.

Contributions of Epidemiologic Surveys

Advantages

Epidemiologic surveys have the potential of making a substantial contribution to our understanding of suicidal behavior in the population. Because the respondents are selected by a probability sample drawn from the community, not the clinic, they are representative of the population. The findings can thus be generalized to the population. Since the respondents are not limited to clinic patients and controls, the biases frequently associated with clinical studies (Feinstein, 1977) are avoided. The large sample sizes, relative to clinical studies, increase the power of the study. If the sample size and number of cases are large enough, analyses can go beyond two-way tables to detailed multivariate analyses and identification of independent risk factors.

Disadvantages

The main disadvantage of any properly conducted epidemiologic survey is its expense, in both time and money. Surveys are major efforts that must be carefully planned and executed by multidisciplinary teams of investigators. An analytic disadvantage of a large-scale survey is the complexity of the analyses required. If the probability sample for a survey is other than a simple random sample, and adjustment or weighing procedures are necessary, the analyses may be beyond the resources of some investigators. This disadvantage can be overcome, however, by the sophisticated analytic software that is currently available. There are two scientific disadvantages generally associated with surveys. One is the inability to collect data on the worst cases, since surveys generally do not sample institutions. In addition, it may not be possible to collect data in very great detail, because of the necessity to limit the amount of time taken by the household interview. These disadvantages, too, can be overcome, by including institutions in the sampling universe and by using multistage combinations of screening and interview techniques.

Role of the Epidemiologic Survey in the Study of Suicide and Suicidal Behavior

Can the epidemiologic survey play a meaningful role in the study of suicide and suicidal behavior? It can indeed. Estimates derived from a well-conducted survey can provide policy makers with a clear idea of the scope of the problem in the population. Despite the range of estimates found in the six studies reviewed here, we can be reasonably confident that the lifetime prevalence of suicide attempts in the general population is less than 5%, and that the 1-year prevalence is less than 1%. The large numbers of respondents to a survey permit exploration of a greater number of risk factors with more rigorous analyses than are possible in clinical studies. Based on multivariate analyses, several independent correlates of suicidal behavior have been identified, including psychiatric symptoms or psychiatric diagnosis, female gender, youth, white race, disrupted and/or single marital status, lower socioeconomic status, and social isolation. These correlates augment findings from clinical studies, and can serve as a basis for identification of high-risk groups in the population.

Epidemiologic surveys can also serve as the vehicle for improving the methods used to collect data on suicidal behaviors in both the clinic and the community. Case definition remains one of the main difficulties in accurate ascertainment of suicidal behavior. Development and testing of a standardized instrument designed to distinguish among vivid suicidal ideation, self-injury without intent to die, and a genuine suicide attempt can be accomplished with the help of the community survey. The survey population is frequently large enough to permit separation of the relatively small proportion of true attempters from the larger proportion of troubled individuals who use self-injury as a "cry for help," thus increasing our understanding of the association between suicide attempt and completion.

References

Backstrom, C. H., & Hursh-César, G. Survey research (2nd ed.). New York: Wiley, 1981.

Blazer, D., George, L. K., Landerman, R., Pennybacker, M., Melville, M. L., Woodbury, M., Manton, K. G., Jordan, K., & Locke, B. Z. Psychiatric disorders: A rural/urban comparison. Archives of General Psychiatry, 1985, 42, 651–656.

Boyd, J. H., Burke, J. D., Gruenberg, E., Holzer, C. E., Rae, D. S., George, L., Karno, M., Stoltzman, R., McEvoy, D., & Nestadt, G. Exclusion criteria of DSM-III. Archives of General Psychiatry, 1984, 41, 983–989.

Burnam, M. A., Hough, R. L., Escobar, J. I., Karno, M., Timbers, D. M., Telles, C. A., & Locke, B. Z. Six-month prevalence of specific psychiatric disorders: Mexican Americans and non-Hispanic whites in Los Angeles. Archives of General Psychiatry, 1987, 44, 685–694.

Eaton, W. W., Holzer, C. E., III, Von Korff, M., Anthony, J. C., Helzer, J. E., George, L., Burnam, M. A., Boyd, J. H., Kessler, L. G., & Locke, B. Z. The design of the ECA surveys: The control and measurement of error. Archives of General Psychiatry, 1984, 41, 942–948.

Eaton, W. W., & Kessler, L. G. (Eds.), Epidemiologic field methods in psychiatry: The NIMH Epidemiologic Catchment Area Program. New York: Academic Press, 1985.

Feinstein, A. R. Clinical biostatistics. St. Louis: C. V. Mosby, 1977.

Goldberg, E. L. Depression and suicide ideation in the young adult. *American Journal of Psychiatry*, 1981, *138*, 35–40.

Hough, R. L., Landsverk, J. A., Karno, M., Burnam, A., Timbers, D. M., Escobar, J. I., & Regier, D. A. Utilization of health and mental health services by Los Angeles Mexican Americans and non-Hispanic whites. *Archives of General Psychiatry*, 1987, *44*, 702–709.

Karno, M., Hough, R. L., Burnam, M. A., Escobar, J. I., Timbers, D. M., Santana, F., & Boyd, J. H. Lifetime prevalence of specific psychiatric disorders among Mexican Americans and non-Hispanic whites in Los Angeles. *Archives of General Psychiatry*, 1987, *44*, 695–701.

Lilienfeld, A. M., & Lilienfeld, D. E. *Foundations of epidemiology* (2nd ed.). New York: Oxford University Press, 1980.

Mościcki, E. K., O'Carroll, P., Locke, B. Z., Rae, D. S., Roy, A. G., & Regier, D. A. Suicidal ideation and attempts: The Epidemiologic Catchment Area. In U.S. D.H.H.S., *Report of the Secretary's Task Force on Youth Suicide: Vol. 4. Strategies for the prevention of youth suicide*. Washington, D.C. U.S. Government Printing Office, 1988.

Myers, J. K., & Weissman, M. M. Psychiatric disorders in a U.S. urban community: The New Haven Study. In M. Weissman, J. Meyers, & K. Ross (Eds.), *Community surveys of psychiatric disorders*. New Brunswick, N.J.: Rutgers University Press, 1986.

Myers, J. K., Weissman, M. M., Tischler, G. L., Holzer C. E., III, Leaf, P. J., Orvaschel, H., Anthony, J. C., Boyd, J. H., Burke, J. D., Kramer, M., & Stoltzman, R. Six-month prevalence of psychiatric disorders in three communities: 1980–82. *Archives of General Psychiatry*, 1984, *41*, 959–970.

Paykel, E. S., Myers, J. K., Lindenthal, J. J., & Tanner, J. Suicidal feelings in the general population: A prevalence study. *British Journal of Psychiatry*, 1974, *124*, 460–469.

Radloff, L. S. The CES-D Scale: A self-report depression scale for research in the general population. *Applied Psychological Measurement*, 1977, *1*, 385–401.

Ramsay, R., & Bagley, C. The prevalence of suicidal behaviors, attitudes and associated social experiences in an urban population. *Suicide and Life-Threatening Behavior*, 1985, *15*, 151–167.

Regier, D. A., Myers, J. K., Kramer, M., Robins, L. N., Blazer, D. G., Hough, R. L., Eaton, W. W., & Locke, B. Z. The NIMH Epidemiologic Catchment Area (ECA) Program: Historical context, major objectives, and study population characteristics. *Archives of General Psychiatry*, 1984, *41*, 934–941.

Robins, L. N., Helzer, J. E., Croughan, J., & Ratcliff, K. S.: National Institute of Mental Health Diagnostic Interview Schedule: Its history, characteristics, and validity. *Archives of General Psychiatry*, 1981, *38*, 381–389.

Robins, L. N., Helzer, J. E., Croughan, J., Williams, J. B. W., & Spitzer, R. L. *NIMH Diagnostic Interview Schedule: Version 3*. Rockville, Md.: National Institute of Mental Health, 1981.

Robins, L. N., Helzer, J. E., Weissman, M. M., Orvaschel, H., Gruenberg, E., Burke, J. D., & Regier, D. A. Lifetime prevalence of specific psychiatric disorders in three sites. *Archives of General Psychiatry*, 1984, *41*, 949–958.

Schwab, J. J., Warheit, G. J., & Holzer, C. E. Suicide ideation and behavior in a general population. *Diseases of the Nervous System*, 1972, *33*, 745–748.

Shapiro, S., Skinner, E. A., Kessler, L. G., Von Korff, M., German, P., Tischler, G. L., Leaf, P. J., Benham, L., Cottler, L., & Regier, D. A. Utilization of health and mental health services. *Archives of General Psychiatry*, 1984, *41*, 971–978.

Vandivort, B. S., & Locke, B. Z. Suicide ideation: Its relation to depression, suicide and suicide attempt. *Suicide and Life-Threatening Behavior*, 1979, *9*, 205–218.

Index

Accidents, 5, 81
Adolescents
  attempters, 111
  communication of intent by, 70–71
  cross-sectional studies on, 62–63, 64, 65
  disorders in vs. suicide rate, 66
  friends of, 50–51
  in hospitals, 71–72, 91
  rate of suicide, 99, 108
  risk factors, 74, 104, 105
Adults, psychological autopsies of, 44–45
AIDS. *See* HIV
Alcohol abuse, 48–49, 71, 81, 82
Anger in children, 110
Attempters
  dead vs. live, 51
  sex ratio, 90, 99

Beck Depression Inventory, 122
Best-estimate diagnoses, 51
Bipolar disorders and suicide risk, 69, 86–87
Blacks, 101, 103
Bonding problems in children, 93

Certification
  death investigation teams, 10–12
  equivocal cases, 11
  "gold standard" studies, 10–11
  nonsuicides, detection of, 10–12
  sensitivity, 9–10
  specificity, 10
  undercounting of suicide, 10
  yes/no decision about death, 9
Circumstances, getting information about, 52
Circumstances, undetermined, 5
Children
  abuse of, 93, 97, 114
  age of vs. suicidal behavior, 67
  cross-sectional studies, 60–62, 64, 65
  follow-ups on, 69–70
  hospitalization of, 52
  ideation of, 121–123
  lead time of stress before suicide, 52
  prevention of suicide in, 121–122
Clusters of suicides, analysis of
  ages in, 25
  cell methods, 23–24
  data, limits of, 25–26
  Knox statistics, 22, 23
  methods, limits of, 19–20, 25
  Mantel's procedure, 23
  Naus's scan statistics, 24

pair methods, 22–23
reality of, 21–22
reasons for occurrence, 18–19
College students, suicide in
  accuracy in reports, problems with, 126
  cars, hazards of, 124
  college life, factors in, 124–125
  completers, 125–128
  depression, 125
  early studies about, 126
  lifetime suicidal behavior in, 124
  major of study vs. suicidal behavior, 124
  medical students, 127
  parents, loss of, 128
  planned procedures, 124
  psychological predictors, 128
  rates, 127
  students, definitions used, 126
  time of suicides, 127
  undergraduate psychology students, 124–125
Community studies
  attempts vs. suicidal ideation, 133, 134
  Calgary study, 135–136
  ECA study, 136–137
  instrumentation, 143
  Kansas City study, 133, 135
  New Haven study, 132–133
  northern Florida study, 133
  populations studied, and discrepancies, 142
  prevalences found, 132–137
  questions in studies, 132, 133
  representativeness of samples, 143
  response rates, 143
  sampling procedures, 143
  scales used, 132
  self-harm attempts, 136
  structured interviews, 135, 136
  trends, 143
  young adults, 135
Completers, sex ratio of, 90, 99
Contagion vs. clusters, 20, 26–27
Coroners
  certification by, 3–4
  competence of, 83
Corticotropin-releasing factor, 37
Cry for help, self-injury as, 145

D/ART program, vii–viii
Death, finality of, 66–67
Depression. *See also* Corticotropin-releasing factor; Serotonin
  children, 110